The Philosophy of Being in the Analytic, Continental, and Thomistic Traditions

Also available from Bloomsbury

Debating Christian Religious Epistemology, edited by John M. DePoe
and Tyler Dalton McNabb
Four Views on the Axiology of Theism, edited by Kirk Lougheed
Free Will and Epistemology, by Robert Lockie
Kant's Transition Project and Late Philosophy, by Oliver Thorndike
Wittgenstein, Religion and Ethics, by Mikel Burley

The Philosophy of Being in the Analytic, Continental, and Thomistic Traditions

Divergence and Dialogue

Joseph P. Li Vecchi, Frank Scalambrino,
and David K. Kovacs

BLOOMSBURY ACADEMIC
LONDON • NEW YORK • OXFORD • NEW DELHI • SYDNEY

BLOOMSBURY ACADEMIC
Bloomsbury Publishing Plc
50 Bedford Square, London, WC1B 3DP, UK
1385 Broadway, New York, NY 10018, USA
29 Earlsfort Terrace, Dublin 2, Ireland

BLOOMSBURY, BLOOMSBURY ACADEMIC and the Diana logo
are trademarks of Bloomsbury Publishing Plc

First published in Great Britain 2020
This paperback edition published in 2022

Copyright © Joseph P. Li Vecchi, Frank Scalambrino, and David K. Kovacs, 2020

Joseph P. Li Vecchi, Frank Scalambrino, and David K. Kovacs have asserted their right under the Copyright, Designs and Patents Act, 1988, to be identified as Authors of this work.

For legal purposes the Acknowledgments on p. viii constitute an extension of this copyright page.

Cover design by Charlotte Daniels
Cover image © oxygen/Getty Images

All rights reserved. No part of this publication may be reproduced or transmitted in any form or by any means, electronic or mechanical, including photocopying, recording, or any information storage or retrieval system, without prior permission in writing from the publishers.

Bloomsbury Publishing Plc does not have any control over, or responsibility for, any third-party websites referred to or in this book. All internet addresses given in this book were correct at the time of going to press. The author and publisher regret any inconvenience caused if addresses have changed or sites have ceased to exist, but can accept no responsibility for any such changes.

A catalogue record for this book is available from the British Library.

Library of Congress Cataloging-in-Publication Data
Names: Li Vecchi, Joseph P., author. | Scalambrino, Frank, 1976- author. |
Kovacs, David K., author.
Title: The philosophy of being in the analytic, continental, and Thomistic traditions : divergence and dialogue / Joseph P. Li Vecchi, Frank Scalambrino, and David K. Kovacs.
Description: London ; New York : Bloomsbury Academic, 2020. | Includes bibliographical references and index.
Identifiers: LCCN 2020023054 (print) | LCCN 2020023055 (ebook) | ISBN 9781350103320 (hardback) | ISBN 9781350103337 (ebook) | ISBN 9781350103344 (epub)
Subjects: LCSH: Thomas, Aquinas, Saint, 1225?-1274. | Ontology. | Analysis (Philosophy) |
Continental philosophy.
Classification: LCC BD331 .L473 2020 (print) | LCC BD331 (ebook) | DDC 111.09–dc23
LC record available at https://lccn.loc.gov/2020023054
LC ebook record available at https://lccn.loc.gov/2020023055

ISBN:	HB:	978-1-3501-0332-0
	PB:	978-1-3502-1357-9
	ePDF:	978-1-3501-0333-7
	eBook:	978-1-3501-0334-4

Typeset by Integra Software Services Pvt. Ltd.

To find out more about our authors and books visit www.bloomsbury.com and sign up for our newsletters.

*Joseph P. Li Vecchi dedicates this book to
Domenica Pachì Li Vecchi (1927–2019), mother
and* lapis lydiae

*Frank Scalambrino dedicates this book to:
Immanuel Kant (1724–1804)*

*David K. Kovacs dedicates this book to:
The Fordham Philosophical Society*

Contents

Acknowledgments		viii
1	Introduction: Being in Three Traditions	1
2	Being in the Thomistic Tradition: Real Objectivity and the Logic of Existence	7
3	Being in the Continental Tradition: Phenomenological Hermeneutics as Fundamental Ontology	39
4	Being in the Analytic Tradition: The Logic of Existence	83
5	Conclusion: Being in Three Traditions	125
Notes		156
Bibliography & Further Reading		185
Index		196

Acknowledgments

Joseph P. Li Vecchi would like to acknowledge:

I am grateful for the living tradition of Thomism handed down to me at the Roman Dominican *studium*, the Pontifical University of Saint Thomas Aquinas, *Angelicum*, and for the material and spiritual support of my wife Robin.

Frank Scalambrino would like to acknowledge:

I received no outside funding or sabbatical with which to write this book.

David K. Kovacs would like to acknowledge:

Portions of Chapters 4 and 5 were written with the assistance of a Mark and Kathryn Tomasic Research Fellowship.

1

Introduction: Being in Three Traditions

Joseph P. Li Vecchi, Frank Scalambrino, and David K. Kovacs

§1 What Is the Philosophy of Being?

The philosophy of being is as old as philosophy itself; in fact, depending upon your understanding of philosophy, it may even be older. Thus, as long as there will be philosophy, there will always be the philosophy of being. However, books on the philosophy of being have tended to be written from the point of view of, or privileging, just one tradition from the history of Western philosophy.

So, on the one hand, the three of us thought it would be a valuable contribution to the literature regarding the philosophy of being, if we were to write a book that would specifically speak from the different points of view of three major philosophical traditions.[1] On the other hand, we thought an initial introductory section regarding the philosophy of being in general would help orient readers to the context of our book.[2]

§2 Brief History of the Meaning of the Philosophy of Being

It is widely considered standard that Plato (*c.* 428–348 BC) invented the subject of philosophy, as an academic discipline, that Thales of Miletus (*c.* 624–*c.* 548 BC) was the first Western philosopher, and that Pythagoras (*c.* 570–*c.* 495 BC) invented the term "philosopher." Yet, despite the philosophical musings of Heraclitus of Ephesus (*c.* 535–*c.* 475 BC) regarding becoming, the study of the philosophy of being began with the philosophical poetry of Parmenides of Elea (*c.* 515–*c.* 450 BC).

Inaugurating the philosophy of being, then, Parmenides wrote, "That which is there to be spoken and thought of must be. For it is possible for it to be, but not possible for nothing to be."[3] This has often been restated in what may appear to be a rather jejune observation: "Whatever is, is." While interpretations of Parmenides's thought have varied, the influence of his cryptic lines is enormous and undeniable,[4] especially, for example, on Plato, and on Plato's student Aristotle (384–322 BC).[5]

In fact, Plato devoted an entire dialogue—the *Parmenides*—to wrestling, explicitly, with the ideas of Parmenides and his follower Zeno of Elea (*c*. 495–*c*. 430 BC). In addition, Plato also explicitly addresses the philosophy of being in his dialogues: the *Republic*, the *Sophist*, and the *Timaeus*.[6] Moreover, the locus of the disagreement between Plato and Aristotle may have been precisely about how to understand being and existence.[7] Certainly the question was forefront in Aristotle's mind, as he went on to write that the first and the noblest of the sciences—what we standardly call "metaphysics"—is the science of "being as being."[8]

What is more, whereas a number of philosophers working in the Continental Tradition still engage with the writings of Parmenides and Heraclitus, at least one major introduction to Thomas Aquinas's (1225–1274) metaphysics portrays Aquinas as responding to what he took to be the "Parmenidean problem."[9] Thus, the legacy of Parmenides continues to ripple through the history of Western philosophy, as philosophers working in multiple traditions seek: To say something meaningful about being, about what it is to be or not to be.

Philosophers, however, have had complicated and at times strained relationships with each other over the years. For example, the thought of Plato and Aristotle was refined by thinkers Christian, Muslim, and Jewish, among others, and elements of Greek philosophy and monotheistic theology were at times synthesized, reinterpreted, and harmonized. The consequence has been that in recent years Western philosophy is viewed as having fragmented into different "schools" or "traditions." Strangely, it is not always easy to say what separates the different schools of thought. It isn't that our philosophical interests and inquiries are very different. At least part of what separates these schools from each other is that they have each developed their own ways of speaking, almost developing their own languages at times.

In retrospect, it seems inevitable that by the thirteenth century a genius like Thomas Aquinas would be developing what some commentators consider the greatest contribution to philosophy in history, calling it "perennial philosophy." Being has a central place in Aquinas's philosophy.[10] In fact, his followers, known as Thomists, develop and adapt Aquinas's thought to subsequent philosophical trends and problems by returning to core tenets of his philosophy of being. Yet, Aquinas was not the last genius in the history of philosophy.

By 1781 Immanuel Kant (1724–1804) had formulated, what the history of Western philosophy has taken to be, a revolutionary approach to the philosophy of being—the results of which serious philosophers have had to grapple with ever since. For example, his dictum, "Being is not a real predicate," has had reverberations in both the Continental and Analytic Traditions. Interestingly, how predication relates to being is a central issue for each of the traditions discussed in this book. Thus, "Being is not a real predicate" can also be seen as the point of departure for the genius of the Analytic Tradition, Gottlob Frege (1848–1925).

§3 Brief Clarification regarding "Metaphysics" and "Ontology" in the Philosophy of Being

Especially given the above reference to Aristotle's celebrated definition of "metaphysics" as "the science of being as being," a terminological clarification may be helpful for readers. Namely, what is the difference between "metaphysics" and "ontology," specifically in regard to the philosophy of being? On the one hand, this terminological clarification may be helpful since early twentieth-century textbooks of philosophy tended to define "ontology" as "the study of being in general." On the other hand, although the distinction tends to be less relevant to the Analytic discussion of being, each of our three traditions may invoke these terms, and in a slightly nuanced way. Therefore, the following two points should be helpful regarding terminology.

First, though some philosophers may treat these terms as equivalent to one another and completely exchangeable, the Continental Tradition considers ontology to be the more precise term of the two. That is, ontology divides into general ontology and specific ontologies. Whereas the former refers to the study of being as being, the specific ontologies are: the cosmological, the theological, and the psychological (since beings can be divided into those three orders). Therefore, the Continental Tradition precisely distinguishes between these terms such that these four, that is, the three specific ontologies and ontology in general, are understood as constituting and containing all that is studied in metaphysics.

Second, according to the Continental Tradition, it was Kant's *Critique of Pure Reason* that finally realized Aristotle's ambition to articulate metaphysics as a science.[11] In other words, it was not until Kant formulated his Transcendental Method that metaphysics truly became a science—a science which the Continental Tradition calls "transcendental philosophy." Importantly, then, Kant, in fact, considered the terms "ontology" and "transcendental philosophy" as equivalent to one another and completely exchangeable. Thus, even though the terms "ontology" and "transcendental" were already in use within the Thomistic Tradition and may have been considered standard in the vocabulary of Scholastic philosophy, Kant's philosophy standardized these terms differently for the Continental Tradition.

§4 Brief Characterization of the Structure of This Book

The bulk of this book consists of three chapters, each describing a way that one philosophical tradition has dealt with philosophical questions regarding being. We have ordered these chapters in a way that reflects the historical development of the respective tradition. First, the Thomistic Tradition, as influenced by the thought of Aquinas; second, the Continental Tradition, presented as a tradition developing from the work of Kant; lastly, the Analytic Tradition, presented as a tradition developing from the work of Frege.[12] A reader may pick up the book and begin by reading any one of these chapters to get a sense for what that school of philosophy looks like; there is no need to read them in order, although that may provide an excellent sense for the history of Western philosophy over the past 800 years.

The final chapter, however, may be the most important, at least insofar as we seek to promote philosophical dialogue. That chapter does assume that readers have at least some familiarity with the book's previous chapters, since we there engage with each other's theories. Each of us will say what we find problematic about the theory of being proposed in the other two chapters, as well as what may be a strong point that the respective theories make. And we will each make some effort to defend our respective theories from criticisms. How we fare on this front is for readers to decide.

Being in the Thomistic Tradition: Real Objectivity and the Logic of Existence

Joseph P. Li Vecchi

§1 Introductory Remarks

1.1 The Thomistic Wellspring

According to Thomas Aquinas (1225–1274), being shoots through a manifold containing all things actual, possible, and conceptual. We are able to investigate the gamut of this manifold in virtue of the insight that for everything it contains, there is at least one thing that we can know: "It is." This insight is the wellspring of the philosophy of being in the Thomistic Tradition.

1.2 The *Iter Thomisticum*

Aquinas underpins and unifies his entire philosophical system with insights and conclusions about being. These trace a broad path, the *iter thomisticum*, extending from being as the first object of the human intellect[1] to the infinite and self-subsistent being.[2] Aquinas investigates the multifarious aspects of being in over one hundred works amounting to tens of thousands of pages,[3] which over the course of seven and one half centuries have generated innumerable Thomistic interpretations, commentaries, and elaborations.[4]

For Aquinas, the investigation of being begins with the apprehension of material things through the senses.[5] He investigates the proper objects of the "special sciences," or branches of philosophy: being in matter and motion for physics, being that is the quantification of things for mathematics, being that is the origin of all things for rational theology,[6] and so forth for philosophical anthropology, theory of knowledge,[7] philosophical logic,[8] ethics,[9] political theory,[10] and aesthetics.[11] He investigates being that all natural things receive as their actuality, primarily substances, and derivatively, their components, principles, and causes,[12] as well as being that is the proper object of the universal science.[13] Finally, he investigates being in its purest and infinite form, the self-subsistent being from which all other beings come.[14]

Despite the centrality of the consideration of being in his thought, and the evidence of the path along which this consideration develops in his great synthetic works, the *Summa theologiae* and *Summa contra Gentiles*, Aquinas provides no dedicated exposition of the *iter thomisticum*. His "metaphysical primer" *On Being and Essence*, for example, largely focuses on the ontological role of essence in the various kinds of substances. Moreover, his more comprehensive *Commentary on Aristotle's Metaphysics*, which addresses a wider array of his doctrines about being, nonetheless obscures the continuity of the *iter thomisticum* by following the somewhat haphazard order of presentation devised by Aristotle's posthumous editors. While the Thomistic contribution to this book endeavors to draw attention to this continuity, it cannot, within the alloted space, present a comprehensive account of the *iter thomisticum*.

1.3 Goals and Limits

The goal of this book is nothing more or less than to provoke dialogue among three philosophical traditions about their points of divergence on the question of being. Since much of Aquinas's all-encompassing treatment of being only indirectly concerns these points of divergence, the present chapter focuses on two topics in Aquinas's philosophy of being that it takes to be most relevant to this goal. With respect to the Continental Tradition's rejection of the possibility of knowing reality in itself (noumenon), it presents Aquinas's doctrine on the objectivity and ontological value of knowledge. With respect to the Analytic Tradition's rejection of the coherence of discourse about being and existence, it presents Aquinas's doctrine concerning the distinction of mind-dependent being from mind-independent finite being, and from infinite being, which is the ultimate foundation of all being.

By limiting its focus in this way, this chapter provides contemporary readers with the freedom to evaluate these fundamental points of divergence while bracketing Thomistic doctrines aimed at what is arguably the central concern of Aquinas's thought, the divine. Thus, a comprehensive account of Aquinas's philosophy of being, or even a précis of its principal doctrines, doctrines of paramount importance to a general view of his philosophy, falls outside the scope of this chapter.[15] This chapter does not provide, for example, an account of Aquinas's proofs for the existence of God,[16] or of his doctrine of analogy, which he marshals in defense of the possibility of discourse about God.[17] It only briefly addresses Aquinas's account of the participation of finite beings in their common metaphysical principle, and the relation between finite and infinite being.[18]

Given the distinctive goal of this book, the present chapter purposefully avoids a casual juxtaposition of doctrines from different traditions for the sake of a general comparison. Rather, by focusing on specific Thomistic doctrines concerning the objectivity of knowledge and the coherence of discourse about being and existence, this chapter aims to remove obstacles to dialogue with other traditions, and thereby to prompt readers in other traditions to seek out a broader knowledge of the Thomistic philosophy of being.

An adequate presentation of the doctrines treated in this chapter nonetheless requires contextualization within the general structure of Aquinas's philosophy of being. Consequently, after these introductory remarks, this chapter embarks on a general review of relevant Thomistic doctrines. It provides an account of what Aquinas means by the term "being," of knowledge as the mental possession of reality, of the objective and subjective aspects of knowledge, and of the distinction between mind-independent, mind-dependent being, being as received actuality, and being that subsists in itself. More specifically, Section 2, "Being and the Predication of *Being*," indicates the basic definitions, applications, and distinctions, necessary for a general comprehension of Aquinas's philosophy of being and, in particular, of his doctrines concerning the objectivity of our knowledge and the coherence of discourse about being and existence. Section 3, "Our Knowledge of Being," then takes up Aquinas's doctrines concerning the objectivity and ontological value of our knowledge of reality, which rely on his defense of the indubitable being of awareness, and the nature of the relation between the knowing subject and the object known. Section 4, "Being That Constitutes Something in Reality and Being That Does Not," takes up Aquinas's doctrines concerning the coherence of discourse about being and existence, which rely on his defense of the real distinction between a thing's essence and its being, and on the necessity for finite things to participate in being.

1.4 The Middle Path

The history of philosophy is an oscillation between perennial objectivizing and subjectivizing tendencies. The pre-Socratic physicists, for example, looked for the objective cause of things underlying the world of change, without, however, thoroughly considering the impact of the knowing subject on the objects known. By contrast, the Sophists, skeptical of the existence of such an objective cause, or at least of their prospects for knowing it, shifted their attention to an exploration of the nature and subjective projections of the knower. Socrates first recognized that an account of reality must take into consideration both the objective and the subjective pole of knowledge. His quest to obtain definitions for the objects of his inquiries reflects the conviction that an account of a known object cannot be divorced from an account of the subject's mode of knowing.

On the one hand, a perennial tendency to diminish the distinction between reality in itself and reality as known leads to a hyperbolic estimate of the mind's powers of creation. Generally, by adopting a methodology that conflates the object known with the knowing subject, philosophy in the Continental Tradition fails to recognize a fundamental logical and metaphysical requirement of rational inquiry: The mind can apprehend and measure its object only if it is in a relation with that object, and thus is distinct from it. Knowledge is determined not only by the psychological assimilation of mind and object, but also by their logico-metaphysical distinction.

On the other hand, a perennial tendency to exaggerate the distinction between reality in itself and reality as known leads to a hyperbolic estimate of the mind's powers of discovery. Generally, by adopting a methodology that isolates the object known from the knowing subject, philosophy in the Analytic Tradition, fails to recognize the inevitable psychological requirements of rational inquiry. The mind can apprehend and measure an object only if it is in a relation with that object, and thus, assimilates to it. Knowledge is determined not only by the logico-metaphysical distinction of mind and object, but also by their psychological assimilation.

As will be shown in the concluding chapter of this book, Aquinas defends against hyperbolic subjectivism and objectivism by explaining the proper role of subject and object in the foundation of knowledge. The *iter thomisticum* steers a middle path between errors to which other philosophical traditions fall prey.

1.5 The School of Thought

Aquinas's philosophical system has been the subject of centuries of continuous commentary and elaboration, produced by numerous schools of Thomism, beginning with his immediate successors.[19] The school favored in this chapter may roughly speaking be designated as "Scholastic Thomism." This tradition is rooted in the medieval *studium* at the convent of Santa Sabina in Rome founded in 1222, at which Aquinas himself taught from 1265 to 1268. It also identifies with Dominican commentators and manualists of the renaissance such as Tommaso de Vio Caetano (1469–1534) and João Poinsot (1589–1644), better known as John of St. Thomas. Following the general decline of Scholasticism and the birth of Modern philosophy, Scholastic Thomism begins to show signs of rebirth in the second half of the eighteenth century, beginning with Salvatore Roselli (1722–1784) at the Dominican *studium* of Naples and Collegio San Tommaso in Rome, and later with Vincenzo Buzzetti (1777–1824) at the Collegio Alberoni of Piacenza. This rebirth becomes especially self-conscious after the 1879 encyclical *Aeterni Patris* of Leo XIII calls for the renewal of Thomism.[20] At the Pontifical *Gregorian* and *Angelicum* Universities of Rome, the renewal flourishes under the likes of Giovanni Maria Cornoldi (1822–1892), Guido Mattiussi (1852–1925), Édouard Hugon (1867–1929), Martin Grabmann (1875–1949), Réginald Garrigou-Lagrange (1877–1964), Santiago Ramirez (1891–1967), and Cornelio Fabro (1911–1995). These scholars produce critical editions, groundbreaking commentaries on the thought and originality of Aquinas, and manifestos including "The 24 Theses," which aims to codify Thomism's essential contents.[21]

Scholastic Thomism contrasts with other Thomist Traditions, each having a unique tendency to emphasize different aspects of Aquinas's thought. These include Existential Thomism, River Forest Thomism, Lublin Thomism, Transcendental Thomism, and Analytical Thomism. While I am unaware of any comprehensive historiography of Thomism, or of any comprehensive evaluation of these traditions,[22] I think it relevant to note at least Scholastic Thomism's tendency toward a generally non-historical and hermeneutically neutral reading of Aquinas's texts. It aims to elucidate Aquinas's timeless doctrines and arguments concerning the philosophy of being rather than to consider their historical development and contextualization.

1.6 The Question Treated

Most scholars versed in Aquinas's philosophical thought readily recognize the prominent position that his metaphysics has in the history of philosophy. Among these, however, only some appreciate Aquinas's unique contribution to the development of metaphysics, and fewer sufficiently distinguish his metaphysics from his philosophical theology. These are some of the problems encountered in attempting to identify the fundamental question treated in his philosophy of being. The present section identifies this question, and indicates how Thomists have neglected the doctrines concerning objectivity and coherence noted in Section 1.3 in responding to the Continental and Analytic Traditions.

Missing from the "24 Theses," for example, is an explicit defense of the claim that we can objectively know reality in itself. This omission seems to imply that the claim is inessential to core Thomism. Thus, it tacitly licenses philosophers in the Continental Tradition to employ a hyperbolically subjective "transcendental" methodology. Continental philosophy of being uses this methodology to drive a wedge between being, understood as the actuality of phenomena, and the principle of non-contradiction, thereby freeing phenomena from the dictates of logic.

To the contrary, arguments of early revival Thomists, such as Roselli's argument concerning the being of sensory awareness as the "criterion of truth," aim to refute the hyperbolic subjectivizing claims of great Modern philosophers such as David Hume (1711–1776) and Immanuel Kant

(1724–1804).²³ Following Roselli's lead, the present chapter aims to demonstrate how the being of awareness, and in particular, the actualization of what in the intellect represents the object's nature, is the foundation of the objective knowledge of reality in itself, and not merely of phenomena.

Also missing from "The 24 Theses" is an explicit defense of the necessarily subjective aspect of knowledge. This omission similarly seems to imply that the Thomistic "reception dictum,"²⁴ that whatever the human intellect apprehends, it apprehends according to the intellect's subjective mode of apprehending, is inessential to core Thomism. Thus, it tacitly licenses philosophers in the Analytic Tradition to employ a hyperbolically objective "mathematical" methodology. Analytic philosophy weilds this methodology in ways that conflate being and existence, thereby undermining the coherence of discourse about what there is.

To the contrary, the Thomistic doctrine of the mutual epistemic determination of subject and object presented in this chapter aims to refute the hyperbolically objectivizing claims of great Analytic philosophers such as Gottlob Frege (1848–1925) and Bertrand Russell (1872–1970). In light of the Thomistic doctrine of reception, the present chapter defends the Thomistic perspective of diverse modes of being in order to vindicate the coherence of philosophical discourse about being and existence.

Thomistic philosophy of being poses the ontological question in two Anglo-Saxon monosyllables, "What is?" As will be shown below, this approach to ontology contrasts with the Analytic Tradition. Willard Van Orman Quine (1908–2000), for example, poses the question in three Anglo-Saxon monosyllables, "What is there?"²⁵ From the Thomist perspective, what is there corresponds to what *exists*, or being that is independent of the mind, as opposed to being that is dependent on the mind. Consequently, it is possible to coherently predicate *existence* of some beings and not of others.

As will also be shown below, the Thomistic approach to ontology contrasts with the Continental Tradition. Immanuel Kant, for example, poses the ontological question in over 800 pages²⁶ which, addresses the fundamental question, "What is appearance?" From the Thomist perspective, the logic of appearance necessarily involves a relation between that which appears and that to whom it appears. The ontological distinction of the subjective and the objective poles of knowledge vindicates the doctrine of the objectivity of knowledge. It then remains for the knowing subject to interpret the contents of cognition as corresponding to either a mind-dependent or mind-independent object.

1.7 The Interpretation Given

As indicated above in Section 1.3, this chapter's presentation of Aquinas's philosophy of being is intentionally limited in scope to doctrines concerned with substantiating two claims: first, that we know something of reality in and of itself, and second, that it is perfectly coherent to speak of beings that exist and of beings that do not exist. In order to bring Thomistic, Continental, and Analytic philosophy of being into dialogue, this chapter focuses on the Thomistic rationale for these two claims.

Aquinas, like Aristotle before him, never explicitly evaluates the need to defend the objectivity of knowledge or the coherence of discourse about being and existence. Awareness of such a need does not arise, given the multifaceted structure of reality that emerges from the analysis of the psychological process of knowing. Neither Aristotle nor Aquinas foresees the hyperbolic subjectivism of modern skepticism or the hyperbolic objectivism of modern science.

The concluding chapter of this book takes up the task evaluation. Recognizing that every evaluation presumes an interpretation, this section of the present chapter has aimed to introduce the reader to the scholastic interpretation and evaluation of three philosophies of being. Continental philosophy of being contrives to address the ontological question entirely from within the boundaries of subjectivity, minimizing the ontological distinction of the known from the knower, as though a logical account of the actuality of phenomena did not demand their ontological distinction. Analytic philosophy of being contrives to immunize truth and objectivity from all subjective influence, as though the knower could apprehend its object apart from its subjective mode of apprehending. Thomistic philosophy of being steers a middle course between these extremes by admitting the objective and subjective poles of knowledge.

We can answer the ontological question "What is?" only in the context of the question "By what process can we know what is?" According to the Thomistic account of this process, every object of knowledge requires that ultimately some object of knowledge is ontologically distinct from the knowing subject, so that in every mental apprehension we grasp something of reality in itself. This account also shows that every object of knowledge assimilates to the knower's intellect, so that the intellect receives the undeniable objective evidence of being, according to the intellect's mode of receiving.

§2 Being and the Predication of *Being*

This section of the present chapter indicates some of the basic definitions, applications, and distinctions common in the Thomist philosophy of being.

2.1 Two Terms for Being

Aquinas employs two different terms for two distinct meanings that correspond to the single English noun *being*. First and most broadly, he employs the Medieval Latin noun *ens, entis*[27] for anything that signifies the truth of a statement.[28] Given that what signifies the truth of a statement is the affirmation of a fact, or what is the case, by means of the verb *to be* (*esse*),[29] Aquinas acknowledges that anything to which we apply the verb *to be* is a being of some sort.

Aquinas also affirms that we apply the term *being* in virtue of something that has the act of the verb *to be* (*actus essendi*),[30] or *exists*. We apply the term *being* to something either because it has the act of the verb *to be* (exists), or because it depends ontologically on what has this act. Section 3.6 below discusses Aquinas's treatment of the objectivity of our knowledge of things to which we apply this verb. Section 4.4 discusses Aquinas's treatment of the *actus essendi*. Examples of Aquinas's use of the noun *being* include:

> A substance is a being (*ens*) per se.[31]
> The first act is the cause of every being (*entis*) in act.[32]
> The good, which is convertible with being (*ente*), is common to every being (*enti*).[33]
> Whatsoever is in potency is reduced to act by a being (*ens*) in act.[34]
> Some things are called beings (*entia*) that have no essence.[35]

Second and in a more restricted way, Aquinas employs the Medieval Latin verbal noun *esse, essendi*[36] to name the act of the verb *to be* (*esse*) taken as a being in the previous sense. Examples of his use of this verbal noun include:

The actuality of a substance or essence is its being (*esse*).[37]
To be made implies the beginning of being (*essendi*).[38]
Every essence can be understood without understanding anything about its being (*esse*).[39]
Cause is prior to effect in being (*in essendo*).[40]
A creature's potentiality to be (*ad essendum*) is merely receptive.[41]

The act of the verb *to be* is a being in the previous sense because we apply the term *being* to it in virtue of something that exists.

Although the two terms that Aquinas uses for the single English noun *being* have distinct meanings, in both cases he uses the terms to attribute entity to something, so that being in either case is the principle of entity.

2.2 Two Modes of Being and of Predicating *Being*

Among things to which we apply the verb *to be*, Aquinas distinguishes two fundamental ways, or "modes" of being. The first mode concerns what we apply the verb to most properly. This mode of being Aquinas calls *real being* (*ens reale*) since it constitutes something in reality.[42] Real being includes not only substances, which have the act of the verb to be (*actus essendi*), but also their characteristics, their principles, their causes, and their potentialities, whose being depends on the being of substance. Thus, respectively we say, for example,

> "Chalk is a substance."
> "One of its characteristics is whiteness."
> "One of its principles is calcite."
> "Its cause in nature is the accumulation under pressure of marine animal shells."
> "One of its potentialities is to mark slate."
> Section 4 of the present chapter treats real being.

The second mode of being that Aquinas distinguishes concerns what we apply the verb *to be* to because of its relation to the mind. This mode of being Aquinas calls *being of reason* (*ens rationis*) since it does not exist independently, but rather, depends ontologically on the being of the mind. Being of reason includes privations, negations of sentences, impossible objects, and the like. Thus, respectively we say, for example:

"The privation of sight called 'blindness' is in the eye."
"Negation is the opposite of affirmation."
"Round squares are impossible objects."[43]
Section 4 of the present chapter also treats being of reason.

To these two ontological modes of being correspond two distinct linguistic modes of predicating. When a sentence predicates something of a subject, it indicates that the ontological correlate of its subject in some way is the ontological correlate of its predicate.[44] Moreover, Aquinas affirms that the ontological modes of being and the linguistic modes of predicating are proportional to each other.[45] When, for example, a sentence predicates real being of Everest, the sentence indicates that Everest is something by way of its own mind-independent being, or existence. Similarly, when a sentence predicates being of reason of blindness, the sentence indicates that blindness is something, not by way of having mind-independent being, but by way of the being of an existing mind that acknowledges the absence of the power of sight that an eye normally possesses. As the being of Everest is to mind-independence, so the being of blindness is to mind-dependence.

§3 Our Knowledge of Being

This section addresses some aspects of Aquinas's philosophy of being that are especially relevant to theoretical developments in the Continental philosophical tradition regarding the objectivity and ontological value of knowledge. They include: (1) the self-evident nature of being, (2) the priority of being in the logical order, (3) the priority of being in the psychological order, (4) the first principles of reason, (5) the intellect's proper object, (6) the objective knowledge of being, and (7) the formal identity of the knower and the known.

3.1 The Knowledge of Being Is Self-Evident

For Aquinas, a statement is self-evident if the meaning (*ratio*)[46] of its predicate is already included in the meaning of its subject.[47] When we say, for example, "A snub nose is concave," the meaning of the predicate *concave* is already included in the meaning of its subject *snub nose*.⁴⁸ When we say, "Man is an animal," the meaning of the predicate *animal* is already included in the meaning of the subject *man*.⁴⁹ These statements are self-evident in the sense that if we do not already know that a snub nose is concave, then we do not know what a snub nose is; and if we do not already know that man is an animal, then we do not know what man is.

Moreover, for Aquinas, whatever the intellect apprehends, it apprehends as a being (*ens*),⁵⁰ and it attributes to it the meaning of the term *being* (*ratio entis*).⁵¹ For example, the intellect always attributes the meaning of the term *being* to a statement's subject, whether that subject is a mind-dependent being or a mind-independent being.⁵² Therefore, any statement that predicates of its subject that it is a being has the meaning of that predicate already included in the meaning of its subject, and is self-evident.

As Aquinas carefully notes, the term *being* cannot signify whether a thing actually exists independently of the mind:

> Although every finite verb implies being, for "to run" is "to be running," and every infinite verb implies nonbeing, for "to non-run" is "to be non-running," nevertheless no verb signifies the whole, i.e., a thing is or a thing is not. ... Hence, "is" [est] said by itself does not signify what is or is not. ... Being is nothing other than that which is. And thus we see that it signifies both a thing, when I say "that which," and existence [esse] when I say "is" [est]. If the word "being" [ens] as signifying a thing having existence were to signify existence [esse] principally, without a doubt it would signify that a thing exists. But the word "being" [ens] does not principally signify the composition that is implied in saying "is" [est]; rather, it signifies with composition inasmuch as it signifies the thing having existence. ... No verb signifies that a thing exists or does not exist, since "is" said by itself does not signify that a thing exists, although it signifies existence.⁵³

To recognize that the meaning of the term *being* (the *ratio entis*) is included in the meaning of a statement's subject does not make evident whether the ontological correlate of that subject, which is an object present to the mind, has being independently of the mind. Consequently, a Thomistic defense of the existential value of the knowledge of being must derive from a source other than the self-evident nature of statements about being.

3.2 Priority in the Logical Order

For Aquinas, the meaning (*ratio*) of the term *being* is included in the meaning of any intellectual conception whatsoever. He expresses this by saying that this meaning is "logically prior" to any other intellectual conception.[54] Because of this logical priority, Aquinas says that all other conceptions of the intellect resolve logically into the conception of *being*, and generate by adding other rational content to that conception.[55]

3.3 Priority in the Psychological Order

As noted in Section 2.1 above, Aquinas uses the term *being* for anything that signifies the truth of a statement, since that truth is the affirmation by means of the verb *to be* of what is the case. Everything to which we apply the verb *to be* is a being of some sort since it in some way receives the act of the verb *to be* (*actus essendi*). Consequently, whatever we conceive, we always conceive of as a being of some sort,[56] whether a real being or a being of reason. Being is the principle of intelligibility. Aquinas indicates this by saying that whatever we conceive is conceivable inasmuch as it is in act.[57]

Moreover, for Aquinas, whatever psychological operations are necessary for conceiving of a being are also necessary for every other intellectual conception. Aquinas expresses this claim by saying that the intellectual conception of being has "psychological priority" to any other intellectual conception. This necessary psychological priority of the conception of being, however, should be carefully distinguished from the psychological priority of particular conceptions occurring in the mental genesis of a given person.[58]

3.4 The First Principles of Reason

For Aquinas, since the meaning (*ratio*) of the term *being* is prior in the logical order to any other meaning, this meaning is the foundation of what in the scholastic tradition are known as the "first principles of reason."[59] We derive fundamental logical principles such as the principle of non-contradiction, that something cannot both be and not be at the same time and in the same sense, from the opposition of *being* with its opposite, *nonbeing*.[60] Aquinas notes that because of the priority of *being* in the psychological order, anyone who apprehends anything psychologically understands this principle.[61] Aquinas further notes that by applying the principles of reason to sense-based knowledge, we may draw conclusions about the existence of beings not apprehended through the senses.[62]

3.5 The Intellect's Proper Object

By the term *object*, Aquinas indicates what a knowing subject apprehends by means of some capacity or "faculty" for knowing. By the term *subject*, he means that to whom an object is mentally present through some faculty. For Aquinas, the distinction between a knowing subject and the knowledge that this subject possesses is comparable to the distinction between a faculty for knowing and an object that is known.[63] Aquinas expresses this relation by saying that the "proportion" between a knowing subject and a knowable object is like that between a faculty for knowing and that object.[64]

By the expression *proper object* Aquinas means the object under whose *ratio* the subject apprehends anything else by means of that faculty.[65] Color, for example, is the proper object of the faculty of sight since no other faculty apprehends color, and sight apprehends nothing except under the *ratio* of color.

Since being is the first thing that the intellect apprehends, in both the logical and psychological orders, it is the object under whose *ratio* the intellect knows anything else, or the possible differences and species of being.[66] It follows that being is the proper object of the intellect.[67] Moreover, since for Aquinas the bodily senses are the foundation of all knowledge,[68] the proper object of the human intellect in its union with the body is the being of material objects.[69]

3.6 Objective Knowledge of Being

A Thomistic defense of the objectivity of knowledge and of the sense object's existential independence of the mind centers around Aquinas's treatment of three related topics: (1) the process of simple apprehension, (2) the relation between subject and object, and (3) the individuation of material objects.

3.6.1 *Simple Apprehension and the Range of Intellectual Knowledge*

Through the process of simple apprehension, the human intellect forms a concept of a material object by gathering knowledge of the object's essential characteristics through the senses.[70] We call this process *simple* because it grasps a single concept corresponding to an object, and not a complex of concepts, such as in a judgment. We call this process *apprehension* because through it the intellect mentally grasps the object's essence (*essentia*), or that through which it has its being. Aquinas further notes that the object's essence corresponds to a thing's operations, in virtue of which we say it has a *nature*. Essence corresponds to what makes a thing intelligible, in virtue of which we call it *form*. Essence corresponds to a thing's definition because it determines what a thing is.[71]

An account of simple apprehension must explain how from material reality there can arise immaterial knowledge of that reality in the mind of the knower. Simple apprehension moves in three general phases, from the intellect's passive reception of material impact of the object known, to the intellect's activity of dematerializing and activating this passively received material notification, and to the intellect's passive reception of the dematerialized and activated notification.[72]

The first phase of simple apprehension begins with the material impact of a sensory object on the material sense organs. An object's susceptibility of being apprehended intellectually, its *potential intelligibility*, is conveyed through the first stage of simple apprehension, from the material impact on the sense organs to the external part of the intellect, the *external senses*. Each external sense receives notification of certain aspects, or *species*, of the material object's potential intelligibility, according to the sense's proper object. For example, the sense of sight receives species relating to color, the sense of hearing receives species of sound, and so forth.[73] Specified in this way, the material object's potential intelligibility is conveyed to the material intellect and to the internal senses. The first of these internal senses, the *common sense*, receives the species from the individual external sense organs as simultaneous and coordinated. The *imagination* receives the species as a sign, or *phantasm* of the object's essence. The *estimative intellect* receives the species as a preliminary account of the object's essence. The *memory* receives the species as a potentially intelligible record of the estimate of the object's essence.

The second phase of simple apprehension consists of the intellect's dematerializing and actualizing activity. The species conveyed from the external to the internal senses is potentially, but not actually intelligible. If the process of simple apprehension is to result in an actually intelligible concept, then the intellect must possess some faculty that dematerializes the imagination's phantasm, thereby making it actually intelligible. This faculty addresses the potentially intelligible species corresponding to the material conditions of the phantasm, rendering them immaterial and actually intelligible. Aquinas calls this faculty the *agent intellect* because it is the only active faculty of the intellect.[74]

The third phase of simple apprehension consists of the passive reception of the now-dematerialized and actualized phantasm by the *potential intellect*. Through the process of simple apprehension, the potential intellect becomes an actualized universal concept or, *mental word*, corresponding to the object's essence.

Given the results of simple apprehension, the agent intellect may also recombine stored phantasms through memory and imagination. In this way, the intellect can generate new phantasms of objects that it never apprehends directly through the senses, thereby expanding its range of potentially intelligible phantasms and universal concepts. Moreover, the intellect's faculty of reason may employ the phantasms in the intellect to determine the necessary or impossible existential independence from the mind, of objects for which it is not able to contrive phantasms, such as God[75] and contradictory objects, respectively. Through the process of simple apprehension and through the subsidiary use of the intellect's faculties, Aquinas is able to account for the full range of human intellectual knowledge.[76]

The knowledge derived from successive simple apprehensions of the same object, while progressively specific, remains universal in nature.[77] The intellect never knows the individual directly,[78] since through simple apprehension, the intellect knows directly only a universal concept corresponding to the object's essence.[79] Through rational reflection on the process of simple apprehension, however, the intellect is able to determine the individuality and existential status of the object known, as the remaining sections of this chapter endeavor to show.[80]

3.6.2 *The Relation between Subject and Object*

For Aquinas, knowledge requires a relation between a knowing subject and an object known. Evaluating his position on the objectivity of knowledge requires considering both the subjective and objective poles of this relation. In particular, with respect to the universal concept resulting from simple apprehension, it is necessary to distinguish *formal value*, which conveys the essence of the object known, and *objective value*, which attests to its ontological distinction from the knowing subject.

Regarding the *formal value* of the universal concept formed in simple apprehension, Aquinas recognizes the general principle that whatever is received is received according to the mode of the receiver.[81] In simple apprehension, the knowing subject receives notification of the object's essence through the reception of potentially intelligible species. To the extent that the species are received according to the intellect's mode of receiving, however, the universal concept of the object is subjective. For this reason, the formal value of knowledge through the apprehension of species from material objects, while a direct result of simple apprehension, constitutes a representation of the object's essence, rather than a direct presentation of it to the intellect.[82]

Regarding the *objective value* of the universal concept formed in simple apprehension, Aquinas holds that the object known is a singular individual whose being is distinct from that of the knowing subject. Knowledge of the object's individuality and existential independence from the knowing subject is in no way conditioned by the knowing subject's mode of receiving the potentially intelligible species that constitute the phantasm, and thus does not constitute a representation of the object's being, but rather a direct presentation of that being to the intellect.

The basis of the individuality and existential independence of the object is not the actualization of the phantasm in its passage from potential to actual intelligibility, since that actualization derives from the actuality of the intellect and not from the object.[83] Rather, knowledge of the object's individuality and existential independence of the knowing subject derives from the actual presentation of the phantasm to the intellect, as will now be shown.

3.6.3 Knowledge of the Material Object's Individuality

As characterized in the previous section, intellectual knowledge derived directly from simple apprehension is universal in nature. By contrast, the principle of an object's individuation, according to Aquinas, is the quantitatively measurable matter underlying its material accidents, which make the object numerically distinct within a species.[84] This individuating matter, however, is not a principle of cognition, since the immaterial intellect cannot apprehend quantitatively measurable matter, but only abstractions from it. Consequently, Aquinas reasons that the intellect cannot know the individual directly through simple apprehension.[85]

Aquinas recognizes that the intellect, through the senses and imagination, has direct foreknowledge of a material individual object, since the senses and imagination receive the potentially intelligible species from the impression made on the sense organs by the individual material object.[86] Sensation and imagination, however, are not knowledge properly speaking.[87]

For Aquinas, we know the individual object only by referring the universal concept of the object to the particularity of the intelligible species received in sensation. The intellect understands the object as an individual only indirectly, by reflecting on the role of the intelligible species and phantasm in simple apprehension. Through the phantasm, the intellect apprehends the simultaneity and coordination of species corresponding to an individual object.[88] Because the phantasm exhibits this unity and coordination of species, the intellect knows indirectly that the actually intelligible universal concept corresponds to an individual object.[89]

3.6.4 Knowledge of the Existentially Independent Object

In the process of simple apprehension, in order for the intellect to apprehend an essence it must turn to an actually present phantasm. Since, for Aquinas, operation follows being, an object's existential independence from the knowing subject follows from the being of the phantasm that is actually present to the intellect.[90] If there were no phantasm actually present to the intellect, there would be no knowledge. The evidence of the phantasm in this instance cannot be a feature of the object's essence, since the intellect must turn to an actually present phantasm, and not merely to the representation of one.[91] Moreover, the actual presence of the phantasm is distinct from the actualization of the phantasm in its passage from potential to actual intelligibility, since the intellect must have something actually present that is potentially intelligible.[92]

As noted above, however,[93] the intellect may recombine stored phantasms through memory and imagination, so that it can generate phantasms of objects that it never apprehends directly through the senses. A phantasm actually present to the intellect may derive either directly from an act of simple apprehension of real being, or from such recombination and apprehension of a being of reason.[94]

In any particular instance, the intellect's judgment concerning the existential dependence or independence of a particular object may be correct or incorrect, as common experience bears out. It is not possible, however, that all acts of knowledge have as their ultimate foundation anything but objects that are existentially independent of the knowing subject. For any given phantasm, either it is the direct result of simple apprehension, in which case it is the phantasm of an existentially independent object, or it is the product of the recollection and recombination of potentially intelligible species received in simple apprehension. In either case the indubitable evidence of a phantasm's actual presence to the intellect ensures the ultimate foundation of our knowledge of reality in itself.

3.7 The Formal Identity of the Knower and the Known

As noted above,[95] in light of the subjective and objective aspects of simple apprehension, a material object's phantasm simultaneously represents an object's essence to the intellect, and presents its being to the intellect as the actuality of the potentially intelligible phantasm. When the agent intellect actualizes the phantasm, the existentially distinct knowing subject and the object known become formally identical, since, when the intellect abstracts the object's form, the intellect's actuality is nothing other than the immaterial actualization of this abstracted form. Reflection on simple apprehension shows that the potentially intelligible phantasm abstracted from the material object is simultaneously *that by which* it understands the being of the object and *that which* represents the object's likeness.[96]

The formal identity of known and knower justifies the intellect's actualization of the phantasm as the universal concept of an individual object that is existentially independent from the knowing subject. Not only is a thing knowable because it is in act,[97] but everything that the intellectual knows, the intellect is, formally.[98] The being of the object is formally identical with the being of the intellect.[99]

§4 Being That Constitutes Something in Reality and Being That Does Not

As noted above, for Aquinas the term *being* applies most broadly, to whatever signifies the truth of a sentence.[100] Most properly, however, the term is employed for real being (*ens reale*), as opposed to being of reason (*ens rationis*), since only real being constitutes something in reality existing independently of the mind.[101] The present section addresses some aspects of real being as they are treated by Aquinas, which are especially relevant to subsequent theoretical developments in the Analytical philosophical tradition concerning the logical coherence of discourse about being and existence. These aspects include: (1) the distinction between actual and potential being, (2) the nature of substance and accidents, (3) the relationship between a thing's being and its essence, (4) the participation of essence in being as substantial act, and (5) being that does not constitute something in reality.

4.1 Actual and Potential Being

In order to explain the reality of motion and change of things that have being independently of the mind, Aquinas invokes real explanatory factors beyond the fact of the being of a thing. The capacity of a thing to be other than it is does not derive from its actual being, much less from nonbeing.[102] In addition, Aquinas recognizes the real potential of a thing to be other than it is.[103] Accordingly, he divides every genus of being into actual being and potential being.[104]

> Every genus is divided by potency and act. Now potency and act, since they are among the first differences of being, are naturally prior to motion, and it is these that the Philosopher uses to define motion. Consider, therefore,

that something is in act only, something is in potency only, something else is midway between potency and act. What is in potency only is not yet being moved; what is already in perfect act is not being moved but has already been moved. Consequently, that is being moved which is midway between pure potency and act, which is partly in potency and partly in act—as is evident in alteration.[105]

For Aquinas, act, in and of itself, is unlimited. Potency is the principle of limitation on act. Thus, whatever possesses the act of being, either is pure act or arises because potency limits its act of being, as the coalesence of first and intrinsic principles.[106] Things that are in potency are between pure non-being and being in act.[107]

A finite act of being is limited through its composition with potency. Finite beings are multiple and have restricted natures or essences that participate in being.[108] They are contingent and undergo mutation and movement.[109] Motion and mutation are real beings, but not complete in themselves since they do not have their own acts of being. They are a way for finite beings to become complete.[110] Examples of generation and corruption are also real inasmuch as they are necessary for the development of substances or accidents. They are beings in a secondary sense compared to substances, since they have being only by inhering in substances, and since they are accounted for only in relation to privation and negation, which are mind-dependent beings of reason (*ens rationis*).[111] The more ways that a thing is in act, the greater is its actual being, since it has less potential being.[112]

An act of being that is infinite, by contrast, is simple, and pure being, since it is unlimited by any potency. Moreover, it is unique, since there would be no way to distinguish it from any other such being.[113] Such being does not exist in nature, but is divine.[114]

For Aquinas, a thing's potential relates to the thing's formal specifications or essence, which determines its actual or potential accidents.[115] With respect to what a thing actually becomes, act is posterior to potency since what it is not and what it is potentially are prior to the being of what it may become.[116] In the more fundamental sense of a thing's act of being (*actus essendi*), however, act is prior to potency since potency, though real in that it is necessary for the development of substance and accident, does not have its own act of being, but depends on the act of being of something existing independently of the mind.[117] Section 4.3 further treats this fundamental act of being (*actus essendi*) in relation to a thing's essence.

4.2 Substance and Accidents

In addition to actuality and potentiality, Aquinas recognizes other general modes in which real things have being. In this, he follows Aristotle's ten categories of *substance* and nine *accidents*.[118]

4.2.1 *Substances and the Predication of Terms for Substances*

Substances include things such as Socrates, Mount Zion, the sun, and the like. They are the most real things since they are the primary possessors of being, and serve as the ontological foundation of every other kind of being.[119] Non-substantial real being does not have its own being, but depends on the being of substance. Substances are the ontological foundation of both mind-independent accidents that are actual, such as the actual temperature of the sun, and mind-independent accidents that are merely potential, such as the real potential of an acorn to become an oak tree.

Substances are also the epistemological foundation of all non-substantial being. It is in virtue of the being of substances that their related dependent non-substantial beings are knowable.

This is so of real non-substantial beings, such as the real accidents *tallness* and *heaviness*, and of mind-dependent non-substantial beings, such as the privation *blindness*, and the impossible object *round square*. This is so since the proper object of the intellect is being.[120]

Substances are both ontologically and logically independent of every other kind of being. They are ontologically independent in the sense that they exist in their own right independently of other beings.[121] They are not communicable to other things, since they are neither present in anything else as depending on it for its being, nor predicable of anything else as depending on it for its being. Socrates, for example, is neither present in anything else, like shortness or wisdom is present in Socrates, nor predicable of anything, like *man* or *Athenian* is predicable of Socrates. Substances are complete, or undivided in themselves in the sense that they are not missing anything required for their independent existence, but divided from each other as individuals.¹²² They agree with each other in that they possess the same kinds of characteristics while remaining distinct from each other.¹²³ Aquinas also uses the Latin term *res* to mean *thing* in the sense of a real being that is a substance.¹²⁴

Substances are logically independent in the sense that their denoting terms include in their meaning that they exist in their own right, since they are neither present in any other being nor predicable of any other being.¹²⁵ The term *Socrates*, for example, includes in its meaning that Socrates exists in his own right. The term *Socrates* does not denote anything present in anything else, like the term *wise* denotes what is present in Socrates, nor is it predicable of anything, like the term *man* is predicable of Socrates.

4.2.2 Accidents and the Predication of Terms for Accidents

For Aquinas, accidents are real features of substances. They include features such as those listed in Aristotle's most general categories of being:

> of quantity: four-foot, five-foot; of qualification: white, grammatical; of a relative: double, half, larger; of where: in the Lyceum, in the market-place; of when: yesterday, last-year; of being-in-a-position: is-lying, is-sitting; of having: has-shoes-on, has-armor-on; of doing: cutting, burning; of being-affected: being-cut, being-burned.¹²⁶

Accidents are real beings inasmuch as they are positive features of substances, but are a weaker or secondary kind of being than substances, since they are not beings in their own right but require substance as their foundation in being.¹²⁷

Accidents are ontologically dependent in the sense that they do not have being in their own right, but derive their existence from the existence of the substances in which they are present.¹²⁸ Shortness and wisdom, for example, are features that are present in Socrates and depend on Socrates's existence for their reality.

Although what has being accidentally is greater in number than substance,¹²⁹ what is accidentally reduces to what has being in its own right, since it has being after substance.¹³⁰ For example, the accidents *doing* and *being effected*, which Aquinas calls *act* and *potency*, have being after the act of being of a substance (*actus essendi*).

Accidents are logically dependent on substances in the sense that their denoting terms include in their meaning that accidents depend on being present in substances for their being. The term *short*, for example, includes in its meaning that shortness depends on being present in a substance such as Socrates for its reality to the extent that Socrates is short.

4.3 The Relation between Being and Essence

According to Aquinas we can recognize that the real beings revealed in cognition exhibit an ontological composition of *being* and *essence*. The present section of this chapter considers Aquinas's view of the relationship between an object's being and its essence (1) by comparing being and essence to the categories of act and potency, (2) by comparing being and essence to substance and accident, and (3) by presenting Aquinas's argument about the distinction between being and essence.

4.3.1 *Being and Essence Compared to Act and Potency*

Being (*esse*), as principle of a thing's entity and intelligibility, serves to account respectively for the fact that something, whether a real being or a being of reason, in some way has being rather than not, and that as such it is susceptible of intellectual apprehension.[131] Essence (*essentia*), as principle of a thing's distinction, and as that through which every substantial being has being, serves to set specific limits to what otherwise would be a boundless act of being, and to determine what that substance is by establishing it within a particular genus and species.[132]

Aquinas distinguishes the accidents *act* and *potency* respectively from the act that is the being (*esse*) of a substance, and the potency of which a substance is capable in virtue of its essence (*essentia*).[133] Considering the examples *cutting* and *burning* noted above in Section 4.4.2 of the accident that Aristotle calls "doing," which Aquinas calls "act," it is worth noting that the being of a substance is the foundation of this accident inasmuch as being is the metaphysical principle in virtue of which a thing can do anything at all.[134]

Similarly, considering the examples *being-cut* and *being-burned* of the accident that Aristotle calls "being-affected," which Aquinas calls "potency," it is worth noting that the essence of a substance is like this accident inasmuch as essence determines how a substance may be affected. Unlike the accidents act and potency, however, substantial being and essence are not features that a substance may lack and still be that substance.[135]

4.3.2 *Being and Essence Compared to Substance and Accident*

A comparison to the relation between substance and accident also illuminates Aquinas's view of the relation between substantial being and essence.

The relationship between being and essence is in some way like the relationship between a substance and accidents, and in another way, it is unlike this relationship. Like accidents, a substance's essence depends for its reality on the being of the substances in which it inheres.[136] A substance's essence differs from accidents, however, in that essence, as opposed to accidents, constitutes a complex of features that determine what that substance is by placing it within a particular genus and species, and through which a substance has its being.[137] Thus, we can consider or refer to a substance apart from any accidents that it may actually or potentially possess, but we cannot consider or refer to a substance apart from its essence. Although essence like accidents depends for its being on the being of its substance, since it does not have real being apart from that substance, unlike accidents, essence is a necessary point of reference for a substance's intelligibility, since it is through essence that a substance has being.

4.3.3 *The Distinction between Being and Essence*

Aquinas succinctly expresses his argument concerning the distinction between being and essence in the following passage:

> Whatever is not in the concept of the essence or the quiddity comes from beyond the essence and makes a composition with the essence, because no essence can be understood without the things that are its parts. But every essence or quiddity can be understood without understanding anything about its existence (*esse*): I can understand what a man is or what a phoenix is and nevertheless not know whether either has existence in reality. Therefore, it is clear that existence is something other than the essence or quiddity.[138]

We can intellectually grasp characteristics without grasping whether or not they inhere in a substance, either as accidents or as a complex of accidents (essence). Moreover, the complex of features that constitute the essences of finite substances never include the being of the substances. The being of a substance is not an instance of the accident *act* discussed in the previous section, and this being is not a feature contained in the essence of a finite substance.[139] Aquinas concludes from the latter observation that the being of a substance, which is the metaphysical principle that actuates it, is in some sense ontologically distinct from its co-principle, essence. In the case of finite substances, being and essence are not subsisting ontological features. Only substances subsist. Being is the principle of entity and intelligibility of a substance, and essence is the principle of the limitation and distinction through which a substance has being. Being and essence are really distinct, however, since being is not in the essence of a substance, but is a substantial principle outside of a substance's co-principal essence.

4.4 Participation and the Act of Being

As noted above,[140] for Aquinas the term *being* (*esse*), in its broadest sense, affirms a fact, or what is the case. As applied to a substance, the term *being* signifies that the substance is (*an est*). Similarly, Section 3.6.1 describes how for Aquinas the term *essence* (*essentia*) signifies of a substance what it is (*quid est*).[141] In light of the real distinction between being and essence discussed above in Section 4.3, Aquinas explains that essence receives being by participating in it, and that this participation is what accounts for the substance having an act of being (*actus essendi*), and for why it has the act of being. Moreover, he recognizes that the ultimate cause of a substance's participation in being is a being that subsists as a substance. Thus, the present section of this chapter considers the following: (1) the participation of essence in being, (2) the act of being of finite substances, and (3) the being that subsists in itself.[142]

4.4.1 *The Participation of Essence in Being*

For Aquinas being is not a feature that a substance can alternatively possess or lack and still be a substance. Rather, it is the foundation of a substance, so that all other features of substance, such as essence and accidents, including act and potency, depend for their reality, on the being of substance.[143] Moreover, the term *being* does not correspond to any of the conceptual notes that can characterize a finite substance, either essentially or accidentally. It cannot signify whether a thing actually exists independently of the mind.[144]

Beyond admitting a substance's actuality and essence, Aquinas investigates the necessity of inquiring into what accounts for why a substance has being. While essence is the principle of limitation of being in finite substances,[145] for Aquinas, the immediate cause of the actuality of finite substances is their reception of,[146] and participation in[147] a common source of their being, *esse commune*, whose concept is free from all additions or exclusions.[148] Recognition of this reception and participation constitutes the principal originality of Aquinas's metaphysical thought.[149]

4.4.2 *The Act of Being*

In light of his doctrine of the participation of essence in being, Aquinas distinguishes being as the principle of entity thematized by Aristotle,[150] from being as the act arising through participation (*actus essendi*). The term *being*, when it indicates a substance, signifies both the fact of a substance's being and its act of being, or its existence.[151] The consideration of being as the fact that there is a substance is distinct from the consideration of being as a substance's act of participation in being. A substance exists because it has being (*habet esse*).[152] Despite saying that a substance "has being," however, Aquinas does not conflate a substance's act of being with the accident *act*, which a substance may come to have or may lack. Being is the act of every substance and of every feature that a substance may have. Aquinas explicitly warns against conflating the being of the received and the being of the receiver:

> Existence is the most perfect of all things, for it is compared to all things as that by which they are made actual; for nothing has actuality except so far as it exists. Hence, existence is that which actuates all things, even their forms. Whence it is not compared to other things as receiver is to received; but rather as received to receiver.[153]

4.4.3 *Being That Subsists in Itself*

For Aquinas, while the immediate cause of the being of things is their participation in a common source of being (*esse commune*),[154] the ultimate cause of this participation is a substance that is self-subsistent being. This is so because any cause that is not self-subsistent must receive its being from something else, and so cannot be ultimate.[155] Thus, all finite substances receive their being from what is subsistent being in act.[156] Aquinas distinguishes finite substances from pure or unlimited being by noting that finite substances exist in nature, and a substance whose being is infinite does not exist in nature, but is a divine being.[157] Finite beings receive their being through a distinguishing and limiting principle, essence. An infinite being is one whose essence and being are identical.

Self-subsistent being causes the participation of essences in being.[158] Aquinas recognizes this self-subsistent being is the actuality of every act, and the perfection of every perfection.[159] Thus, for Aquinas, while the immediate cause of substances is their participation in being, understood as common to them,[160] their ultimate cause is being, understood as self-subsistent being.[161]

The distinction of being that is the fact that a substance is, from being that is a substance's act of being, arises because Aquinas recognizes that natural substances participate in being. Pure unlimited being, by contrast, subsists in itself as the actuality of every act and the perfection of every perfection. This substance, which Aquinas identifies as God, falls within Aquinas's philosophy of being, not as part of its proper subject matter, since it does not participate in the being that is common to natural things (*esse commune*), but as the ultimate cause of natural things.[162]

4.5 Being That Does Not Constitute Something in Reality

As discussed above,[163] for Aquinas the term *being* applies most broadly to whatever signifies the truth of a sentence. Aquinas divides being in this broad sense into real being (*ens reale*) and being of reason (*ens rationis*), noting that only real being constitutes something in reality independently of the mind.[164] Real being includes what falls into the ten categories, substance in the first instance because a substance possesses its own act of being, and accidents in the second instance because they depend ontologically on substances, and also the processes of generation and corruption because they are necessary for the development of substances or accidents. The present section, by contrast, treats being of reason, which like real being signifies the truth of a sentence, but does not constitute something in reality independently of the mind.

4.5.1 *Being of Reason in General*

Beings of reason are accidents of the mind that arise in acts of will or cognition.[165] By acknowledging beings of reason as a kind of being, Aquinas recognizes that the mind treats all of its objects as beings in order to affirm or deny something about them. They are beings only in the sense that the mind concerns itself with them when it affirms or negates something about them.[166] Aquinas notes that they are the weakest kind of beings because they arise only because of the mind's consideration.[167]

Although there are different types of being of reason, all share the fundamental nature of not positing anything in reality, but of having being only in virtue of the mind's consideration. In contrast to this commonality, beings of reason relate in various ways to the being of what one might call "host" beings.[168] Beings of reason are of two general kinds. One kind concerns the ontological status of substances and includes privations,[169] impossible objects,[170] the future and past,[171] fictions, and the like.

1. Privations relate to the being and properties of their real host beings when one attributes a deficiency to them. For example, holes relate to the real being of their surrounding material as a deficiency of that material, and blindness to the being of the organs of sight as a deficiency of those organs.
2. Fictions relate to the being and properties of their real host beings when one falsely and knowingly attributes other properties to them. For example, unicorns relate to horses and to the property of being horned, by falsely and knowingly attributing other properties to those real beings.
3. Erroneous judgments relate to the being and properties of their real host beings when one falsely but *unknowingly* attributes other properties to them. For example, the judgment that "Every person is a parent" may relate to the real being of every person and the real property of being a parent, by falsely and unknowingly attributing to each person the property of being a parent.
4. Negations relate to the being and properties of their real host beings when one denies other properties of them. For example, the judgment that "The earth does not have a second moon" relates to the real being of the Earth and the Moon, by denying of them that they relate to a real second moon.

5. Impossible objects and self-contradictory statements relate to their real host beings when one affirms that these real beings cannot simultaneously coexist as one real being, or simultaneously be affirmed of the same being. For example, a circular square and the statement that "The square is circular" relate to a real square and a real circle by simultaneously describing them as having, or affirming them to have, the property of being circular and of being square.

A second kind of being of reason concerns logical intentions and definitions. It includes things such as the intentions *species, genera, difference,* their *relations of affirmation and negation,* and *relations of inclusion and exclusion,* which are the proper subject matter of logic.[172] For example, the following claim exemplifies the relations of affirmation and inclusion among genus, species, and individual: If a certain species falls within a certain genus, and a given individual falls within that species, then the individual falls within the given genus.

4.5.2 *Being of Reason, Objectivity, and Subjectivity*

A being of reason relates immediately either to another being of reason or to a real being as its host. All beings of reason, and all forms of being generally relate, either directly or indirectly, to real being. For example, a fiction such as a fairy's wing immediately relates to another fiction, the host fiction, fairy, but ultimately relates to some real being such as a bird's wing. The ultimate relation of all beings to real being constitutes the foundational objective dimension of all knowledge.

The dependence of beings of reason on the real being of the mind contrasts the independence of real being from the mind. The necessary relation of all reference to being, whether real being or being of reason, however, tempers this contrast. As emphasized above,[173] acknowledging a being as real cannot entail denying its necessary relation to the mind. It is not possible to refer to any object, whether it is a real being or a being of reason, without entailing a relation to the mind. The act of referring necessitates that the intellect receives its object according to the intellect's mode of receiving.[174] This inevitable relation of the intellect's objects constitutes the foundational subjective dimension of all knowledge.

Not only does the object known determine the knowing subject's act of knowledge, but also the knowing subject, in virtue of its mode of receiving, and only to that extent,[175] determines the object known in the act of knowledge. In light of this mutual epistemic determination of knowing subject and object known, Aquinas also recognizes truth and reference as being intentional in nature. His definition of truth as the conformity of reality and the intellect implies not only that the intellect conforms to reality, but also that reality, in virtue of the intellect's mode of apprehending it, and only to that extent, conforms to the intellect.[176] Similarly, not only does the referring subject conform to the object referred to, but also, the object referred to, in virtue of the subject's mode of apprehending it, and only to that extent, conforms to the knowing subject.

4.5.3 *Beings of Reason and Intentionality*

Aquinas recognizes two levels of intentionality in the act of knowledge. First intentions are objects of knowledge inasmuch as we apprehend them through features that are actually present to the intellect. A first intention attests to an object's indubitable nature and proximate or remote foundation in reality discussed above.[177] By contrast, second intentions are features that the intellect attributes to objects as a natural and necessary result of the knowing subject's mode of exercising an act of knowing, but that are not present in first intentions.[178] They are denoted by terms of second imposition such as those mentioned below, but become first intentions when the knowing subject takes them as its objects.

Second intentions accrue to objects taken first intentionally in each of the three acts of the intellect.[179] For example, in acts of simple apprehension the second intentions *genus*, *species*, and the like accrue to objects thereby justifying statements like "All cats are animals."

4.6 The Consideration of Being from Diverse Perspectives

Being shoots through the manifold of all things actual, possible, and conceptual. As is stated at the beginning of this chapter, we are able to investigate the gamut of this manifold in virtue of the insight that for everything that it contains, there is at least one thing that we can know: "It is." As the foregoing chapter has endeavored to show, Aquinas employs this insight as a criterion for distinguishing diverse kinds of being, and perspectives on being. These include the following: (1) the being of a substance as fact, (2) the being of real accidents, (3) real possible being, (4) the being of what is dependent on the mind, (5) a substance's act of being, (6) the being in which substances participate, and (7) the being that is the ultimate cause of their participation in being.

For Aquinas, only substances, and derivatively, their accidents, exist, because only substances have their own act of being. Aquinas similarly recognizes substances as the immediate ontological foundation of beings of reason. Beings of reason neither possess their own act of being nor depend as material accidents on the existence of material substances. For Aquinas, we can apply the term *being* to beings of reason because anything we can say "is" of, is a being of some sort.[180] Beings of reason do not exist independently of the mind, but rather, depend ontologically on the being of the mind in which they inhere as immaterial accidents.

We can coherently claim of different beings, either that they exist, as in the case of substances, and derivatively accidents, or that they do not exist, as in the case of beings of reason. As will be discussed in the Thomistic section of the concluding chapter of this book, discourse about being and existence avoids incoherence in virtue of the various modes of being. Recognizing this coherence depends on recognizing being, as it shoots through the manifold of all things actual, possible, and conceptual.

Being in the Continental Tradition: Phenomenological Hermeneutics as Fundamental Ontology

Frank Scalambrino

§1 Distinguishing the Continental Tradition

Few people alive today could provide an "exhaustive account" of what is known as the Continental Tradition in Western philosophy. Moreover, by its very nature, there would be disagreement as to what would constitute an "exhaustive" account and how various aspects of the Continental Tradition should be articulated. Yet, we can cut through the knot of these disagreements by taking what essentially differentiates the Continental Tradition from all other traditions as our point of departure. In fact, what distinguishes the Continental Tradition *from all other traditions* can be stated in one word: methodology.

Ultimately, what constitutes the Continental Tradition, and differentiates it from all other traditions, is the use of the Transcendental Method. This method, of course, was first formulated by Immanuel Kant (1724–1804) in his revolutionary: *Critique of Pure Reason* (1781). Only the Kantian, that is, Continental Tradition uses the Transcendental Method, and to use the Transcendental Method is to participate in the Continental Tradition. Thus, the methodology of the Transcendental Method, and its application toward solving problems in philosophy, distinguishes the Continental Tradition from *all* other traditions.

According to Kant, applications of the Transcendental Method may be divided into its use as an "instrument of scientific discovery" and its use as a transcendental logic to provide "rules of inference" with which to guide our thinking. Kant referred to the first way to apply the Transcendental Method as its use as an "organon," and he referred to the second as its use as a "canon." As a canon, then, Kant's Transcendental Method may be understood as revolutionary because it established a new transcendental logic for philosophy, a logic which goes beyond what is traditionally known as "general" or "formal" logic. As an organon, the Transcendental Method discovers the forms of perception and the forms of judgment, which are the conditions for the possibility of human experience.

What is more, the Transcendental Method can be used as a canon to think about the results of its use as an organon. When applied in this way, the Transcendental Method reveals that the relations between the conditions for the possibility of human experience form a system. Thus, in regard to the elements of this system, Kant referred to the organic products as modes of "cognition," that is, perception and judgment, and the canonic products as "concepts." This is the proper context in which to understand Kant's explicit statement from the *Critique of Pure Reason*: "A *system* of such concepts would be called *transcendental philosophy*" (A 12/B 25).

Now, as noted in the Introduction to this book, Kant considered the terms "ontology" and "transcendental philosophy" as equivalent to one another and completely exchangeable. Furthermore, as was also noted, according to the Continental Tradition a precise (quadripartite) clarification can be made regarding ontology, that is, *general* ontology, or the order of "being in general" and its immediate division into three *specific* orders of being: the cosmological, the theological, and the psychological. Thus, the philosophy of being in the Continental Tradition can be stated, here, in summary form.

That is to say, human experience happens in time and in an environment. On the one hand, both the things in the environment and the human having the experience may be considered parts of the cosmological order of being; in other words, each thing and each human *is* in the cosmos. On the other hand, the psychological order is unique in that it refers to the human who *is* applying the Transcendental Method. Moreover, the revelation, brought forth through the science of transcendental philosophy, *is* happening in time. Hence, organically, through the uniqueness of the psychological order, the Continental Tradition has direct methodological-access to the revelation of being *as being*.

Furthermore, transcendental philosophy provides canonical clarification by *clearing* away the non-transcendental elements in the experience of being in time; thus, the Continental Tradition has access to the metaphysical meaning of being.

How these aspects of ontology differ from one another is important. Whereas the former accomplishes the ultimate goal of Western metaphysics by methodologically inducing the revelation of "being as being," the latter accomplishes the goal of providing a scientific understanding of "being in general." Just as Aristotle's ambition distinguished between these two inquiries regarding metaphysics as the science of being, Kant's transcendental philosophy provided the truth of their scientific solution. Therefore, it is not simply the case that only the methodology of the Continental Tradition can bring forth these truths in the philosophy of being; rather, it is also the case that these truths are the actual solutions to the very inquiries that constitute the philosophy of being.

In addition, then, to clarifying, and providing context to, the above summary-introductory statements, this chapter is designed to articulate *the philosophy of being* in the Continental Tradition, specifically, so that readers may accomplish, at least, three goals. First, after reading this chapter, readers should have a general understanding of how Kant's Transcendental Method functions as the methodology of the science of metaphysics. Second, readers should gain a deeper understanding of how the Continental Tradition understands being. In addition to logical clarification regarding the science of metaphysics, this means a sketch of the history of the initial explorations of the Continental Tradition's developments of transcendental philosophy. Lastly, after reading this chapter, readers should be in a position to more easily understand what distinguishes the philosophy of being in the Continental Tradition from all other traditions, especially the Thomistic and the Analytic.[1]

1.1 On the Importance of the Concept of Incommensurability and the Organization of This Chapter

This chapter is divided into five major sections. This first section is devoted to two tasks. First, clarification is provided regarding what is meant by "the Continental Tradition." It is especially important that readers recognize the difference between "continental philosophy" and "the Continental Tradition." On the one hand, the principle that essentially distinguishes the latter from the former is, of course, the Transcendental Method. On the other hand, this distinguishes the transcendental philosophy of the Continental Tradition from both the Thomistic and, importantly, the Cartesian[2] traditions, though all three may technically be referred to as examples of "continental philosophy."

Second, this section of the chapter is devoted to introducing the concept of incommensurability. The use of the concept of incommensurability is perhaps the best way to identify traditions as distinct from one another, because it can be used to precisely distinguish them in terms of their uniqueness. The term "incommensurability" was popularized by Thomas Kuhn's (1962) *The Structure of Scientific Revolutions*.[3] An example that is both easy to understand and was used by Kuhn is the difference between theorizing in regard to pre-Copernican Worldviews and theorizing in regard to post-Copernican Worldviews. As we all should know, Nicolaus Copernicus (1473–1543) is credited with the hypothesis that perhaps the sun does not revolve around the earth; rather, the earth revolves around the sun. Notice how, in a way, we could say that hypothesis both groups and distinguishes all the theories regarding the cosmos that came before it from all the theories that come after it.

In other words, that hypothesis provides a uniqueness with which to *essentially distinguish* all the theories before it from all the theories after it. Another way to articulate this accomplishment: It provides a different way of seeing the context, rather than the content. That is to say, when making measurements, pre- and post-Copernican astronomers may be looking at the same stars, that is, the same content; however, pre-Copernican astronomers understood that content, and the elaboration of its various meanings, within a specific context. Copernicus changed the context, and it was by changing the context that he changed our view and our understanding of the content and the various meanings which could be elaborated regarding the content. Thus, despite being about the same content, pre-Copernican theories are *incommensurable* with post-Copernican theories. Ultimately, they involve essentially distinct worldviews, and, so, they have fundamentally different ways of gaining insight regarding, what may be, otherwise, considered the same—content—across worldviews.

In the same way that incommensurability functions in astronomy—illuminating essentially distinct worldviews and theories by way of what distinguishes them—it functions in the philosophy of being. In this way, (1) the Continental Tradition is essentially distinct from all other traditions; (2) likewise, the scientific solution of Western philosophy's ultimate metaphysical inquiries can only be revealed through the Transcendental Method and are, therefore, exclusive to the Continental Tradition; (3) in this way, the Continental Tradition may legitimately claim to be the only tradition to properly *contextualize* being in the philosophy of being. Thus, the "Kantian Copernican Revolution" (cf. Kant, 1998: B xvi) is what essentially distinguishes the Continental Tradition from all other traditions, and that "Revolution" is, of course, methodological.

Because the meaning of the term "science" has differed throughout Western history (cf. Losee, 2001; cf. Scalambrino, 2018a), we will discuss the meaning and relevance of this term in Section 1.3 below. However, in regard to the philosophy of being, then, Kant's methodological revolution in the history of Western philosophy may be characterized in terms of his "demarcation of the human-existential rules of inference" regarding metaphysics. That portion of this chapter is Section 1.4. Moreover, it is in this way that Kant himself understood his accomplishment. That is why Kant considered his *Critique of Pure Reason* to have accomplished the *Prolegomena to All Future Metaphysics*.

In other words, Kant—rightly—believed that no philosopher would be able to work on metaphysical questions after him, that is, in the future, without first making an inquiry into the method being applied and how that method relates to Kant's method, specifically as an organon and as a canon. Thus, as noted above, the fact that the transcendental logic of Kant's Transcendental Method differs canonically[4] from general or formal logic is a central part of what makes his methodology unique. In Section 1.4 this insight is stated in terms that may be more often found in other traditions. That is, the Continental Tradition takes the principle of actuality to be more primordial than the principle of non-contradiction.

The second major section of this chapter, then, begins to explicitly answer the question: What is the meaning of being in the Continental Tradition? Given the overall project of this book, it is important to keep in mind the fact that the Continental Tradition historically originated in the middle, that is, between the Thomistic and Analytic Traditions. As a result, the application of Kant's Transcendental Method to determine the meaning of being in the Continental Tradition is articulated in the second section of this chapter in terms of Kant's "Critique of Metaphysics."

To assist its comparison with other traditions, especially the Thomistic, Kant's methodology is articulated there as a kind of response to the metaphysical writings of Aristotle (384–322 BC).[5] This articulation should not be controversial, since the philosophy of being can be traced back, at least, to the puzzles and theses formulated by Aristotle in his *Metaphysics*, among other works. Moreover, it may be helpful to reiterate here that it is not in terms of the problems or the questions (the content) of philosophy that the Continental Tradition is distinguished from other traditions; it is in terms of the method (the context) with which the Continental Tradition approaches the problems and questions of philosophy that makes the philosophy of the Continental Tradition incommensurable with other traditions.

The third major section of this chapter, "From Apprehension-in-Time to the 'Transcendental Unity of Apperception' as Being," explicates the Continental Tradition's answer to the two ultimate questions in the philosophy of being. These were noted above already; first: "what is being *qua* being?" which may be formulated also as "what is being as being," "what is being in terms of being," "what is metaphysical being," or "what is the be-ing of beings?" Second, "what is the meaning of being?" That is to say, on the one hand, Section 3 of this chapter indicates how the philosophy of the Continental Tradition methodologically reveals metaphysical being—also known as "transcendental being."[6] On the other hand, Section 3 deepens the Continental Tradition's critique of the metaphysics of both the Thomistic and the Analytic Traditions in that the canonical application of Kant's Transcendental Method takes *time* to be the ground of the *meaning* of being.

In the fourth major section, the focus shifts toward the history of the Continental Tradition. Especially given the commercialization of Western philosophy, this focus may be what most readers of a chapter regarding the philosophy of being in the Continental Tradition initially expect. Yet, as noted at the very beginning of this chapter, only a sketch of such an account is possible here: on the one hand, for the obvious reason of space constraints, and, on the other, because an "exhaustive account" may not even be possible.

Therefore, the fourth major section of this chapter has been designed to sketch the history of the Continental Tradition with two principles in mind.

First, because the parameters of what movements are possible within the Continental Tradition are set by the limits of Kant's transcendental philosophy, and because there are only two ultimate questions in the philosophy of being, it is widely considered true that all of, what may be called, the "major moves" in regard to Kant's "system" of transcendental philosophy have already been made. In fact, there is a deep truth in Heidegger's offhand remark that Nietzsche was the last *metaphysician* in the Continental Tradition. In other words, the last of the possible moves in regard to Kant's system of transcendental philosophy may have already been made by Nietzsche.

The second, closely related, principle, despite the fact that the focus of this section is historical, is to articulate these historical moments for the Continental Tradition as developments of transcendental philosophy. This was, of course, avowedly the project of philosophers after Kant, at least, up to and including Schelling and Schopenhauer, and constituted a kind of "Homeric Contest" to complete the system of Kant's transcendental philosophy. Thus, the styles of characterizing being, and the elements of transcendental philosophy, may be used to distinguish all of the movements possible within the Continental Tradition.

On the one hand, this is precisely why we hear philosophers in the Continental Tradition of philosophy speak of "the end of philosophy." On the other hand, this is why a portion of the concluding section will focus on the special question of subjectivity. For, subjectivity indicates merely one style of characterizing Kant's Transcendental Unity of Apperception (TUA). Many interpreters fail to realize that the use of the idea of "subjection" originally belongs to a specific historical period and so forth. These interpreters seem to believe that because the term "subject" may logically apply to a being, it necessarily applies to transcendental being—yet, that is a mistaken belief. In order to illustrate the possibilities developed in the Continental Tradition, subjection will be contrasted with individuation and differentiation.

Lastly, then, the fifth and final section of this chapter provides a concluding, summary, statement regarding the philosophy of being in the Continental Tradition. Section 5.1 addresses three common ways in which being in the Continental Tradition is misunderstood, and, as just noted, one of these ways is in terms of "naïvely" characterizing transcendental apperception in terms of subjectivity. These common misunderstandings often stem from the failure of readers to distinguish between continental philosophy and the Continental Tradition. That is to say, be-ing is not to be understood merely as cognition, as a subject, or as an object.

For, though there are many senses of the term "being,"[7] ultimately this chapter focuses on the "metaphysical" sense of the term as it is understood in the Continental Tradition, that is, as "transcendental being." In addition, then, to providing this essential clarification and providing a concluding summary of this chapter, the concluding section should also allow for a deeper appreciation of the celebrated phrase often used to characterize the Continental Tradition's unique understanding of metaphysical being, that is: "Being as the be-ing of beings."

1.2 Differentiating "The Continental Tradition" from "Continental Philosophy"

"Continental philosophy" refers to a kind of Western philosophy. In its most original and general sense, the term "continental" indicated a geographical distinction, that is, philosophy of the European "continent." Geographically, then, "continental" contrasts with "Anglo-American" philosophy. Though it would not be an incorrect use of the term "tradition" to speak of the difference between the Continental Tradition and the Anglo-American tradition, the term "philosophy" is standardly used to distinguish one geography-based group of philosophers from another. Thus, we speak of "continental philosophy" in contrast to "Anglo-American philosophy."

Rather than geography, another standard, and general, use of the term "continental" is to group philosophers giving priority to their writings. This use of the term includes a large list of philosophers across diverse geographies, histories, and even writing styles. For example, philosophers such as Plato (427–347 BC), Marsilio Ficino (1433–1499), René Descartes (1596–1650), Friedrich Nietzsche (1844–1900), Simone de Beauvoir (1908–1986), Gilles Deleuze (1925–1995), Jacques Derrida (1930–2004), and Wilhelm Wurzer (1948–2009) may accurately be referred to as "continental philosophers." Thus, despite their differences, the term "continental philosophy" may be accurately and standardly used to group such a list of philosophers because of the philosophical concerns they invoke in their writings.

Though writing style is the most aesthetically striking difference between continental and non-continental *philosophy*, methodology is ultimately the best factor for differentiating the various "Traditions" within continental philosophy. Especially insofar as continental philosophers may use the aesthetic of their writing itself to advance an argument, the writings of continental philosophers include a wider rhetorical range than those of non-continental philosophers. Whether considering Nietzsche's use of aphorisms and epigrams, Heidegger's discussion of poetry, or Deleuze's discussion of painting, it would be quite rare to find the philosophical writings of a non-continental philosopher praised for "passionate lyricism." Yet, beyond writing style, topics in "phenomenology," "hermeneutics," and "existentialism" tend to be exclusive to "continental" philosophers. Thus, in sum, the general category of "continental philosophy" may be further specified in regard to geography, history, methodology, topic or subject matter, and style. Yet, the most essential way to differentiate the "Continental Tradition" from other traditions is in terms of methodology.

1.3 Introducing Kant's Revolutionary Transcendental Methodology: The Prolegomena to Any Future Metaphysics That Will Be Able to Present Itself as a Science

In what way did Kant see transcendental philosophy—and, thereby, the metaphysical study of being in the Continental Tradition—as a "science"? In general, he thought of transcendental methodology as a science; in particular, he thought of sciences as methods with certain features. He listed these features in the second part of the *Critique of Pure Reason*; however, the terminology he used can be a barrier to our understanding his insight, so a few words of clarification may be helpful. The first part of the *Critique* is the "Doctrine of Elements," and the second part is the "Doctrine of Method." In this latter part, there are two points Kant clarifies that we should note.

First, Kant's methodology limits its domain to impure reason, which means reason in combination with content from sensory experience. Second, his "canon," that is, the rules for making inferences in his articulation metaphysics as a science, is transcendental logic. We will have more to say about this later; however, this is how Kant initially characterizes his "science." A domain plus a canon produces an "organon," which means "an instrument of scientific discovery." Thus, for the Continental Tradition, the proper way to engage in metaphysical investigations is to be involved in metaphysics methodologically limited by those parameters. In whatever sense, either the Thomistic or Analytic Traditions may be thought of as a "science," neither of their methodologies are constituted by this domain determination, canon, or organon.

The two methodological innovations that develop out of Kant's science of metaphysics, that is, his ontology or transcendental philosophy, are (1) Kant's *approach* to "cognition" and (2) his *approach* to "judgment."[8] Whereas Kant's first innovation refers to what is known as the "Kantian Copernican Revolution" (Kant, 1998: B xvi), the second innovation points to Kant's infamous critique that "Being" is "not a real predicate" (Kant, 1998: A 596/B 624).

Now, Kant's *Critique of Pure Reason* is indeed a watershed in the history of Western philosophy. On the one hand, his work provides a criticism of *all* prior Western philosophy, specifically in regard to methodology and metaphysics. On the other hand, there is a profound sense in which all Western philosophy after Kant may be characterized in relation to his philosophy. For example, this latter insight is famously reflected, first, in the title of the book Kant subsequently wrote for the sake of clarifying the *Critique of Pure Reason*, that is, the *Prolegomena to Any Future Metaphysics* (1783), and, second, in the provocative Lewis White Beck quip "There is a saying among philosophers, 'You can philosophize with Kant or against Kant, but you cannot philosophize without him'" (Beck, 1950: 1).

1.4 The Canon of Transcendental Logic versus The Canon of Formal Logic: The Principle of Actuality versus The Principle of Non-Contradiction

It would be a mistake to think that the Continental Tradition somehow denies the principle of non-contradiction. For, the logical forms of judgment are not in question here; what is in question here is the *application* of the forms of judgment. By focusing on the application of judgment (within the domain of experience), we can clarify that there are different modes to the power of judgment. For this clarification, we can look to Kant's *Critique of the Power of Judgment* (1790) to see the difference between the determining and the reflecting power of judgment.

> The power of judgment in general is the faculty for thinking of the particular as contained under the universal. If the universal (the rule, the principle, the law) is given, then the power of judgment, which subsumes the particular under it ... is *determining*. If, however, only the particular is given, for which the universal is to be found, then the power of judgment is ... *reflecting*. (2000: 66–7)

In sum, experience invokes a determining judgment when we already have the universal in mind and are merely applying it to a particular. With a reflecting judgment we experience a particular, and, by reflecting, we must look for, or create, a universal to apply to it. In the former case, we adhere to the principle of non-contradiction, and in the latter, we cannot help but adhere to the principle of actuality.

In terms of transcendental philosophy as a science, a reflective judgment forces us from the use of the Transcendental Method as a canon to its use as an organon. We move from the mode of demonstration and logical analysis to the mode of discovery. Since we must remain within the domain of impure reason, our "search for the universal" amounts to an application of transcendental logic to the *experience* of the particular regarding which we are not yet aware of its universality. The trajectory of this "reflective" judgment goes from cognition of the particular through the unity of the judgment *in the experience of the particular*, and forces an awareness of the transcendental dimensions of the *experience*.

In other words, we experience some particular through the human-animal body, and the mind's ability to use judgment to determine the identity of the particular fails—or, at least, is not successful in its usual everyday way. As a result, the mind is forced into a reflective relation to the particular it is experiencing, and the domain of that reflection—according to the science of transcendental philosophy—is the experience itself. Therefore, the universality available for the mind to discover is not a concept governed by the principle of non-contradiction, per the mind's usual ability to determine the identity of particulars; rather, the mind is reflectively forced through the failure of the determining power of judgment into the transcendental dimensions of the experience, and the transcendental dimension is governed by the principle of actuality. That is, the transcendental dimension is governed by the actual sensory capacities and powers of judgment through which the experience of a particular *can* manifest. As we will discuss extensively below, this distinction between reflecting and determining uses of judgment helps clarify how the Continental Tradition has methodological-access to metaphysical being.

§2 The Kantian Critique of Metaphysics, Articulated Regarding Scholastic Philosophy: "Being Is Not a Real Predicate"

Kant's *Critique of Pure Reason* (1781) is the first of his three critiques, the other two being: the *Critique of Practical Reason* (1788) and the *Critique of the Power of Judgment* (1790).[9] As discussed in the Introduction, "critique" means "to set limits to." Kant's critical project is epistemological, then, in that he limited the methodological use of reason to arrive at *knowledge*.[10] As was also already stated in the Introduction to this book, Kant's critique makes clear that the "being" predicated in existential judgments by the Thomistic and Analytic Traditions is logical, not real, being. Beyond this "critical" accomplishment is the "transcendental" side of Kant's project, and Kant himself emphasized that the project of "transcendental philosophy" is metaphysical.[11]

Thus, for the sake of both introducing and distinguishing the Continental Tradition, the following presentation of Kant's methodology is articulated in terms of what the Thomistic Tradition refers to as "Predication and Modes of Being."[12] This articulation should help readers more easily discern the sense in which Kant's transcendental philosophy was "revolutionary." The context, then, for the following articulation of Kant's "Critique of Metaphysics" involves what is standardly referred to in the history of philosophy as the "*noetic process*." In other words, how does the relation between things in reality and human cognition both influence and limit metaphysics? As we will see, Kant's *approach* to "cognition" shifts the focus of metaphysics from modes of being in terms of predication to modes of being in time. In order to establish the proper context, then, for understanding Kant's "Critique of Metaphysics," we will briefly invoke Aristotle regarding the role of "cognition" in metaphysics.

2.1 The "Peripatetic Axiom" and the *Noetic* Process

The ultimate source of knowledge for both Aristotle and Aquinas is "induction." Recall the "Peripatetic Axiom," which Aquinas formulated in regard to the work of Aristotle: "Nothing is in the intellect that was not first in the senses."[13] Of course, generally speaking, the Peripatetic Axiom is in line with Kant's concern to limit metaphysics to the domain of the "impure" use of reason. However, this axiom involves *several important distinctions*, and in considering these it becomes clear how Kant's relation to this axiom differs from that of Aristotle and Aquinas. Stating this difference in terms of methodology: whereas Aristotle and Aquinas understood the "Peripatetic Axiom" in terms of "formal logic," Kant understood it in terms of "transcendental logic."

To be clear, when we speak of "induction," we are discussing how an experience happens. Thus, when an experience happens, we say that the content of the intellect in the experience derives from the interaction between the senses and things in the environment.[14] The first distinction to consider, then, is between "in reality" and in "the soul."[15] This distinction, of course, may subsequently be used to organize other terms. For example, the term "thing" refers to things "in reality," and the products of the intellect are said to be "in the soul." Next, a distinction may be made between "the senses" and "the intellect." Notice that this distinction is between powers in the soul. In other words, even though we understand sensation to be a process that happens in natural physical bodies, the recognizable products of the process of sensation appear within "the soul."

Through induction, then, knowledge produced by the intellect is intended to be about things "in reality." In other words, we may say that knowledge produced by the intellect is *in* "the order of the intellect" but *about* "the order of nature."[16] Furthermore, the order of nature, in general, and "things," in particular, may also be described as "extra-mental" or as located in "mind-external" reality. Thus, we may say that in order for the intellect to be directed toward reality it must be directed toward the senses. To capture this "directionality" of the intellect, Scholastic philosophers used the term "intention," which means "to go toward," since it is as if the intellect is going toward mind-external reality when it produces knowledge through a natural experience.

The next relevant distinction, then, is between "first intentions" and "second intentions." Though *both are intellectual*, first intentions involve the senses and second intentions are *purely* mental. Importantly, notice that this distinction is different from the second distinction noted above between "the senses" and the "intellect." In order to better contextualize the distinction between "first" and "second intentions," consider Aristotle's distinction between the "passive" and the "active intellect." Passive and active, here, do not coincide with first and second intentions; rather, the distinction between passive and active explains how we can move *from* "in the senses" *to* first intentions "in the intellect."[17]

In Aristotle's Greek, the passive intellect and the active intellect are called *nous pathētikos* and *nous poiētikos*, respectively. The former term means "capacity to receive," hence "passive," and the latter term—importantly— means "capacity to make," hence "active." Thus, on the one hand, when we encounter some "thing" "in reality" it affects our passive bodily "senses" and "phantasms" (images—"animal spirits") are produced in the soul from the senses being affected. On the other hand, whereas the production of "phantasms" constitutes the activity of the bodily senses, it is through a process of *noēsis* that the passively informed senses are *intentionally* changed by the "operations of the intellect," from first to second intentions.

Until the act of *noēsis* the passive intellect is said to contain a "phenomenal representation" which is only "potentially intelligible." Through the act of *noēsis*, then, the active "productive" intellect makes the *potentially* intelligible "phenomenal representation" in the "passive intellect" *actually* intelligible *as* a "first intention." How is it then that "passive" and "active," here, do not coincide with first and second intentions? This is because before the act of *noēsis* occurs the intellect is said to be in "potency," and when the act occurs the intellect is said to be in "act." That is to say that when the passive potential intellect (*nous pathētikos*) is activated, its activation "creates" the "first intention," so the intellect (*nous*) is then the productive active intellect (*nous poiētikos*). Importantly, the act of *noēsis* is, generally speaking, called "abstraction" by Aquinas and "cognition" by Kant.

Here's an example with which to make all this more concrete. When my senses come into contact with some "thing" in the environment, my passive intellect contains "phantasms" in relation to the thing. These phantasms—supposing, for this example, the thing is a sandwich—would be images of the slices of bread and whatever is between them. These images are not merely visual; the phantasms function to aggregate the five senses, so there may be olfactory, gustatory, and so on aspects represented by the phantasms "in my soul." When these images of the thing are "recognized" in my soul, it is because the potential for these images to be recognized in my (passive) intellect is activated, and thus the "active" intellect "creates" a "first intention" in regard to the images.[18]

Now, this first intention is placed into a predication, such that, through a *determining* judgment and reasoning, a "second intention" can be created, and in this way, the intellect is supposed to be able to *determine*, and thereby know, the "nature" of the "thing." Namely, in this example, the intellect is supposed to know that this thing in front of me *is* a sandwich, and because the intellect can understand the definition of "sandwich," the intellect is supposed to know the nature of this sandwich-thing in reality. For our purpose, the Kantian critical question we should ask here is: Even if this process allows us to know the nature of the sandwich-thing in reality, does it also allow us to know the nature of "being" in reality? Kant's response to this question would be, "No." Only through the methodological changes proposed by Kant can we gain methodological-access to metaphysical being in "the order of nature," that is, "in reality."

Finally, the last distinction we need to mention points to what is standardly referred to as the "three operations of the intellect." These operations are (1) "Apprehension," (2) "Judgment," and (3) "Reasoning." Accordingly, we say that the intellect *apprehends* the "thing" through the senses, placing it, as a first intention, into a *judgment*, and developing second intentions through further judgments and *reasoning*. Though most of the terminology used in making these distinctions comes from Scholastic philosophy, all of the above distinctions may be understood as originating from Aristotle's *Posterior Analytics*, Book II §19 (99b30-100b6) and *De Anima*, Book III §§3-6 (427a16-430a25). Thus, if we briefly consider a portion of Aristotle's *Metaphysics*, we will have sufficiently characterized the logical and philosophical context out of which Kant's "Critique of Metaphysics" emerged.

2.2 The Aristotelian-Context of Kant's "Critique of Metaphysics"

Since a complete discussion of Aristotle's *Metaphysics* is, of course, beyond the scope of this chapter, the following will suffice for our purpose. We may say that Aristotle's *Metaphysics* represents his search to state "the meaning of being in terms of being" (cf. *Metaphysics* IV §1, 1003a20). In other words, we are looking for—what just above we called being "in reality"—what it means "to be." Now, of the fourteen "Books" comprising Aristotle's *Metaphysics*, by the time he reached "Book 6" he was able to summarize the four most viable answers to the question of the meaning of being. After providing his summary, he systematically eliminates all but one of those four possibilities; as a result, in Book IX he affirmatively states the fourth possibility as the answer to his question. It is this answer, then, that he spends the rest of the *Metaphysics* using to solve various metaphysical puzzles.

Now, the four possibilities are: (1) "the accidental," (2) "the true," (3) "the categories," and (4) "potentiality and actuality." His reasons for eliminating the first three are: (1) there can be no science of the "accidental" (cf. *Metaphysics* VI §2, 1026b22-24), and (2) because it is *predications* and *judgments* that are "true," and the true "depends on combination" (cf. *Metaphysics* VI §4, 1027b18-29). In other words, something must first *be* before it can *be combined* through predication or judgment. Next, Aristotle eliminated "the categories" (3) because: "A particular this can be destroyed, a definition cannot"[19] (cf. *Metaphysics* VII §15, 1039b20-24). In other words, though a thing may be categorized in multiple ways, we are not interested in the meaning of *being categorized* in any way; we are not interested in the meaning of "being in a category." We are interested in the meaning of "being as being." We want to know what it means *to be* "in reality," not what it means to be *categorized* "in the soul."[20]

One of the ways Aristotle illustrates this difference between, on the one hand, "being" and, on the other hand, the eliminated "predicated being" and "being categorized" is to note: were Socrates to change somehow in the category of quantity, that is, in terms of *some quantification* of him, he would still *be* Socrates. Were this not true, then every time Socrates ate a sandwich, he would be different from himself, since "the quantity" that was Socrates previously would have changed. Of course, in terms of quantity it *is true* that Socrates may gain and lose weight. It may even be true that Socrates *is* "obese," and hence *true* to say "Socrates represents an instance of obesity." However, despite the truth of such a judgment, we are not interested in investigating when a concept *is instantiated*. To investigate the sense in which an abstract concept is represented concretely is to remain within the "order of the intellect" and to consider some *logical being*.

Of the final possibility, "potentiality and actuality," Aristotle affirmed that the meaning of being for which we have been searching is "actuality" (*Metaphysics* IX §8, 1050b1). Now, we can produce an even more precise statement of the meaning of being if we formulate Aristotle's answer in terms of the Scholastic distinctions noted above. That is to say, to be is to be an actuality in reality, regarding which we form judgments in the soul. Thus, we *apprehend* some actual "thing" through "the senses," and as a subject in a *judgment* this "first intention" is combined with a "second intention" as the judgment's predicate. Finally, for Aristotle, the third operation of the intellect "reasoning" allows us to recognize that an actual "thing" *activated* our passive potential intellect, and so, for Aristotle, being "in reality" means actuality.

We have now discussed enough of Aristotle's comments to sufficiently characterize how Kant accomplished a "Critique of Metaphysics," and to state, within the context of this characterization, how the Continental Tradition is essentially different from the Thomistic and the Analytic Traditions. That is to say, on the one hand, by examining the beginning of the *noetic* process in Aristotle ("abstraction" in Aquinas and "cognition" in Kant), Kant's "Critique of Metaphysics" differentiates the Continental Tradition from the Thomistic and Analytic Traditions by making time—not logic or language—the proper ground on which to do metaphysics. On the other hand, by examining the conclusion of the *noetic* process Kant's "Critique of Metaphysics" differentiates the Continental Tradition from the Thomistic and the Analytic Traditions by showing that the "being" upon which they focus is "in the order of the intellect."

For Kant, "Being is not a real predicate" may be understood in a twofold way. First, "being" that is predicated is logical being, not real being. Second, real being, that is, being in reality, is not a predicate; it is the ultimate condition for the possibility of all predication. For, not only must we be and must something be, but there must also be an intellect, if there are to be the intellectual formations known as "predications." As will be made clear in the next section, contrary to an idea that may be a foundational premise for the Analytic Tradition: language is not the only "mirror." Thus, it would be a metaphorical use of language to describe apperception as a "mirror," and, moreover, though, methodologically speaking, ap-perception manifests "reflectively," its manifestation is non-discursive.

2.3 Kant's Alternative to Thomistic "Abstraction"

Kant is not skeptical of Aristotle's use of the term "actuality" as much as he is skeptical that any product of the intellect can tell us what actuality means by itself. In other words, there is a difference between knowing some "thing" in the intellect and knowing a thing "in reality." For to know a thing "in reality" would be to know "the thing-in-itself." And, Kant's position that we cannot know the thing-in-itself is infamous (Kant, 1998: A 239). On the one hand, this is the general criticism of both the Thomistic and Analytic Traditions, namely, that they ultimately do not consider being in itself; they consider logical being. Again, this is captured in Kant's claim that "Being is not a real predicate." Insofar as these other traditions are considering some predication—whether that is in terms of logical abstraction or the analysis of language—they are not considering extra-mental being, aka, being-in-reality or metaphysical being.

On the other hand, as previously mentioned, the two methodological innovations with which the Continental Tradition can be essentially differentiated from other traditions, in regard to the meaning of being, are (1) Kant's *approach* to "cognition" and (2) his *approach* to "judgment." Whereas Kant's first innovation refers to what is known as the "Kantian Copernican Revolution" (cf. Kant, 1998: B xvi), the second innovation points to Kant's infamous critique that "Being" is "not a real predicate" (Kant, 1998: A 596/B 624). Furthermore, this latter criticism of the other traditions is twofold.

First, there is the part of the criticism the explication of which we just concluded at the end of Section 2.2; that is, the other traditions do not have methodological-access to being "in reality." Second, there is the part of the criticism which we will complete in the next section, namely, providing an answer to the question: What is the meaning of being? Thus, we will end this section of the chapter by stating Kant's "Copernican Revolution" in regard to "cognition" to conclude our discussion of the *noetic* process and to transition into the next section where the discussion of cognition turns from a discussion of time and judgment to a statement of the meaning of being in the Continental Tradition.

Though, of course, entire books could be written on "Thomistic abstraction," since the focus here is Kant's alternative, the following juxtaposition of Aquinas and Kant should sufficiently illuminate Kant's "Copernican Revolution" as an alternative to "abstraction." Question 85 of Aquinas's *Summa Theologica* regards "The mode and order of understanding," and Article 1 asks: "Whether our intellect understands corporeal and material things by abstraction from phantasms?" Aquinas concludes his answer, noting,

> [T]herefore, it is proper to it [the human intellect] to know a form existing individually in corporeal matter, but not as existing in this individual matter. But to know what is in individual matter, *not as existing in such matter* [emphasis added], is to abstract the form from [the objects, that is,] individual matter which is represented by the phantasms. Therefore, we must needs say that our intellect understands material things by abstracting from the phantasms. (Aquinas, 1964: *S. th.*, q. 85 a. 1 ad 1)

It is clearly also with the noetic process in mind that Kant constructed the following statement at the beginning of the *Critique of Pure Reason*.

> Up to now [e.g. the Scholastic Tradition] it has been assumed that all our cognition must conform to the objects; but all attempts to find out something about them *a priori* through concepts that would extend our cognition have, on this presupposition, come to nothing. Hence let us once try whether we do not get farther with *the problems of metaphysics* [emphasis added] by assuming that the objects must conform to our cognition. (Kant, 1998: B xvi)

As will be explained in the next section of this chapter, the above passage from Kant signals a "revolution" in metaphysics by taking the "a priori intuition of time," what Kant also calls "inner sense," to organize the first phase in the *noetic* process. Thus, all the various modes of cognition are grounded in time, and this actually accomplishes what Aquinas hoped to accomplish in regard to the *noetic* process. That is, Aquinas wanted to mathematize the origin of the *noetic* process, such that when the process is complete the "math stamp," so to speak, of quantification would still be on the object produced through the process, which is why Aquinas named the process—of apprehension from the passive senses—"abstraction."

However, a major concern regarding "abstraction" follows from the realization that it was only one of the ways Aristotle used to characterize the relation between the active and the passive intellect. Aquinas attempted to mathematically universalize this relation by reducing the creative activity of the *nous poiētikos* to "abstraction"—Aristotle's term for merely the mathematical use of the *nous poiētikos*, not the "theoretical" and "practical"[21] modes. According to Aquinas, "the object of mathematics is real quantity, either discrete quantity in arithmetic or continuous quantity in geometry. The mathematician considers the essence of quantity in abstraction from its relation to real existence in bodily substance" (Maurer, 1993: 43).

Kant circumnavigates the concern regarding over-generalizing in Aquinas and universalizes the relation by making it temporally-universal. According to Kant, "I call all cognition transcendental that is occupied not so much with objects but rather with our mode of cognition of objects insofar as this is to be possible *a priori*" (1998: B 25). Kant placed primary focus on the mode, or way, in which a human is capable of experiencing the object of an experience, that is to say: whatever time-stamped cognitive object is produced in the soul through the *noetic* process. This effectively shifts the focus of metaphysics in continental philosophy from "predication and modes of being" to "being and modes of cognition and judgment." With Kant now, all creative activity of the intellect (*nous poiētikos*), whether theoretical, practical, or mathematical, takes place *in time*.

§3 From Apprehension-in-Time to the "Transcendental Unity of Apperception" as Being

For Kant "space" and "time" are neither subsistent beings nor mere concepts; rather, they are the forms of sensible intuition[22] (cf. Kant, 1998: A 26-30/B 42-5, A 32-48/B 49-73). That is to say, "space" is the form of "outer sense" and "time" is the form of "inner sense." As the senses are affected, the passive intellect forms first intentions in terms of space and time. I am looking at that thing *over there* (right now). It is time, however, and not space that is the universal-ground because both outer and inner awareness is accomplished in the form of time. Every thought, memory, and fantasy we have occurs in a "now." Thus, whereas for Aquinas mathematical-quantification was the original condition for intelligibility through the *noetic* process, for Kant it is time.

Just as the senses contain a multiplicity, time functions to unify—allowing the active intellect to make intelligible—sensory content. The senses contain a multiplicity in that there are multiple senses *and* in that sensory and muscle memory can contribute to the content of our "bodily-grip" on things in reality—that is, the mind-external environment. To signify this multiplicity, Kant suggests the senses contain a "synopsis," since it is as if the senses were "seeing all of that content together." Furthermore, this is Kant's solution to what he calls the "problem of heterogeneity."[23] Namely, how can the content of the senses be combined with the content of the intellect when they generate from different kinds of origin? For Kant, the "manifold" of sense can be brought to the various operations of the intellect by being indexed in time.

In regard to the first operation of the intellect, then, sensory data are "apprehended" in time, as the active intellect makes the cognitive object of experience intelligible through the *noetic* process (cf. Kant, 1998: A 120). Thus, as this section of the chapter will make clear: because time is the universal-ground of being, all being will be expressed through time, and so the Continental Tradition will understand time (especially as "History" after Hegel's reading of Kant) as providing the "meaning of being." Furthermore, and most importantly for explicitly differentiating the Continental from the other traditions, the activity of the active intellect—understood through Kant's transcendental methodology—"points" directly to being in reality.

What "points" here means is that Kant's Transcendental Method shows the position of being in reality in relation to the active intellect's contributions to the *noetic* process. According to Kant, the position known as the Transcendental Unity of Apperception is the position to which the active intellect's contributions "point"—or may be "traced-back to" through transcendental reflection—as a point of unity *outside* the *noetic* process. That is, insofar as the transcendental elements conditioning (contributing to) the *noetic* process are not within that process, the TUA turns out to be being in reality, aka "in the order of nature." Though more will be said to clarify this point, because Kant's Transcendental

Method reveals the TUA as a necessary condition for the *noetic* process, the TUA indicates being in reality in a methodologically certifiable way.[24]

3.1 What Is the "Transcendental Unity of Apperception"?

We arrived at the conclusion that time is the universal-ground of being by considering Kant's alterations to Aristotle's discussion of the *noetic* process. The truth of this conclusion notwithstanding such an examination considers experience as "static." For it is as if we are freezing a single experience *in time* and examining it in isolation. Thus, a distinction arises between "unity in time" (synchronic unity) and "unity across time" (diachronic unity), and whereas the former refers to "static" temporality, the latter—as we will see—shall refer to "ec-static" temporality. In fact, in this way we will clarify a difference which at this point may still be vague, namely: What is the difference between "the meaning of being" and "being in reality"?

Considering the *noetic* process in relation to a static experience, time unifies the various elements of the *noetic* process in that they all refer to some activity of the intellect in regard to the content of the senses, *now*. When we reflect on multiple experiences across time, though the meaning of the unity of those experiences is grounded in time, the unity reveals an ec-static position. As Kant explained, the posit-ing of this posit-ion is necessary, and the structure that reveals its necessary position also indicates that it is being in reality. This unity is, of course, called the Transcendental Unity of Apperception (TUA). Hence, these are the Continental Tradition's answers to the two ultimate questions in the philosophy of being. Because for the Continental Tradition judgments determining being primordially occur in time, (a) time is understood as the meaning of being, and because apperception through the unity of reflecting judgments reveals being in the psychological order of *reality*, (b) the answer to the question "what is being in reality?" or "what is metaphysical being?" is the TUA.

In order to clarify that this is not a merely "logical" being, Kant made two comments. First, "it is true that this principle of the necessary unity of apperception is itself merely an identical and hence an *analytic* proposition [emphasis added]." (B 135). Second, indicating that the "analytic" proposition depends on a synthetic one:

The thought that these representations given in intuition all together belong *to me* means, accordingly, the same as that I unite them in a self-consciousness, or at least can unite them therein, and although it is itself not yet the consciousness of the *synthesis* of the representations [across time], it still presupposes the possibility of the latter, i.e. only because I can comprehend their manifold in a consciousness do I call them all together *my* representations. (B 134)

Concluding, Kant noted, "Synthetic unity of the manifold of intuitions, as given *a priori*, is thus the ground of the identity of apperception itself, which precedes *a priori* all *my* determinate thinking" (B 134). In other words, I myself am that being—outside of the *noetic* process—brought into focus through the apperception of transcendental reflection, that is, the TUA.

In Kant's words, on the one hand, there is the "flow of inner appearances" *within* the *noetic* process called "inner sense or empirical apperception," and on the other hand, "there is the numerical identity across the appearances in the flow, i.e. the unity which means all these appearances relate to me" (A 107). Because this unity "precedes all cognition of the object" (A 129), it *is*—it has being—*prior* to the activity of the *noetic* process. The term "prior" does not mean prior in the order of experience. It means that the TUA must *be* prior to the manifestation of the meaning of experience within the *noetic* process.[25] Thus, we may say that the TUA has "ontological priority"[26] in that it is *a priori* within the order of being; yet, this priority is not temporal (rather, the TUA is ec-static) because time-determination takes place—per Kant's "Copernican Turn"—in the order of experience, that is, inductive intuition, initiating the *noetic* process.

To conclude, notice that if we are to have an experience, then *prior* to that experience there *must be* some "thing" to experience, and we *must be* to be able to experience it. Recall from above how Kant operationalized Aristotle's Actuality/Potentiality distinction: If I am actually seeing red, then I must have the potential to see red. Kant described apperception as, "The supreme principle for the possibility of all intuition in reference to understanding," and noted that "everything manifold in intuition is subject to conditions of the original synthetic unity of apperception" (B 136). Thus, on the one hand, Kant could say, "in every judgment I am always the determining subject [indicated as the TUA] of that relation that constitutes the judgment" (B 407). And, on the other hand, he could say perception "is properly only a determination of apperception" (A 368).[27]

3.2 Through the Systematic Development of the Transcendental Method's Application to Reality, the TUA Indicates Being in Reality

Though we have already stated above how the TUA provides methodological-access to being in reality, this brief section is important for differentiating the TUA from other potential contributors of transcendental unity to the *noetic* process. Ultimately, there are two other potential contributors of transcendental unity to the *noetic* process, and both will be ruled out by Kant's criteria against the use of "pure reason." Those two potential sources are (a) the world and (b) God. In order to differentiate the TUA from these other potential sources, it is important to remember that the Transcendental Method revealed the TUA by considering the diachronic unity across multiple instances of the *noetic* process.

In regard to the *noetic* process Kant noted, "All our cognition starts from the senses, goes from there to the understanding, and ends with reason, beyond which there is nothing higher to be found in us to work on the matter of intuition" (Kant, 1998: A 298/B 355). Whereas the TUA was revealed as the *actuality* which could be said to contain the *power* of both sensibility and understanding in a methodologically certifiable way—I *am* that be-ing which is *apperceived* in the unity of transcendental reflection, in contrast: understanding either the world or God as a source of transcendental unity requires the method of pure reason. This is because neither the unity of the world nor the unity of God can be immediately *apperceived*.[20]

For Kant the logical quantifiers of "one, some, and all"—or "unity, plurality, and totality" (A 80/B 106)—may be used diachronically in regard to experience. Thus, the TUA indicates the unity of a multiplicity of experiences. However, whereas the TUA indicates this unity by *being* it, this is not the case regarding the world and God. According to Kant, "the world" is a "pure" *idea* of reason because it refers to an idea supposed to contain a plurality of experiences without itself being a necessary component of the experiences. The (unknowable-in-themselves) "things" affecting sense may be considered necessary for static experiences.[29] However, grouping some plurality of these "things" such that the unity of that plurality is supposed to signify the reality of the concept "the world" does not make the unity necessary. There are many possible ways to characterize the world; however, it is necessarily the case that each of those possible ways is determined by you. Hence, a necessity belongs to the TUA that does not belong to the "world."

According to Kant, the same critique will apply to the *idea* of God. Kant suggested that *thinking* of "God" results necessarily from the consideration of the *totality* of synchronic experiences. In this way, for example, we may look for the instantiation of God as omnipresent. Ultimately, however, the unity of grouping "the totality" of all experiences *in the intellect* is critiqued in two ways. First, as noted above, supposing such a grouping were possible, a necessity belongs to the TUA that does not belong to the idea of "God." Second, there is no sensory content that makes the experience of some "thing" an instance of the experience of "God." It is for both these reasons that Kant suggested "faith" is required to access that to which "God" is supposed to refer, not the *noetic* process or the use of pure reason.

3.3 Being Expresses-Itself through Time; Time Is the "Meaning of Being"[30]

In this section we will provide a summary conclusion of the insights gained into metaphysics by Kant. Reflecting on synchronic experience with the idea of the relation between actuality and potentiality, we came to realize that the *noetic* process conditions experience and that the universal-ground of the *noetic* process is time. Yet, upon further reflection regarding diachronic experience, we realized the necessary unity of the TUA, and, thereby, we came to understand that the TUA has ontological priority in regard to the *noetic* process. When we combine these insights, we are able to envision being in reality, that is "in the order of nature," and as not yet "in the intellect," this transcendental being expresses-itself—its meaning—through time. Put in a more poetic phrasing, as being is be-ing itself, it activates—through time—the *noetic* process, which is the meaning-making process for humans.

The meaning-making process, then, regarding "experience in general," may be characterized by saying: The active intellect uses logical categories of being to *noetically* coincide, so to speak, with some time-determination; in other words, according to Kant, "the succession of the manifold insofar as it is subject to a rule" (A 144/B 183). Thus, the logical categories function as "rules" regarding how to quantify the manifold "in the senses" as a time-determination. There are two important conclusions to draw from this insight. First, notice that reversing the trajectory of this *noetic* process asks if some instance (time-determination) meets the criteria of the logical rule (concept). Notice further that this logical quantification, so to speak, does not point to the TUA; rather, it is a logical operation of the intellect *within* the *noetic* process.

Second, in the wake of Kant's accomplishment, the Aristotelian-Scholastic understanding of the term "transcendental" and, more importantly, "being as a transcendental" is retained, while methodologically establishing the "order of being," and taking the human capacities for experience as a methodological point of departure. Of course, the Aristotelian-Scholastic term "transcendental" meant "to climb across"[31] the categories of reality. Thus, being was considered a "transcendental" because it had ontological priority in regard to the categories of being. This is directly analogous to Kant's TUA and the *noetic* process. Yet, it was not until Kant, however, that we gained methodological-access to a systematization of the categories of being derived from their possible use regarding modes of cognition *as time-determinations*.

§4 Explorations of the Continental Tradition: From the Canonic to the Organic Ends of Transcendental Philosophy

Recall how Kant began the *Critique of Pure Reason*, "I call all cognition transcendental that is occupied not so much with objects but rather with our mode of cognition of objects insofar as this is to be possible *a priori*" (A 11/B 25). And, further, "A *system* of such concepts would be called *transcendental philosophy*" (A 12/B 25). Because the terms "system" and "transcendental philosophy" aroused so much suspicion and controversy in both the nineteenth and twentieth centuries, it is important to return to the meanings of these terms as they were originally construed by Kant along with the Transcendental Method itself. In this way, it may be said that *transcendental philosophy provides the proper context and point of origin for the Continental Tradition*.

Because the Continental Tradition is a living tradition that continues into the future, it is not possible to formulate it as a completed totality. Thus, the value of this section of the chapter comes not from its ability to characterize the totality of the Continental Tradition; rather, the value of this section comes from its depiction of how philosophers have articulated various aspects of the Continental Tradition—within the context of, and with the insights gained by, Kant's paradigm-shifting philosophy. This section is unique, then, in that all of the other sections take being as their primary focus, and this section takes the Continental Tradition as its primary focus.

4.1 The "Homeric Contest" to Complete the System of Transcendental Philosophy: The Birth of German Idealism and German Romanticism

The two philosophical "movements" which quickly developed out of Kant's transcendental philosophy were "German Idealism" and "German Romanticism." Though it is beyond the scope of this chapter to provide an exhaustive account of these movements or the history of their textual influence, it is important to note the manner in which each movement relates to Kant's revelation. If we examine these movements in terms of their development of elements in Kant's system, then we find that their development is constrained by Transcendental Method, that is, by the ways in which the elements *can be* developed. Put another way, as was self-consciously and historically made explicit by the German philosophers in Kant's wake, these movements are constituted by the organic and canonical applications of the Transcendental Method, which function as the *conditions for the possibility of* the development of the transcendental elements toward a complete system.

Secondary to the methodological constraints, then, there are a limited number of points in the uncompleted system that can be developed toward the system's completion. Given all that was said above, it should come as no surprise that these points are time and the TUA. On the one hand, the concept of history became such a staple in the Continental Tradition in precisely this way, that is, by developing the element of time in terms of a concept of history. On the other hand, the traditional developments of the TUA fall into three different styles of characterization: subjection, individuation, and differentiation. Lastly, there are, of course, multiple ways in which the developments of the time and TUA elements of the system may be combined to articulate novel attempts to characterize the system and to use the system as a point of departure for characterizing mind-external reality, while still remaining within the Continental Tradition.

Thus, the following German philosophers contributed significantly to both the completion of Kant's system of transcendental philosophy and the raising of the project of its completion to the level of a "Homeric Contest": Karl Leonhard Reinhold (1757–1823), Johann Gottlieb Fichte (1762–1814), "Novalis" (1772–1801), the brothers August Wilhelm Schlegel (1767–1845) and Friedrich Schlegel (1772–1829), the "Tübingen Three" Georg Wilhelm Friedrich Hegel (1770–1831), Friedrich Hölderlin (1770–1843), and Friedrich Wilhelm Joseph Schelling (1775–1854), and, last but not least, Arthur Schopenhauer (1788–1860).

4.1.1 *The Opening of the Homeric Contest*

The initial reception of Kant's transcendental philosophy was thoroughly polemical and negative. As a kind of response, Karl Leonhard Reinhold constructed a series of articles in letter form—hence, the *Letters on the Kantian Philosophy*—between August 1786 and September 1787. Because these letters functioned as the catalyst for the Homeric Contest, it is worth asking: What was Reinhold's motivation for writing them?

In multiple ways, Reinhold's letters may be read as prompted by the publication of a set of letters directed, not at Kant's philosophy but, at the philosophy of Baruch Spinoza (1632–1677). These letters, published in 1785, written between Friedrich Heinrich Jacobi (1743–1819) and Moses Mendelssohn (1729–1786), popularized the idea that the Rationalist philosophy of the "Age of Reason," or the "Enlightenment," ultimately leads to "nihilism." On the one hand, Jacobi took Spinoza's philosophy to be the most systematically coherent of the all the Rationalist philosophers. On the other hand, just as Spinoza's philosophy was understood to culminate in "pantheism" and, thereby, "atheism"—because it is the most representative of the Rationalist-Enlightenment project—Jacobi concluded that *all* rationalistic philosophy is ultimately atheistic and nihilistic.

Reinhold (the former Catholic priest and later Freemason) recognized the rationalistic philosophy of Kant's *Critique of Pure Reason* as the exception to Jacobi's accusations. The idea may be helpfully paraphrased that Kant's philosophy "critiques reason to make room for faith." Thus, Reinhold emphasized two aspects of Kant's philosophy, which helped its previously dismal reception greatly. First, Kant's philosophy is rational without leading to atheism and nihilism. Second, as trivial as it may sound to anyone who has not attempted to read Kant's *Critique of Pure Reason*, Reinhold suggested the *Critique* should be read "backwards." (cf. Reinhold, 2005). This latter suggestion led readers to initially encounter Kant's thoughts on God, freedom, and immortality, rather than begin with the steep climb into Transcendental Logic.

Reinhold's "apology" for Kant's *Critique of Pure Reason* concluded with his attempt to provide a "foundation" for Kant's transcendental philosophy. Regardless of Reinhold's exact motivations for attempting to articulate such a foundation, it had the significant historical consequence that it explicitly motivated Fichte's attempt to work Kant's transcendental philosophy into a "Transcendental Idealism" (cf. Breazeale, 1982). Thus, Fichte set out in his 1794/5 *Foundation of the Entire* Wissenschaftslehre [*Theory of Scientific Knowledge*] to accomplish Reinhold's task of developing an ontological foundation for Kant's philosophy, since—as we have seen—it is actually methodologically grounded. Importantly, Fichte focused on the TUA; that is to say, Fichte's attempt to develop a foundation emphasized the way in which knowledge relates to the TUA.

In an earlier, and much shorter work, *Aenesidemus* (1792) Fichte had already formulated the essential idea. There Fichte famously claimed that representation of mind-external reality through the *noetic* process is *not a fact* of consciousness; *it is an act* of consciousness. How representation as an action of consciousness relates to the TUA is precisely the question, then, that ignited a kind of "Homeric Contest" among the German philosophers to complete the system of transcendental philosophy by articulating an ontological foundation for it. Toward merely providing a sketch, here, we may conveniently divide the different understandings of the ontology of the action by which mind-external reality is re(-)presented, and, thereby, the developments of Kant's revelation into two groups, the *noetic* and the *poetic*. Whereas the former relies primarily on the canonic application of the Transcendental Method, the latter relies primarily on the organic.

Thus, because the action by which mind-external reality is re(-)presented is also the ground by which transcendental apperception is reflectively accomplished, we may go so far as to say that it is Idealistic to conceive of the *action* as *noetic*, and it is Romantic to conceive of the action as *poetic*.[32] Of course, what is at stake between these two conceptions is the question of how to articulate an ontological foundation for Kant's Transcendental Method. In other words, on the one hand, if the action is *noetic*, then it logically follows that a kind of Absolute Idealism may be developed out of Kant's philosophy. For, if spirit-in-time—or history as the revelation of being—has a rational structure to it, then it may be possible to think into that dimension by using the action of the revelation of the TUA as a kind of portal into the Absolute. Perhaps the most succinct statement of this position can be found in Schelling's *System of Transcendental Idealism* (1800) where he characterized it noting, "History as a whole is a progressive, gradually self-disclosing revelation of the Absolute" (2001: 211).

On the other hand, if the action is *poetic*, then it logically follows that consciousness is a consciousness of alienation. Per such an understanding, judgment does not reveal an ultimately rational transcendental dimension; for, recall that though both German Idealism and Romanticism tend toward an interpretation of the transcendental dimension as Absolute spirit, Kant's original relation to the transcendental dimension was methodological and things-in-themselves are ultimately mysterious. In other words, the Romantic conception of the TUA is not the revelation of spirit finding its home in the world or its identity in rationality; rather, the Romantic conception of the conscious awareness of the TUA is the revelation of spirit's homelessness-in-the-world. Thus, the *poetic* truth of transcendental revelation is an awareness of loss and a kind of longing for the Absolute exemplified by home-sickness.

Now, regarding the Homeric Contest, though it was Schelling who provided the first exposition of Fichte's attempt at an ontological foundation with his 1794 *On the Possibility of a Form of Philosophy in General*, it was Hölderlin who first identified the problem with Fichte's attempt *and* offered a viable way to resolve the problem; thus, the work of Fichte and Schelling, on the one hand, and Hölderlin, on the other, provided the original development of the Methodological-revelation of Kant's transcendental philosophy into Idealistic and Romantic conceptions, respectively. It is helpful, when formulating any kind of narrative regarding the Homeric Contest, to treat Hölderlin's contribution in 1795 as a kind of anchor point, because the number of figures and characterizations multiplies quickly afterward.

In 1795, Hölderlin wrote "On Judgment and Being" [*Über Urtheil und Seyn*] in which he makes the distinction between identity and unity,[33] and attempts to ground Kant's Transcendental Method in the *action* of "judgment." This, of course, directly relates to the idea of transcendental subjectivity, because Hölderlin's distinction calls into question that the apperceptive-revelation of the TUA actually reveals "a subject." Indeed, Hölderlin claimed that *being* is a "whole of which object and subject are the parts"[34] (2003: 192). Notice, then, that even though Hegel's attempt to complete the system came after Hölderlin's, by characterizing the TUA in terms of judgment as *poetic* action, Hölderlin is the first to reveal a style for characterizing the TUA that later became important for combating Hegel's style of characterizing the TUA.

The problem that Hölderlin highlights can be stated as a question: How can the TUA, for example, as Fichte's Absolute "I," interact with the "Not-I" of mind-external reality? On the one hand, Hölderlin's distinction between identity and unity subsequently allows for a conception of the TUA as indicating *being* in an Absolute dimension, without setting up a "metaphysical dualism." On the other hand, by taking the *poetic action* of judgment to be responsible for the subject-object dichotomy, he retains the revelation of Absolute being and characterizes the poetic action of judgment as the primordial indicator of the Absolute. Thus, the poet is now truly the mouthpiece of divinity.

How this relates to—what I continue to refer to, here, as the "styles for characterizing the TUA"—is that Hölderlin allows for a conception of the being to which the TUA points in terms of individuation and differentiation, instead of subjection. Of course, the work of thinkers such as Descartes and Hobbes led to subjection becoming a central concept of "Early Modern philosophy." Moreover, despite the fact that Hölderlin had already indicated the problem with simply incorporating the Early Modern concept of the subject into the context of transcendental philosophy, as we will see, Hegel's style of characterizing the TUA can be distinguished from other post-Kant characterizations in that it relies on a concept of "the subject" that does *not necessarily* follow from the use of the Transcendental Method to complete the system of transcendental philosophy.

At the same time, that is, 1795, Schelling also attempted to go beyond Fichte's philosophy with two different works: *Of the I as Principle of Philosophy or on the Unconditioned in Human Knowledge* and *Philosophical Letters on Dogmatism and Criticism*. Building off Hölderlin's work, Schelling sought to characterize the Absolute ground indicated by the TUA as Nature. In the attempt to reconcile another possible "metaphysical dualism"—between nature and freedom or the laws of nature and God—Schelling characterized Absolute Nature as pantheistic, as if to make Spinoza's philosophy transcendental. Thus, despite his initial canonic emphasis toward an Absolute Idealism, this more organic emphasis would be the groundwork toward the *poetic* conceptions more commonly associated with Schelling's Romantic "Nature philosophy" [*Romantische Naturphilosophie*] and the "Positive," or "Existential," phase of his later philosophy.[35]

Now, in regard to the Romantic development of Kant's revelation and the conscious awareness of the transcendental dimension, the role of Novalis cannot be overlooked. In 1790, though he was not yet known by the pseudonym "Novalis," Georg Philipp Friedrich Freiherr von Hardenberg became a student at the University of Jena, where he studied history with Friedrich Schiller (1759–1805) and philosophy with—none other than the Kantian "apologist" whose work sparked the Homeric Contest—Reinhold. It was, then, also in 1795, when Novalis met, and conversed with, Fichte and Hölderlin at the home of Friedrich Immanuel Niethammer (1766–1848). Though Hölderlin had been consistently attending Fichte's lectures at the University of Jena, this was their first introduction to Novalis.

After this meeting, Novalis went on to write the *Fichte Studies* in 1795/6, contributing, in 1797, to the *Athenaeum*, the literary journal, produced by the Schlegel brothers, considered the founding publication of German Romanticism. Moreover, Novalis' Romantic conception of the action through which the TUA is revealed as *poetic* is important for understanding the transition from Romanticism to Existentialism; that is to say, Novalis' work regarding the revelation of being stands out in the Continental Tradition as a kind of "theurgy" or "philosophical alchemy,"[36] in that he emphasized "philosophical enlightenment" and an individual's discovery of the revelation of transcendental being as a kind of philosophical quest, culminating with ascendance into the Absolute dimension. Hence, Novalis' style of characterizing the TUA is Romantic, poetic, and does not depend on the concept of subjection.

Though the philosophies of Fichte, Schelling, Hölderlin, and Novalis open the Homeric Contest in the Continental Tradition, it is the philosophies of Hegel, Schelling, and Schopenhauer that close it. Moreover, since many older textbooks, having not considered Romanticism sufficiently philosophical or Existentialism sufficiently transcendental, may have too hastily deemed Hegel the "winner" of the Homeric Contest, we will begin the discussion of the closing of the Homeric Contest, here, with him.

4.1.2 *The Closing of the Homeric Contest*

As emphasized in his 1807 *Phenomenology of Spirit* and clarified in his 1817 *Encyclopedia of the Philosophical Sciences*, Hegel envisioned *the system* of transcendental philosophy as a whole consisting of three parts:[37] Logic, Philosophy of Nature, and Philosophy of Spirit.[38] Hegel, then, divided Philosophy of Spirit into Subjective, Objective, and Absolute. Finally, *Subjective* Spirit is divided into Anthropology, Phenomenology, and Psychology. Thus, recalling that Phenomenology and Psychology, in transcendental philosophy, correspond to the *noetic* process and the TUA, respectively, one immediately sees Hegel's style of characterizing the TUA, that is, in terms of subjection.

In other words, by emphasizing the following two points in Hegel's Speculative Idealism it is possible to distinguish his attempt to complete the system of transcendental philosophy from the other contestants, so to speak, in the Homeric Contest. On the one hand, characterizing the TUA as *subjective* spirit provided him sufficient grounds *in terms of general logic* to immediately posit objective spirit, and to continue his logical climb into the Absolute. It is in this way that Hegel was able to depict *a whole system*: the parts of which could all be conceptualized and the logic of which could systematically refer to all of the parts. Moreover, because Hegel's Speculative Idealism allows for these two latter aspects of *his* system, Hegel has often been lauded as the winner of the Homeric Contest.

In fact, it is for this reason that so many, if not all, of the subsequent phases, or movements, in the Continental Tradition have been historically articulated as reactions to Hegel's philosophy; not just the later philosophy of Schelling or the philosophy of Schopenhauer, but the philosophies of Karl Marx (1818–1883), Søren Kierkegaard (1813–1855), and Friedrich Nietzsche (1844–1900), among others, are often articulated as reactions to Hegel. It is important to note this for two reasons. First, historically speaking, and often according to these philosophers, their philosophies were articulated specifically as a reaction to Hegel's completion of "the system." Second, despite the sense in which their philosophies may be reactions to Hegel, the context in which they were operating and the goal in relation to which they were working were not Hegelian. It was Kantian; they were the Continental Tradition and the system of transcendental philosophy, respectively.

In this way, the work of Schopenhauer and the later work of Schelling, despite often being thought of as mere reactions to Hegel, are actually *both* polemics against Hegelianism *and* contributions toward completing the system of transcendental philosophy. Moreover, by emphasizing the ways in which they approached completing Kant's system, it is possible to see how all of the possible major "moves" in the Homeric Contest may have already been made after Schelling and Schopenhauer offered their solutions. Hence, we can speak of the closing of the Homeric Contest with the work of Hegel, Schelling, and Schopenhauer, and because Schelling and Schopenhauer provide a shift in focus for the Continental Tradition from Philosophy of History to Philosophy of Mythology and Philosophy of Life, respectively, we will discuss these in the next section.

4.2 Positive Philosophy and Philosophy of Life, beyond Systematic Totality: Toward the Mythical and Mysterious Nature of Being Individuated

Keeping in mind that the completion of Hegel's system and the revelation of its systematic totality rely on the characterization of the TUA in terms of Subjective Spirit, we can directly distinguish the contributions to the Homeric Contest of Schelling and Schopenhauer from Hegel in terms of Nature. That is to say, the later work of Schelling and the work of Schopenhauer differ from Hegel by characterizing the action constituting the revelation of the TUA as *poetic*, rather than *noetic*, and placing emphasis on Nature, so as to not fall into a style of characterizing *being* in terms of subjection. It is in this way that both Schelling and Schopenhauer may be understood as Romantics—the former optimistic and the latter, infamously, pessimistic.[39]

Thus, it is possible to state a case for Hölderlin, Schelling, or Schopenhauer—rather than Kant, Fichte, or Hegel—as the first to complete the transcendental system. The case for Hölderlin would highlight his distinction between identity and unity as the first to employ the style of Romantically characterizing the ground of the system as poetically ineffable. The case for Schelling would invoke the development of his *Romantische Naturphilosophie* through his *The Ages of the World*—the first version of which is believed to have been constructed in 1811—into his final philosophy of characterizing the ground of the system of transcendental philosophy in terms of the mythical revelation of individual existence, that is, individuated being. Finally, the case for Schopenhauer would invoke his two volumes of *The World as Will and Representation* from 1818 and 1819, respectively. There Schopenhauer also takes the Romantic approach to Nature; the TUA points to individuated Nature as poetically deceived by the universal will of Nature.

Schelling's later philosophy is unique in its ability to characterize transcendental, mind-external, reality in terms of differentiation, that is, in addition to individuation. This can be seen by his emphasis of the distinction between positive and negative philosophy. For Schelling, Hegel's philosophy is the ultimate accomplishment of a negative philosophy. Negative philosophy is a philosophy of mere reflection; its focus is on attempting to characterize the truth of itself; thus, it can be systematically total and complete because it does not focus on transcendental, mind-external, reality. For Schelling, it is positive philosophy that focuses on attempting to characterize the truth of reality.

In what may be understood as a characterization in direct contradistinction from Hegel's philosophy, Schelling developed a philosophy of Nature— indicated and arrived at through the TUA—as more primordial than time. His motivation for this should be clear given all that was said about regarding the view of time according to transcendental philosophy. With Nature more primordial than time and, thereby, history, Schelling was able to point to mythology and revelation as the modes of *individuated* Nature's *existence*.[40] This flung the door open and set the stage for "existentialism," and indicated a way to complete the system of transcendental philosophy without following Hegel into a merely negative philosophy.

At the same time, Schelling's later, positive, philosophy may be seen as the systematic development of Hölderlin's insight regarding unity, and this allows for an understanding in terms of differentiation of that to which the TUA points. For, the "I" of the mind may be understood as resulting from the structure with which one negatively and reflectively relates to (the whole of) Nature's existential positivity—of which one *is*, of course, a part. What is more, because this existence is more primordial than the structures of time which ground negative characterizations of it, transcendental philosophy may envision its dynamic ineffability as pure difference. That is, transcendentally speaking, it may be the case that the eternal flux of primordial Nature's dynamic ineffability can only be ontologically comprehended as a difference that is different from itself, or as Difference in Itself.[41]

Finally, to be clear, it may be tempting to read Schopenhauer's style of characterization in terms of subjection to the universal will of Nature, rather than individuation; however, if we keep in mind Schopenhauer's commitment to freedom as the very life blood of the individual's dissatisfaction with universal Nature—and especially in light of his later clarifications of individuation by way of concepts from Hinduism and Buddhism—it is clear that the ontology of Schopenhauer's philosophy of life is ultimately characterized in terms of individuation. On the one hand, then, Schopenhauer's philosophy is distinguished from Hegel's in a number of ways: most notably, in terms of his characterization of the TUA and his explicit statements against Hegel and "Hegelianism."

On the other hand, it is for this reason that Schopenhauer's case for being the winner of the Homeric Contest is strong. That is to say, Hölderlin did not produce a systematic exposition of what may have been his view of the system of transcendental philosophy grounded in poetic ineffability, and Schelling's "grounding of positive philosophy" as his grounding of the system of transcendental philosophy in mythology and revelation was never actually published; moreover, it arguably wasn't completed until his Berlin lectures delivered in the 1840s. Thus, if the contest comes down to the first to publish, at least a sketch of, the complete system of transcendental philosophy, then the contest may be stated in terms of the question of Idealism versus Romanticism, canonic-emphasis versus organic-emphasis, and Hegel versus Schopenhauer.

Thus, the Homeric Contest may be understood as providing a sketch of all the possible moves that can be made in regard to "completing" or "grounding" what Kant referred to as the system of transcendental philosophy. By considering how philosophers in the Continental Tradition characterize the TUA, that is, in terms of subjection, individuation, and differentiation, it is possible to provide further evidence of the—completion or ground-work development—limits to transcendental philosophy. In fact, it is for this reason that philosophy is often compared to a game, such as chess, and that the idea of "endgame" is invoked in regard to the Continental Tradition. That is to say, Kant finally organized philosophy into a canonical science, and either Kant's revolution itself or the gestures toward the completion of its ground-work made through German Idealism and Romanticism are understood as entering us into *the final stage* of philosophy.

The ends of philosophy—from the point of view of the Continental Tradition—can only be characterized in so many ways, and each of those characterizations must result from the application of the Transcendental Method. Since the Transcendental Method can only be applied in a finite number of ways, there are actual ends of philosophy. There are a limited number of ways transcendental philosophy can be characterized and developed. External reality may be an eternal flux; however, the canonical-philosophical science that reflects on it is not. Thus, there is an actual end to philosophizing, and we are living in those end times.

In this way, then, just as, generally, all of the philosophical movements within the Continental Tradition are constrained by the Transcendental Method, so too all of the various ways to characterize being are also constrained. Thus, the various styles with which philosophers in the Continental Tradition characterize the TUA are important, indeed. For example, central to Existentialism and Philosophy of Difference are the styles of characterizing the TUA in terms of individuation and differentiation, respectively. Moreover, this insight provides a point of departure for an archaeology of the major movements in the Continental Tradition, such as "German Idealism," "German Romanticism," "History of Philosophy," "Existentialism," "Phenomenology," "Hermeneutics," and "Philosophy of Difference."

4.3 The Quest to Discover, and Live in the Light of, Transcendental Apperception: From Decidability as Existential Freedom to Philosophies of Difference as the Necessity of Intensity and Undecidability

There are only two major points to be made in this subsection of the chapter. First, existential philosophies and philosophies of difference may be seen as direct developments and responses to the contributions to the Homeric

Contest made by all the philosophers just noted. Second, though it is beyond the scope of this chapter to enumerate them, all of the later innovations in the Continental Tradition—insofar as they actually participate in the Continental Tradition—are formulations of the elements of transcendental philosophy and applications of the Transcendental Method. Even the twentieth-century notion of "phenomenological hermeneutics as fundamental ontology" is really a summary restatement of Kant's use of the Transcendental Method to lay the groundwork for all future metaphysics.

Thus, in regard to "existentialism," we may ask: Of what does transcendental *reflection* make us aware regarding existence? And, especially in a way that can only be asked in the first person: What does transcendental reflection bring to awareness regarding this individual existence that is "mine" to live? For existentialists, being is not something to be simply *determined*, it requires the highest powers of our mind to honor it; that is to say, we must take a *transcendentally-reflective* relation to it, if we are to become aware of its transcendental dimension, and it is only by honoring its transcendental dimension that *each of its individuations* can be brought to the revelation of its own existence.

Just as it is standard to characterize the philosophies of Søren Kierkegaard (1813–1855) and Friedrich Nietzsche (1844–1900) as reactions against Hegel's totalizing vision of existence and as an affirmation of freedom, so too it is standard to recognize how their visions of individual existence relate to Kant and the German Romantics. For, even if we master the system of transcendental philosophy such that we can reflect on the existence of our life with transcendental clarity, we still have life to live. Thus, existentialism may be characterized as the awareness of life as a quest to discover the transcendental reality, out of which we each have our own individuated existence. Of course, the moment at which we accomplish this existential quest is the moment at which we accomplish the apperception which can only be made possible through transcendental reflection.[42] In fact, all of "Existentialist philosophy" may be characterized as stemming from *that* moment in the system of transcendental philosophy.

Moreover, as was noted in the previous section regarding the moment in which an individual gains a reflective awareness of its own being in the transcendental dimension, there is a "dreaded freedom" involved in the very characterization of the identity of that which is apperceived, since—according to transcendental philosophy—that which is apperceived is, ultimately, the dynamic ineffability of transcendental reality. Within such a context, philosophies of difference emphasize "undecidability" regarding the ineffable intensity of transcendental being. In the same way, among philosophers such as Martin Heidegger (1889–1976), Albert Camus (1913–1960), Jean-Paul Sartre (1905–1980), and Simone de Beauvoir (1908–1986) the emphasis on time, freedom, and ambiguity may be traced back to Kant's delimiting of the ways in which transcendental being may be characterized.

Thus, the inescapability of freedom is common to both existential philosophies and philosophies of difference because it is a feature of the primordial element of transcendental philosophy indicated by the TUA. *Time* passes, and—because we do not have a systematically total view of existence, despite Hegel's dream—we cannot escape making a choice. In other words, since choosing not to choose is still having made a choice, we cannot escape making a choice; yet, given the Nature of transcendental being as ineffable and in flux, the identity and meaning of our choices, just like the identity of our transcendental being—be-ing as becoming—call for such characterization as ultimately undecidable. Yet, rather than point to anarchy, for existentialists, this points to a fundamental responsibility and the question of integrity regarding one's decisions.

Thus, as standardized by Heidegger's *Being & Time*, the difference between determining the identity one's being in terms of "everyday" decidability, rather than in terms of its transcendentality, may be understood as the difference between being "inauthentic" and "authentic," respectively. Furthermore, recalling that the TUA has "ontological priority" in regard to temporal experience, the being to which the TUA refers is ec-static and free in relation to time. Whereas existential philosophies emphasize the ecstasy of being and the "inescapable freedom" of deciding, philosophies of difference emphasize the intensity of that ecstasy and the necessity of undecidability.

§5 The Philosophy of Being in the Continental Tradition

The final section of this chapter is divided into three parts. The first part provides clarification by emphasizing that the Continental Tradition's understanding of metaphysical being is neither as cognition nor as subjectivity or objectivity.

In other words, transcendental being is not a cognition, we gain awareness of it through transcendental apperception; transcendental being is neither a subject nor an object, it is the condition for the possibility of being a subject or an object. The second part of this section provides a shorthand summary characterization of being in the Continental Tradition toward clarifying a distinction that often remains vague in other traditions, namely that there is in fact a difference between the two ultimate questions in the philosophy of being. Lastly, the main insights of this chapter are summarized.

5.1 Neither Cognition Nor Subjectivity or Objectivity: From Ontological Unity in the Power of Judgment to Beauty and Goodness (Harmony) as the Revelation (Truth) of Transcendental Being

This section emphasizes two points stated above. The first was stated explicitly, though not summarily, and the second needs to be stated explicitly. Were the first point to be a section of its own, that section title might be: The Revelation of an Individual's Organic-Transcendental Reflection Exceeds All Canonical Subjection: On Transcendental versus Naïve Subjectivity. Were the second point to be a section of its own, that section title might be: Kant's Implicit Re-articulation of the Scholastic Theory of Transcendentals.

The first point should be re-stated summarily here because it is my sincere belief that it is the number one mistake made by those who participate in traditions other than Kant's, whenever they approach and attempt to understand transcendental philosophy. The Thomistic portion of the Conclusion to this book provides just such an example.[43] Helpfully, the use of the term "naïve" to modify subjectivity comes from Edmund Husserl (1859–1938). It is intended to refer to pre-Kantian—mainly Cartesian—understandings of subjectivity, and, technically, the contrast is between the TUA and some empirically or rationally derived concept of a subject.[44] Yet, as was emphasized above, it is not necessary to use the concept of a subject. Subjection can be contrasted with individuation and differentiation.

In sum, then, if we are to understand being in the Continental Tradition correctly, we must understand that transcendental being is not cognition. It is the condition for the possibility of a cognition. Also, we must understand that transcendental being is neither an object nor a subject.

In regard to the second point, then, notice that the title of this section contains all of the so-called Scholastic Transcendentals: Unity, Truth, Beauty, Goodness, and Being. Briefly, the TUA is the transcendental unity of the power of judgment and the reflective point at which the transcendental dimension comes into focus. As was noted above regarding the difference between determinative and reflective uses of judgment, when we experience a particular for which we do not have a universal we are forced into the reflective use of judgment. Kant spoke of this most explicitly in his *Critique of the Power of Judgment*. In such instances, the trajectory of this "reflective" judgment goes from cognition of the particular through the unity of the judgment *in the experience of the particular*, and forces an apperceptive-awareness of the transcendental dimensions of the *experience*.

Kant spoke of this in the context of judging beauty in an experience. For Kant, there is no *a priori* concept of beauty; if there were, then we could enumerate the criteria and every experience of beauty would need to conform to those criteria. In contrast to this, Kant recognized that the experience of particular beauty forces us to discover the universal, and since there is no concept of beauty, Kant explains that the universality that we identify with beauty stems from the psychological experience; that is to say, the experience of "the free play of the imagination," as we search for a concept, is universal to the human species, and, therefore, provides the very universality that is otherwise absent as a concept (2000: §9).

Notice, then, on the one hand, the trajectory of the reflective power of judgment is the trajectory of the TUA. On the other hand, Kant's conclusion about beauty is actually twofold, that is, about beauty and harmony. In other words, as Kant makes explicit, the universality of the pleasure of the free play of imagination is both a transcendental resonance between the subject and the beautiful object and a resonance across all individuals with the human-species specific conditions for the possibility of experience. Therefore, though Kant does not make this explicit, we can notice his re-working here of the Scholastic theory of Transcendentals.

In other words, the Transcendental Method illuminates the transcendental *unity* of apperception, *beauty* and *goodness* (as harmony) along the trajectory of the reflective power of judgment, and *truth* as the revelation of *being* at the end of the trajectory. Thus, Kant's philosophy may be articulated as formulating a theory of Transcendentals. Just as the unity of transcendental reflection brings the transcendental dimension into focus for Kant, it is in that dimension that he locates the Scholastic Transcendentals. Notice, again, the appropriateness of the Copernican metaphor: Kant is looking at the same philosophical content; however, he has established a scientific context for understanding that content.

5.2 Being as the Be-ing of Beings

The convention of writing "being" with a hyphen emphasizes the term's use as the participle of the verb "to be," as opposed to a noun (cf. Wilhelmsen, 1956: 59). Thus, in order to signify the *activity* of being in regard to each individual being, we emphasize the "ing" by writing "be-ing." In this way, even though being is not a genus, we can refer to the activity of its dynamic ineffability generically as be-ing, rather than as Spirit or Nature. In this way, since being can be said in many ways, it can be clarified that there is an "ontological difference" between be-ing and beings, and whereas the Thomistic and the Analytic Traditions focuses on beings, the Continental Tradition focuses on be-ing.

Thus, with this convention, the following phrase may be articulated: It may be said that metaphysics in the Continental Tradition studies "Being as the be-ing of beings." This phrase is valuable, since, on the one hand, lowercase "being" refers to particular beings, such as cosmological, theological, and psychological beings. On the other hand, the phrase is valuable because it provides a succinct response to the two ultimate questions in the philosophy of being. That is to say, the study of metaphysical being involves the study of (transcendental) "be-ing," and the meaning of "Being" is time. Thus, this convention helpfully keeps distinct and clarifies the often-vague difference between "the meaning of being" and "being in reality."

5.3 Concluding Summary

Recall that what distinguishes the Continental Tradition *from all other traditions* can be stated in one word, and that word is: methodology. In other words, what constitutes the Continental Tradition, and differentiates it from all other traditions, is the use of the Transcendental Method. This method, of course, was first formulated by Immanuel Kant (1724–1804) in his revolutionary: *Critique of Pure Reason* (1781). In this way, only the Kantian, that is, Continental Tradition uses the Transcendental Method, and to use the Transcendental Method is to participate in the Continental Tradition. Hence, the methodology of the Transcendental Method, and its application toward solving problems in philosophy, distinguishes the Continental Tradition from *all* other traditions.

The Transcendental Method can be applied organically or canonically. When applied organically, it functions in accordance with the Kantian "Copernican Revolution" by hypothesizing that "objects must conform to our cognition" (B xvi), that is to say, the object of our cognition is limited by our ability to cognize it. Thus, through the application of the Transcendental Method, we immediately see that the thing *is* different from the object of our cognition.

Furthermore, recall that the two ultimate questions in the philosophy of being are: "What is being?" and "What is the meaning of being?" Because there are many ways in which being can be said, it would be more precise to ask the questions as: "What is metaphysical being?" and "What is the meaning of metaphysical being?" Furthermore, given the Continental Tradition's understanding of metaphysics, we would clarify these questions by replacing the term "metaphysical" with "transcendental."[45] At the same time, it may be easier to engage in dialogue initially with participants of other traditions by using the terms "metaphysical" or "ontological."[46]

Now, the being of the thing—as opposed to the ways in which being may be said regarding the object of our cognition—*is* the existing individual. Hence, organically applied, the Transcendental Method "extends our cognition," that is, allows us to apperceptively envision, to become aware of, and to think into the transcendental dimension. Because transcendental being is metaphysical being, the organic application of the Transcendental Method reveals the true answer to the question: What is being? That is to say, through transcendental reflection each individuated being—with the conditions for the possibility of experience which are universal to the human species—can use the Transcendental Method to accomplish transcendental apperception. In other words, I myself am that being brought into focus through the apperception of transcendental reflection, that is, the TUA. That is how we answer the question: What is being?

When applied canonically, the Transcendental Method provides the rules governing the validity of inferences made when thinking transcendentally—so long as our thinking does not fall into "transcendental illusion" by leaving the domain of impure reason. On the one hand, the canonic use of the Transcendental Method, therefore, provides clarification to its organic use. On the other hand, it provides us with the elements of Transcendental Aesthetics and the Transcendental Logic with which to analyze them. In doing so, we recognize time as the primordial *a priori* element in the constitution of experience (i.e., not merely sensation). In other words, it is by conforming to the human intuition of time that things become objects of cognition. Thus, the canonic application of the Transcendental Method answers the second ultimate question in the philosophy of being: What is the meaning of being? This is because time constitutes the ground of all existential meaning-making. Put another way, how humans make meaning of being is, ultimately, in terms of time. No other tradition approaches the meaning of being in this way.

In sum, by showing the Continental Tradition's answers to these questions and revealing the (scientific) method with which to induce a revelation of the transcendental dimension, this chapter has elucidated *the philosophy of being* in the Continental Tradition. In light of this chapter, then, readers now should be able to accomplish, at least, three goals. First, readers should have a general understanding of how Kant's Transcendental Method functions as the methodology of the science of metaphysics. Second, readers should have a deeper understanding of how the Continental Tradition understands being.

Finally, in addition to logical clarification regarding the science of metaphysics, this insight is twofold. On the one hand, this means the ability to understand German Idealism and German Romanticism as developments in a "Homeric Contest" to complete Kant's system of transcendental philosophy. On the other hand, this means the ability to understand philosophy in the Continental Tradition—as differentiated from continental philosophy—as functioning within the confines of transcendental philosophy as a science. In this way, readers should be in a position to more easily understand what distinguishes the philosophy of being in the Continental Tradition from all other traditions, especially the Thomistic and the Analytic. Readers should also be in a position from which to more easily appreciate the genius of Kant.

Being in the Analytic Tradition: The Logic of Existence

David Kovacs

§1 Introducing Analytic Philosophy

What is Analytic philosophy? How is it characterized? And what insights have Analytic philosophers offered concerning the nature of existence? In this chapter, I will address those questions. Before turning directly to the nature of existence, I will say something about what Analytic philosophy is. I will do this by first telling you something about its historical origins. Then, I will try to give you a sense of the major characteristics of Analytic philosophy by describing a famous example of it. Then, I will have something to say about a philosopher who is important for the history of Analytic philosophy especially as it pertains to the topic of this book.

1.1 Historical Origins

By the end of the nineteenth century, the dominant philosophical school in Great Britain was a tradition called "British Idealism." This was a collection of related philosophical theories largely influenced by the German philosopher G.W.F. Hegel (1770–1831). The most influential and highly regarded British Idealist (at the time) was F.H. Bradley (1846–1924). Idealism, in general, is a view that questions or denies the existence of a world independent of the mind; that is, idealists tend to believe that reality (insofar as reality can be spoken of at all) is reducible to mind or thought or ideas.[1] In addition to this central belief, the British Idealists also tended to be monists, which is to say that they denied any real divisions or distinctions in reality. According to monists, everything can be reduced to some single indivisible and fundamental "thing" (for lack of a better word), which Bradley and others labeled "The Absolute."[2]

Analytic philosophy was born as a rejection of British Idealism. G.E. Moore (1873–1958) and Bertrand Russell (1872–1970) are two philosophers who were trained in, and who rebelled against, British Idealism. Moore defended the common-sense view that there is a mind-independent world.[3] Indeed, Moore tried to argue that a significant problem with British Idealism was its rejection of what he called a "common sense view of the world," that the error of the British Idealists consisted in a sort of arrogance by which they think that nearly every human who has ever lived has been mistaken in some of their most fundamental beliefs, such as the belief that there is an external world.[4] Against the monist view of reality, Russell thought that the universe is made up of many independently existing items, and this belief formed the basis of his theory called "Logical Atomism."[5] These were some of the earliest theories in Analytic philosophy.

Why do I mention the historical origins of Analytic philosophy? Obviously, studying the history of a philosophical movement is a fine way of learning about it, but is there any lesson in the origins of Analytic philosophy that would help us answer the question, "What is it to be an Analytic philosopher?" I think that there is. I think this because today there is no central doctrine that everyone who is grouped under the label "Analytic philosophy" adheres to. There is no creed, no binding maxim such that, once someone accepts it, she is then guaranteed admission to the Analytic "club." Instead, there are just certain habits that Analytic philosophers take pride in, and there are styles of writing and ways of thinking that we tend to agree to characterize this tradition. Analytic philosophy is like a flavor that one recognizes when one tastes it. One such characteristic of Analytic philosophy is seen in the early rejection of British Idealism.

Many Analytic philosophers like to deal with clear, concrete ideas that can be expressed using common, ordinary language. While there is occasionally a need to invent some new jargon (this is especially the case in Analytic Metaphysics), Analytic philosophers often try to de-mystify philosophy. This desire for de-mystification is present, for example, in the rejection by

Moore and Russell of British Idealism, especially some of British Idealism's more obscure doctrines concerning monism and "the Absolute." To see how this rejection takes place, let's look at a comment by A.J. Ayer (1910–1989) regarding the famous British Idealist F.H. Bradley.

Ayer was one of the main representatives (perhaps *the* main representative) of a group of Analytic philosophers known as "Logical Positivists." One of the central tenets of the Logical Positivists was that, for the most part, a sentence is meaningful only if one can specify what sort of observation would confirm the truth or falsity of it.[6] If a statement is such that it cannot be confirmed or disconfirmed by empirical observation, then the Positivists said such a statement was neither true nor false, but meaningless; it was a mere pseudo-statement. To drive this point home, Ayer selects what he claims is a "random sentence" chosen from Bradley's *Appearance and Reality*: "The Absolute enters into, but is itself incapable of, evolution and progress." Since there is no way of even imagining how to empirically confirm what is meant by this statement, Ayer says that its author "fails to communicate anything to us."[7] This tenet of Logical Positivism, that (in general) a statement must be verifiable to be meaningful, I should note, is generally now held to be untenable.[8] And, I should add, there may be good reason to think that Ayer did not give Bradley a charitable reading. Nevertheless, there is a legacy that still thrives in Analytic philosophy that praises this hard-nose kind of approach. The statement "The Absolute enters into, but is itself incapable of, evolution and progress" is the sort of statement that Analytic philosophers will rarely be happy with, and it is one which they will demand that one who utters it clarify and refine it until it becomes very clear what such a statement means. I cannot even begin to understand such a statement without analyzing each of its component terms: "The Absolute," "entering into evolution," and so on.

1.2 An Example of Analytic Philosophy: Gettier Cases

The sort of analysis mentioned in my previous sentence is, in fact, where Analytic philosophy gets the "Analytic" part of its name from. To get a sense of how such analysis proceeds, it may be helpful here to briefly consider the history of epistemology in Analytic philosophy. Epistemology is the part of philosophy that considers questions about the nature of knowledge, especially the question "What is knowledge?" The first thing that Analytic philosophers typically do when confronted with such an abstract question is to convert it to a question that is less abstract. "Knowledge" is an abstract term; "A person who knows" is not. For example, if the philosophical question were "What is love?" an Analytic philosopher would exchange that question with the statement "Someone loves something (or someone) when ..." and then proceed to list the conditions that have to be satisfied for the statement to be true. If the question were "What is beauty?" the Analytic method would prescribe trying to determine how to complete the statement "Something is beautiful if and only if ...."

So Analytic philosophers would handle the question "What is knowledge" by trying to analyze the statement "Someone knows something." Notice that the "something" here is necessary; while it might be meaningful to say "Jack knows" if one means something like "Jack is the sort of thing that knows things (unlike that kitchen blender which knows nothing)," we typically make knowledge claims that are (as philosophers say) "*intentional*." That just means that knowledge takes an object; all knowledge is knowledge *of* something or other. And, in English, what we know is typically expressed in the form of a statement, such as "The cat is on the mat" or "The Pope is from Argentina" or "Water is H2O."[9] For convenience, any one of these statements can be reduced to the single letter p (when Analytic philosophers want to represent non-specific statements with single letters, they start with lowercase p, q, r, etc.).[10] So with that said, we are now in a position to analyze the statement "Someone knows p."

First, it seems that anyone who claims to know anything must admit to believing the statement she claims to know. If I do not believe that Cleveland is north of Akron, I certainly cannot know that Cleveland is north of Akron. But I believe lots of things, and not all of my beliefs are bits of knowledge. Importantly, some of my beliefs throughout my life have turned out to be false. When I was in college I had a professor who, whenever he was in need of an example to illustrate some difficult point, would refer to his cat, Mr. Whiskers. And so I believed that my professor had a cat. I later learned that he had never had a cat and that Mr. Whiskers was a fictitious feline that he made up years earlier and had been using ever since. So my belief was false. And it would be very strange, therefore, to say that I *knew* that my professor had a cat named

Mr. Whiskers. So we now have a second criterion for knowledge: Someone knows *p* when they believe *p* but also when *p* is true.

Still, this cannot be the whole story. Sometimes we have beliefs that are true but which do not constitute knowledge. People who consult astrologers will sometimes point to instances where the astrologer got something right; Terry's astrologer said that Terry was adopted by a couple other than Terry's biological father and mother; Terry believes it and later gets a confession from the couple who raised her that this is in fact the case. Now, assuming that astrology is pseudoscientific nonsense, it would seem strange to say that Terry *knew* that she was adopted based on the word of the astrologer. She believed it, and it later turned out she had a true belief, but it seems like she was not warranted to have that belief; the belief was not sufficiently justified. And so Analytic epistemologists often stipulate a third condition that has to be met for someone to possess some knowledge: They must have a true belief that they are *justified* in holding; knowledge is true justified belief.

For a long time, Analytic philosophers considered this definition of knowledge, that is, as true justified belief, to be a good one. They saw it as unproblematic. But I want to tell you about a further development in the history of Analytic epistemology because I think that it illustrates something else about the methods of Analytic philosophers. The development which I have in mind has to do with what is now called "The Gettier Problem."[11] The basic idea here is that it is not too difficult to come up with instances of someone having a true justified belief, but where we would not call the belief in question "knowledge." Such cases are called "Gettier cases." The Gettier Problem is a good example of two things that Analytic philosophers do: They try to find counter-examples to claims (often by means of thought experiments), and they rely on our intuitive, common sense for what words like "knowledge" mean.

To see what a Gettier case is, consider the unfortunate fellow Pauley who is summoned by his employer for random drug testing. Pauley takes the test and his employer receives the report that afternoon that says that Pauley tested positive for cannabis. Of course, any reasonable person would believe the result of a highly sophisticated test, and Pauley's boss likewise formed the belief "Pauley has been using cannabis." Planning to call Pauley into the office in the morning and confront him about the matter, however, became unnecessary when the lab called the employer shortly before the end of the day to inform her that, due to a lab malfunction, Pauley's test result might not have been accurate. So now unfortunate Pauley is actually fortunate Pauley, for it turns out he really was a habitual marijuana smoker. Pauley's boss dropped the matter rather than putting time and resources into a new test, but the point is that there was a period of time when she believed "Pauley uses cannabis," and moreover her belief was true and justified! The belief was justified because it is reasonable to believe the results of drug tests. Yet, given that the justification was the result of a sort of luck, most people would be reluctant to describe her belief as an instance of knowledge. (Another example of a Gettier case would be someone who judges what time it is based on a broken clock without knowing that the clock is broken, but who happens to look at it at the very hour and minute corresponding to when it stopped working.) Gettier cases seem to show that knowledge is not merely true justified belief after all.

The history of epistemology in Analytic philosophy has largely been an attempt to deal with the Gettier problem, and a survey of how philosophers have attempted this task is not what concerns me here.[12] For now I wish to draw your attention to what I think makes this analysis of knowledge an especially perspicuous example of Analytic philosophy.

1. It begins by attempting to answer a question about a word that we use on a normal, daily basis. In this case, the word is "knowledge." Other ordinary words that Analytic philosophers have been concerned with include "love," "truth," and even "number" and "art." This aspect of Analytic philosophy is sometimes called "ordinary language analysis." The ordinary words with which this book is concerned are "existence" and "being" (which appear, to my eye, roughly synonymous; I see no reason, as opposed to some thinkers in other traditions, to distinguish between the two).

2. Analytic philosophers consider these questions first by converting the abstract form of the question into a concrete one. "What is knowledge?" becomes "What does it mean to say that someone knows something?" In this book, I am concerned with answering the question "What is existence?" by considering the question "What does the word 'exist' mean?" which is just to ask "What sense can be made of saying that something exists?"

3. Intuitions are accorded serious respect by Analytic philosophers. For example, when I asserted that a belief cannot count as a bit of knowledge unless it is a belief that is true, I offered no further evidence of this claim except to note that you probably already intuitively use the words "knowledge" and "know" in such a way. Likewise, Gettier cases, for example, are meant to provide examples where we intuitively would say that someone *doesn't* have knowledge, despite meeting all the conditions we stipulated for knowledge. Yes, our intuitions can be wrong. But when a counter-intuitive claim is made, Analytic philosophers typically expect strong arguments for such claims. You will see that in a good deal of this chapter, I am defending the counter-intuitive claim that the statement "Kovacs exists" is a bit of gibberish; it has no meaning. I defend this by trying to show that it conflicts with intuitions that we consider more fundamental to our belief structure.
4. Insofar as possible, Analytic philosophers prefer the familiar over the abstruse. Consider this definition of knowledge from a decidedly non-Analytic philosopher: "The truth of knowledge consists in the conformity of the mind with the thing."[13] Now it might be that this definition has something going for it.[14] However, on its face, it appears very obscure. Just what does it mean for "mind to conform with the thing"? Furthermore, such a definition would have to do some work saying what is meant by "mind." These problems are not insurmountable, neither for Analytic philosophers nor for thinkers in other traditions, but they are problems that Analytic philosophers generally try to steer away from.
5. As the scientist tests hypotheses in a lab with controlled experiments, Analytic philosophers test claims in the laboratory of the mind with thought experiments, keenly on the lookout for counter examples.

While this list is not exhaustive, these are some of the features which characterize philosophy as it has been done in the English-speaking world for the past century. Analytic philosophy has consequentially sometimes been called "Anglo-American Philosophy." But this label is misleading. One reason that it is misleading is because some philosophers outside of the English-speaking world could have their work characterized in much the same way.[15] Another reason that it would be misleading is that it overlooks the influence of Gottlob Frege (1848–1925).

1.3 Frege and the Turn to Mathematics

Frege was a German thinker whose training was primarily mathematical (the title of his doctoral dissertation, translated into English, is "On a Geometrical Representation of Imaginary Figures in a Plane"). His interests in mathematics led him to study logic, however, and Frege was for some time interested in showing that all the truths of arithmetic (e.g., "1+1=2") could be deductively proved from a few logical axioms (a logical axiom would be something like "If statement p is true, and if p entails q, then infer q"). In this endeavor, he found inspiration from another German philosopher who had died nearly two centuries earlier, Gottfried Wilhelm Leibniz (1646–1716). Frege took Leibniz to have shown that the task of deducing arithmetic from logic is not a task that could be done using ordinary language. Just as you cannot get very far in explaining calculus to someone without having to rely upon (or invent, as Leibniz himself did) a different system of unusual looking signs, logic would have to develop its own language: a logical calculus. This is exactly what Frege did.[16]

Readers who wish to read Frege's own writings on this topic (as well as responses written by other early Analytic philosophers) will want to keep in mind that a central concern of Frege's thinking on logic was the distinction between sense and reference. What do I mean by "sense"? And what do I mean by "reference"? Consider the terms "morning star" and "evening star." In fact, both of these terms refer to the same object: the planet Venus. Nevertheless, the two terms have distinct senses; the first has the sense of (roughly) "the bright celestial object visible in the morning," the latter has the sense of (roughly) "the bright celestial object visible in the evening." That sense and reference are distinct is obvious when one considers that the statement "The morning star is the evening star" is true because "Venus is Venus" is necessarily true. Yet, if I say "Jack did not know that the morning star is the evening star," am I implying that Jack did not know that Venus is Venus? Of course I am not. The upshot this distinction is that a term can have a sense, as "Sherlock Holmes" does ("The famous detective who lives at 221B Baker Street") and yet have no reference. The distinction between sense and reference left early Analytic philosophers with a mystery: What can a statement like "Sherlock Holmes does not exist" mean? Readers interested in these historical issues can consult Section 3 ("History and Further Details").[17]

I mention Frege in this introduction for one other reason: Because he, perhaps more than anyone else, accounts for a tendency one finds among Analytic philosophers: a tendency toward a fascination with mathematics.[18] You will see in Section 2.1.8 that it was Frege's attempt to define certain numbers, most especially the number "zero" (insofar as it is rightly called a number), that led him to make a startling claim about existence: That there is no such property rightly called "existence" or "being." To say that something exists is just to say that the number of things that correspond to that something (whatever that something might be) is not zero, that it is at least one. "Black holes exist" just means "The number of black holes is not zero; there is at least one black hole." This deflationary view of existence (I call it "deflationary" because it deflates, so to speak, the view that existence is some sort of property) has come to be common among Analytic philosophers; for Analytic philosophers who haven't thought especially about the matter of existence, it might even be a sort of default view. The Fregean reasons for thinking about existence this way constitutes the bulk of the remainder of this chapter.

But as I said already, there is no central tenet that all Analytic thinkers hold. And so some philosophers have put forth arguments meant to show that Frege and his defenders on this matter are mistaken, and that existence is a property that individuals have, just like color is a property that apples have. Since I want you to have a sense for how Analytic philosophers engage with each other, I have, therefore, also included at the end of this chapter summaries of the arguments that three detractors of the Fregean thesis have given in recent years. I believe that all three are good samples of what it means to think about *being* or *existence* in the Analytic Tradition. Nevertheless, I think that Frege's original view is the correct one, and when you turn to our concluding chapter, you will see me give my reasons for thinking this.

§2 Analytic Philosophy and Being

Let me begin by using a lot of the jargon that Analytic philosophers use when talking about existence, or being.[19] Then, with all of the technical and (to perhaps some of you) unusual vocabulary "out on the table" (so to speak), I will explain what it all means. To begin, the slogan "Being is not a real predicate," and others similar to it, is commonplace in Analytic philosophy. The view of most philosophers in this tradition is that existence is not what they call a "first-order property" of individuals. Gottlob Frege is usually credited with providing this analysis of existence. However, the most robust defense of the Fregean analysis has come from C.J.F. Williams (1930–1997).[20] Therefore, this chapter will be first concerned with summarizing Williams's arguments about existence and explaining what it is that Analytic philosophers mean when they claim that it is not a real predicate or first-order property. In the brief second part of this chapter, I will provide some history and also consider a dispute in Analytic philosophy regarding how to properly understand what is called the "existential quantifier." This dispute is more technical and some readers may want to initially skip it. As I pointed out in the Introduction, there is no dogma that all Analytic philosophers adhere to in virtue of which they can be called analytic, so it will not surprise you to learn that the Fregean view advocated by Williams has had its share of challengers. The last part of this chapter, therefore, turns to three critics who have aimed to show that Williams is wrong about existence. Whether any of their criticisms are decisive, I will leave to the reader to decide and to the discussion in the concluding chapter of this volume.

2.1 Williams's Defense of Frege on Existence

Frege and Williams can be thought of as denying what might be called a "naïve view" of existence. What is the naïve view? It is, perhaps, the most intuitive view of existence given how we use the word "exists." In the Introduction, I told you that Analytic philosophers are big fans of how words get intuitively used, and that these intuitions are only discarded if it turns out that they conflict with other, more fundamental intuitions. So, first I will tell you about the intuitive, naïve view of existence, and then I will tell you why Frege and Williams thought that the naïve view conflicts with other, more fundamental intuitions.

2.1.1 The Naïve View of Existence

The naïve view of existence, which most of this chapter will give reasons for thinking is flawed, is that existence is a real property that individuals have. On this view, the statement "Pope Francis exists" is on par with the statement "Pope

Francis is from Argentina." Both statements have an individual (the person of Pope Francis) for their subject and purport to tell you something about that individual by means of attaching a predicate to the subject term. To see this, let's look at some basic features of language.

2.1.2 *Things and Words; Properties and Predicates*

Suppose you asked me about myself. I might tell you that I am 5',10", weigh 180 pounds, and I am lazy. When I do this, I would be telling you about a thing, myself, by telling you about my properties: my height, weight, and behavioral disposition. I could even have told you that I am a human. And then I would have had to tell you about an additional property that I have: my humanity.[21]

So it seems like this is the kind of world we live in. There are things, that is, particular individuals that can be touched and moved and pushed and studied, and there are the properties of these things.[22] The difference between things and properties is this: Properties can be repeated, individual things cannot.[23] People, trees, and marbles can all be 5'10"; but at most one thing can be me. There can be lots of people, which is why we can think of humanity as a property, too; but you know the difference between me and every other person that you know.[24]

This distinction between things and their properties, between what cannot be repeated and what can, is reflected in our language when we speak of subjects and predicates. In the sentence, "Kovacs is a human that is 5'10", 180 lbs, and lazy," the word "Kovacs" is a subject that refers to the thing that is writing this sentence. And the words "human," "5'10"," "180 lbs," and "lazy" are predicates that refer to my properties.

But surely this is too simple. If a property is just something repeatable, what do we do with sentences like "Kovacs was remembered by his students?" Lots of things, hopefully, can be and have been remembered by my students, and so in that sense being remembered is repeatable. Yet being remembered by students seems different from other things that can be repeated, like being a human or being green or being literate. These latter repeatables all tell us something meaningful about an individual. And why talk about properties at all if not to give information about an individual? Yet being remembered by students tells us nothing except, perhaps incidentally, about the students themselves. My grandparents have been dead for a long time; when I tell you

"My grandparents are remembered by Kovacs" it is impossible that this will give you new information about them since they are not alive anymore.

This is why some philosophers distinguish between real properties and what they call "Cambridge properties." What, exactly, a Cambridge property amounts to is difficult to say, and at any rate not everyone agrees where to draw the lines, but for our purposes we can say that *real properties* are those that, when expressed as predicates, provide meaningful information about individuals considered in themselves. Cambridge properties, on the other hand, do not. They make no difference to the subject of which they are predicated. My students can remember me a hundred times a day and I won't be modified in any way by this fact. The importance of the distinction between real properties and Cambridge properties will play an important *role* in the objections to the Fregean view of existence below.

2.1.3 *Verbs as Predicates and an Account of the Relation between Words and Properties*

So far all the properties we have been considering are ones expressed by adjectives. But we can also consider actions as properties and take verbs and verb phrases to be predicates. So, in the statement "Sally laughs" we predicate "laughs" of Sally. Examples of more complex verb phrases turned into predicates and expressing properties would be when we predicate something like "likes watching television more than listening to opera" of Sally to form the sentence "Sally likes watching television more than she likes listening to opera." So, talk of properties is not limited to adjectival properties; verbs can be predicates and express properties just as well.

So far, then, things look straightforward. It looks as if any time you take some phrase that refers to an individual (whether you do so with a name, such as "Kovacs," or with a description, such as "The author of the present paragraph") and make a grammatically acceptable sentence out of it, what you have done is used predicates to say that the individual has the properties named by those predicates (with the above-mentioned exception for Cambridge properties). Conveniently, language provides a map to how things in the world are.[25]

2.1.4 *Predicates and Predicables: A Warning*

Williams thought that questions about existence would be in large part resolved by reflecting on philosophy of language.[26] Thus, I have been trying to explain some of the nuts and bolts, so to speak, of how subjects and predicates work and what they might tell us about individuals and their properties. Yet a superficial understanding of what I have said so far might lead to a confusion when identifying a term as a predicate or a subject. In particular, one might be tempted to think that any term that can be identified as a noun serving the *grammatical role* of a subject is the subject being talked about, and whatever else the sentence appears to say about that subject can be identified as a predicate that picks out a property for the subject. But sometimes the grammatical and logical structures of sentences come apart. The importance of this "coming apart" and its relevance to our discussion of existence will become clear below, but it is important to get ourselves straight on this issue right away.

I need here to introduce a distinction between a predicate and a predicable.[27] This distinction may serve no purpose to the grammarian, but it will prove very useful for us. A predicable is any term that *can* be used as a predicate (i.e., as a term that tells us about some property that a subject has), even if it is not so used in every such instance. When we learn to diagram sentences as children, we were trained to divide the sentence "No drug is safe" into its grammatical subject, "No drug," and its grammatical predicate, "safe." But logically, this won't do. If logical predicates denote the properties that individuals have, then what individual am I talking about when I tell you "No drug is safe?"

A more robust demonstration of the distinction between predicates and predicables is available if we reflect on the logical operation of negation. Logicians negate statements by placing "It is not the case that" before the statement that they wish to negate.[28] The negation of "Kovacs is lazy" is "It is not the case that Kovacs is lazy." And the negation of "No drug is safe" is "It is not the case that no drug is safe." No statement and its negation can be simultaneously true.

There are more natural sounding ways of forming negations in English, but we need different means of doing so for different kinds of statements. The difference between predicates and predicables is seen when one sees why we need different means for forming natural-sounding negations. In statements that predicate a property of an individual, a more natural way of forming a negation is to simply find a word that is antonymous with the predicate. Thus, the negation of "Kovacs is lazy" becomes "Kovacs is industrious." If our language lacked a suitable word to oppose "lazy," we have plenty of prefixes to resort to, and one might say "Kovacs is not lazy" (or, more awkwardly, "Kovacs is non-lazy"). If you believe either of those two statements, you cannot, no matter how hard you try, simultaneously believe the original sentence "Kovacs is lazy."

But this procedure falls apart when we start talking about the safety of drugs. We cannot move from the wordy "It is not the case that no drug is safe" to "No drug is unsafe." If you were to protest your doctor's prescription by insisting "No drug is safe!" he might reply, seeking to negate your claim, "It is not the case that no drug is safe; for this antibiotic is perfectly safe." However, not even Dr. Timothy Leary was brazen enough to declare that "No drug is unsafe," for some are quite deadly. Rather, if we want to negate statements that have quantifying terms (a quantifying term is a word like "some," "no," or "all") we must modify, not the predicate term, but the term that we have been treating as the subject. Thus, "It is not the case that no drug is safe" becomes "Some drug is safe," which is why your doctor prescribes antibiotics.

The reason that statements with quantifiers like "some" and "no" cannot be negated by the same process as others is that in, for example, "No drug is safe," the logical (as opposed to grammatical) *role* of predicate and subject is reversed. The full importance of this will have to wait. For now, I merely want to draw your attention to a nuance in how subject-predicate statements work: With quantified statements such as "Some senators are honest," the logical subject cannot be "senators" or even "some senators." This has devastating impact for the naïve view of existence, as I will explain below. For now, however, the time has come to see how all of these observations from the philosophy of language apply to views about existence.

2.1.5 *The Naïve View of Existence Explained*

Here are some sentences that, whether true or not, many people would say at least make sense and are meaningful: "Pope Francis exists," "The Loch Ness Monster does not exist," "The Library at Alexandria used to exist but does not anymore." Each of these statements consists of a subject followed by a verb, the denial of a verb, or (in the third case) an assertion that the verb once truly applied but now does not. According to the above account of the relation between language and properties, then, each of these statements should be predicating properties (or denying them) of a subject, namely the property called "existence." Pope Francis, in addition to having the property of being from Argentina, also has the good fortune of having the property of existing. The Library at Alexandria once had a lot of properties, including that of existing, but now that is one property that it does not have.

(You may already be wondering what to do about the phrase "The Loch Ness Monster does not exist." What object could I possibly be saying lacks that property if I were to utter such a statement? Surely such a statement runs into problems where other statements of denial, such as "This pear is not ripe," do not. Nevertheless, the statement appears acceptable. More on this in a moment.)

If you also find these statements inoffensive, it may be because you already intuitively held the naïve view of existence. You might think existence is a property which things have that is expressed by the predicate "exists."

But let us now subject this view to the crucible.

2.1.6 *The Traditional Analytic View of Existence*

The predominant view of existence among Analytic philosophers is that existence is never a property of individuals. In particular, the Fregean view which I will be laying out, as explicated and defended by C.J.F. Williams, makes the bold claim that any statement of the form "_____ exists," where the blank is filled in with the name of an individual, is a "meaningless string of words."[29] I offer three arguments for this theory.

2.1.7 *First Argument: Plato's Beard*

"Plato's Beard" is the name of a simple argument against the naïve view that existence is a property of individuals and it hinges on the problem of trying to talk about things that do not exist.[30] We can think about this argument by returning to an example from a previous section. What are we to do with the sentence "Nessie does not exist" when we think about The Loch Ness Monster? I am going to assume that, in fact, there is no such beast living in the Loch Ness. But let's compare "Nessie does not exist" to sentences with a similar structure but which do not use the word "exist" or any of its synonyms. The comparison sentence will be "Kovacs does not own a motorcycle." This sentence is true. Grammatically, the two sentences look similar: Both appear to consist of a subject term and then a denial that the subject in question has a certain property.[31]

But what does the second sentence mean? I take it that it just means that if you examined the thing, Kovacs, represented by the subject term, and could list all its properties, ownership of a motorcycle would not be on the list.

Now let's assume that the naïve view of existence is correct, and that the first sentence, "Nessie does not exist," functions not only grammatically the same as the second, but also logically the same. The problem is clear: What is it we are talking about when we say that, among the properties Nessie has, existence is not one of them? It seems that there is simply nothing there for us to talk about. Yet, on the naïve view, it is difficult to find any other way to analyze the sentence "Nessie does not exist." If the sentence is not telling us about The Loch Ness Monster (by telling us that there is some property it lacks), then what is it telling us? One possibility is that "Nessie" isn't meant to be a referring term, the way "Pope Francis" is in "Pope Francis is from Argentina." But then it is difficult to figure out a better way of analyzing subject-predicate statements generally. Yet the term "Nessie" in "Nessie does not exist" certainly cannot be telling us about Nessie, for as I said, there isn't one for us to be told about.[32]

Plato's Beard forces us to see a problem that comes from considering existence as a property of individuals or "exists" as a meaningful predicate that describes individuals. For on the naïve view, negative existential statements like "Nessie does not exist" come out self-contradictory. Conversely, true positive existential statements like "Kovacs exists" turn out tautologous: They are true not because of how the world is but because of how the words in the sentence function. But *that* can't be right. Normally, we consider a statement to be self-contradictory because, upon analysis, we find that it entails two statements which are not capable of being consistent. Suppose you heard someone say "I am thinking of an odd number divisible by two." You would realize at once that there was something self-contradictory about such a statement. If asked to say why, you might point to the fact that the statement entails these two incompatible claims: "I am thinking of a number not divisible by two (for that is all an odd number is)" and "I am thinking of a number divisible by two."

But what pair of inconsistent statements does "Nessie does not exist" yield? Perhaps, by mere mention of Nessie as a subject, one might think we are entitled to the statement "Nessie exists." And so the contradictory statements would be "Nessie exists" and "Nessie does not exist." But this runs into two problems: First, if existence is a property of individuals, the first statement is still tautology (if it is true, it *must* be true) and the second is still self-contradictory. Moreover, the second statement just is the same as the original statement which we are trying to analyze. We would have to again explain why the second statement is self-contradictory, leading to an infinite regress.

In the next section I am going to propose a reason that statements involving existence don't fit the pattern that we've come to expect from other subject-predicate sentences. However, first I wish to draw your attention to an exception to the Plato's Beard examples we have been considering: Statements that assert the existence of a plurality.

Consider the claim "Happy philosophers exist." This statement seems innocent of the sort of problems I accused the statement "Nessie exists" to be guilty of. The reason for this is that, if you were to hear someone say "Happy philosophers exist," you would not take him to be saying that any particular individual has the property of existence. Rather, you would understand the claim to be that, among philosophers, at least some of them are happy. In fact, if you learned of Smith that she is a philosopher and that she is happy, you would be entitled to the claim "Happy philosophers exist," and it would be difficult to imagine that your claim could be reduced to a tautology in the way that the naïve view of existence has forced us to think about existence claims referring to individuals. Maybe you thought the philosopher, Smith, was happy, and so inferred "Happy philosophers exist." Upon learning how miserable Smith really is, you would not then decide "Turns out there are no happy philosophers after all."

So the word "exists" behaves more strangely than we might have first supposed. When we try to use it as a predicate like any other predicate that refers to a property of an individual, we find ourselves in awkward paradoxes. Nevertheless, we can refer to the existence of pluralities with no problem because when we do so we are not trying to predicate a property of any individual. So, what is the truth about existence? To try to answer that question, I now turn to the solutions proposed by C.J.F. Williams.

2.1.8 Second Argument: Statements of Existence Are Analogous to Statements of Number

So it seems that when "exists" is attached to the names of individuals, like "Nessie," it leads to paradoxes. These paradoxes disappear when "exist" is attached to pluralities, like "happy philosophers." Why the discrepancy? To answer that question, consider that "exists" is hardly the only word which functions this way. Statements about number, naturally enough, also only comfortably work in sentences where the grammatical subject is plural.

Williams cites Frege as being the first to have a certain insight regarding statements of number.[33] For it was Frege who noticed a peculiarity about answers to questions of the sort "How Many?" To use his own example, suppose you were to ask "How many horses draw the king's carriage?"[34] And suppose I were to answer "The king's carriage is drawn by four horses." On the surface such an exchange might be thought to resemble one where you asked me what sort of horses draw the king's carriage and I replied "The king's carriage is drawn by thoroughbred horses." But, of course, the two are really not much alike at all. When I tell you that the king's carriage is drawn by thoroughbred horses, I am telling you that each particular horse drawing the carriage has a property, namely that of being thoroughbred. On the other hand, when I tell you that the king's carriage is drawn by four horses, I am not telling you anything about any horse at all. I am answering a "How many" question.

Why is it that "thoroughbred" in "thoroughbred horses" and "four" in "four horses" do such different work? That is, why is thoroughbred a property of individuals yet four never is? The reason, Frege tells us, is that "the content of a statement of number is an assertion about a concept."[35] In other words, numbers are not properties of individuals; rather, they are properties of properties. They tell us *how many* times a property is instantiated. "Four horses draw the king's carriage" is just a way of saying "The property 'Horse that draws the king's carriage' is instantiated (or can be found) four times."[36] And that is what philosophers mean when they speak of second-order (or second-level) properties: First-order properties are properties that tell us about individuals; second-order properties are properties that tell us about properties or concepts.

To see this point about number statements more clearly, and to point to how it relates to statements about existence, consider number statements where the number in question is zero (assuming that zero is a number). What am I saying if I say "The Pope has zero children?" On the Fregean account, I must be ascribing a property to the concept "children of the Pope," namely the property of having nothing falling under such a concept. The alternative is this: Each object has the property "one." And agglomerations of objects have other numbers as properties, each agglomeration having the number corresponding to how many objects are within it, as a Roman Triumvirate would have the property "three" since it contains three members. What then, of zero? Is it the number ascribable to no object at all? How can we predicate a property of that which does not exist? To do so gets us entangled in Plato's Beard once again.

We can now state the traditional Analytic view of existence with some precision: Existence can be thought of as a kind of number-statement, or at least be thought of as being very much like one.[37] So existence is never a property of individuals, but is only a higher-order property. It applies to concepts and tells us that the concept it is applied to is instantiated at least once. This is why we see no problem making existential statements about objects in the plural. "Happy philosophers exist" tells us that at least one philosopher is happy; the number of happy philosophers is not zero; the concept "happy philosopher" has instances. None of these statements amount to the tautology threatened by the Plato's Beard line of thought. For the same reason, the statement "Dragons do not exist" is not self-contradictory; all it is saying is that the concept "Dragon" has no instances, it is a concept corresponding to nothing real.

2.1.9 Third Argument: "Wrapping Around" and the Word "Some"

Perhaps the claim that existence is not a real property seems scandalous in light of everything I said about language in everything I wrote previously about language. The sentence "Ken likes drinking soda" means one of Ken's properties is his fondness for drinking soda; and "Juanita cries" tells us about a first-order property of Juanita, namely that she cries. So, given the very claims I have made about language, why shouldn't the statement "The Hope Diamond exists" do the same sort of thing and tell us about one of The Hope Diamond's properties? Let's look at another of Williams's defenses of Frege regarding statements kike "The Hope Diamond exists." Here we will have to recall my warning about statements involving words like "some."

Williams seeks to show that "some" is a second-order predicable. Recall that a predicable is an expression that can be used as a predicate, regardless of whether or not it is being used as a predicate in any given sentence. For Williams's argument here to succeed, he thinks he must show that this premise is true: If "some" is only ever a second-order predicable (i.e., never first-order), then the same is true for "exists." To see how this argument unfolds, I need to introduce a new bit of terminology, that of "wrapping around."

Let's start with the sentence "Some philosophers are happy." We already saw how this sentence differs from "Smith is happy." The logical structure of the latter sentence is the same as its grammatical structure: "Smith" refers to the subject, the person Smith, and "happy" is a (first-order) predicate that tells us about Smith. However, in the first sentence, our considerations about negation led us to observe that the logical rôles are reversed: "Happy" does the logical work of a subject-term, while "some philosophers" does that of a predicate.[38] Following a convention established by A.N. Prior (1914–1969), Williams describes the logical work of each part of a sentence in terms of which part is "wrapped" around the other.[39]

With this in mind, we can consider the second sentence by seeing that we have started with a name, "Smith," and then wrapped around that name an incomplete expression, "— is happy." Whereas there may be some instances where "Smith" is a complete expression (as when I am asked "Who let the dogs out?" and I answer, "Smith"), "— is happy" is by its nature incomplete; like a piece of wrapping paper waiting for the stick of gum that it will be wrapped around, it is empty until we couple it with something like a name, such as "Smith." We can even wrap the complete sentence "Smith is happy" into other wrappings, including "It is not the case that," which, as we have seen, is equivalent to "Smith is not happy."

Since we have seen how the subject and predicate *roles* get reversed in statements that involve quantified terms, that is, statements modified by words like "some" or "all" or "none," we will not be surprised to see the order of wrapped and wrapping also gets reversed in sentences like "Some philosophers are happy." Here we must start with the expression "— are happy" and wrap "some philosophers" around it to get our complete sentence. So in such statements, "some" is the logical predicate; and since every predicate is also a predicable, "some" is a predicable. But is "some" a first- or second-order predicable?

We can answer that question by noting the symmetry between what happens when we wrap predicables around names and when we wrap predicables around other predicables. A predicable, like "happy," when wrapped around a name, like "Smith," produces a complete sentence where the predicate in question is first-order. But when a proposition is formed by wrapping a predicable around a first-order predicable, the predicable that wraps around the first-order predicable is a second-order predicable.

Williams's evidence for this comes from considering what happens whenever we attempt to deal with other second-order predicates.[40] Take a statement like "Four philosophers are happy." We know from Frege's example of the horses drawing the king's carriage, discussed in Section 2.1.8, that "four" is a second-order predicable. And we know that "happy" is a first-order predicable because I have predicated it of Smith. Moreover, the negation of the statement "Four philosophers are happy" is not "Four philosophers are unhappy" but rather "There are fewer than four philosophers who are happy." So if all that we have said about wrapping around checks out, what is happening here is that we start with the first-order predicable, "happy," and wrap "Four philosophers" around it. The negation comes when we wrap "It is not the case that—" around both. And we see the same process at work with any second-order predicate you can think of: The negation of an expression where a predicable is wrapped around a first-order predicable always requires us to alter the term that is the grammatical subject; this is never true when a first-order predicable is wrapped around a name. And so it seems that "some" is indeed only a second-order predicable.

What remains for Williams to show then is that his conclusion about "some" applies with equal force to "exist." And he does this by saying that many second-order predicables which have the appearance of grammatical adjectives (as "some" does in "Some philosophers") can be replaced with verbs without losing any meaning. So, "Many philosophers are happy" can be expressed as "Happy philosophers abound." In the same way, the work done by "some" is done by "exist": "Happy philosophers exist" tells us nothing about any philosopher, predicates nothing of any individual, but instead expresses the same thought as "Some philosophers are happy." Likewise, the statement "No philosophers are happy" tells us happy philosophers do not exist.

This brings us to Williams's conclusion about the absurdity of attaching "exists" to names of individuals. I can form a valid argument from premises like "All happy philosophers read Aristotle" and "Smith is a happy philosopher" and reach the conclusion "Smith reads Aristotle." This is because "—reads Aristotle" is clearly admissible as a first-order predicable. But when we try to make valid arguments using terms which we have seen can be only second-order predicables, we get nonsense: "Happy philosophers abound" and "Smith is a happy philosopher" should not lead us to believe that Smith abounds, whatever that could mean. And just as "Smith abounds" is not a meaningful sentence, so we ought to conclude the same of "Smith exists." Tempting though it is, premises like "Happy philosophers exist" and "Smith is a happy philosopher" cannot lead us to conclude "Smith exists."

So, on the Fregean view, for all the sentences we have that use the word "exists," we can discard those which attach the word to names of individuals: For existence is never a property that an individual has and, therefore, never a meaningful predicate about an individual. It can only ever be used, according to these arguments, as a second-order predicate, one which tells us about a property of a concept and which can answer "How many?" type questions. This view has been widely held among Analytic philosophers.

§3 History and Further Details

Hopefully the preceding has helped you understand what Analytic philosophers mean when they say things like "Being is not a real predicate" and why many of them make such claims. In short, since there is, on their view, no real property of individuals called "being" or "existence," it cannot be expressed using any real predicate. Now I want to show you, by exploring the history behind these claims, some further debates that surround existence. This section will be a little more technical than the last one, and beginners in philosophy may want to skip directly to Section 3.4, where I discuss Analytic philosophers who have proposed alternatives to Williams's arguments discussed in Section 2. However, if you are comfortable with the technicalities, these are some details that you will want to know about when you talk with Analytic philosophers about some of their central existential concerns.

3.1 Meinong's Unusual Ontology

When philosophers want to refer to the things that they believe in, they use the word "ontology." Aquinas admitted angels into his ontology; Bertrand Russell, whose ideas about existence you will become acquainted with momentarily, did not. Perhaps one of the most unusual ontologies ever proposed was that of Alexius Meinong (1853–1920). For Meinong, whatever can be thought of should be admitted into the philosopher's ontology. (I am leaving aside Meinong's complicated theories regarding objects like square circles; his thought on these issues, while interesting, is tangential to the present topic.) So Meinong's ontology includes not only you, this book, and penguins, but also ghosts, Sherlock Holmes, golden mountains, and, famously, a present king of France.[41] The former objects, according to Meinong, exist, and the latter subsist. By subsistence Meinong appears to mean a kind of quasi-existence, an intermediary state between something that you can interact with (like this book and penguins) and something that you can merely think of (like golden mountains).

The intuition fueling this theory is not outlandish. In order to be thought of, there must *be* something to be thought of. (Philosophers sometimes use the word "intentionality" to describe the feature of thought whereby it must be about something: Thought is intentional). Otherwise you are left with pure nothingness, and so subsisting objects like the present king of France might be thought of as somewhere in between pure nothingness and what we typically say exists. Suppose I did not know that France lacks a king; perhaps my education in European history was especially inadequate. I could have some thoughts about the present king of France. I could wonder what he likes to eat, whether he is married, or how old he is. I could pray for him or hope his health is in good condition. If, while doing these things, you asked me "What are you thinking about?" I would surely be wrong to say "Nothing." It was considerations like this that led Meinong to posit that a complete ontology must include anything whatsoever that can be thought of.

For a time, Meinongianism was a popular view among philosophers. Today it is not. I once heard a philosopher say that he had adopted a particular theory regarding the nature of mental properties because, he claimed, it seemed that every other theory would end up entailing Meinongianism. Meinong's philosophy of mind is actually still accepted in some circles, but his theory regarding non-existent objects has acquired such a bad reputation that many Analytic philosophers go out of their way to avoid anything that could lead to it. The historical reason that this has come to be the case has to do with a problem proposed by Bertrand Russell. Russell had himself once accepted Meinong's theory, but came to reject it because of logical paradoxes that the theory seems to generate.

3.2 Trouble for the Present King of France

If there is one paper that should be read by anyone interested in the historical origins of Analytic philosophy, that paper would be Bertrand Russell's 1905 "On Denoting." There Russell was concerned with the supposedly subsisting present king of France. If it is the case that he could think of this monarch only because he was, in some sense, real, then, according to Russell, it would make sense to wonder whether the present king of France is bald. But one thing Russell could not be content with was violating the law of excluded middle: According to this law of logic, for any meaningful statement, either it is true, or its negation is true, but both cannot be true. And you will hopefully recall from above that in statements where a property is predicated of an individual, as in "The present king of France is bald," one can obtain a negation by negating the predicate. So the negation of "The present king of France is bald" is "The present king of France is not bald." But which of these two sentences is the true one?

Russell's solution to this problem can be understood in two steps. In the first step, he proposes a logical analysis of statements like "The present King of France is bald." According to this logical analysis, this seemingly simple seven-word English sentence is telling us three things:

(1) There is presently a king of France.
(2) There is presently only one king of France (this is captured by the English article "the").
(3) For everything whatsoever, if that thing is the king of France, then it is bald.

If you have ever taken a logic class, you might recall that one of the first things that you had to learn is that if you have a long sentence made up of a number of shorter sentences connected by the word "and," then unless every one of the shorter sentences was true, your whole long sentence was false. So, if the "The present king of France is bald" is in fact a short-hand way of expressing (1)—(3) above, with "and" after (1) and (2), then we can know that "The present King of France is bald" is false as soon as we read "There is presently a king of France."

But, you may ask, does that mean that law of excluded middle commits Russell to believing that the present king of France is not bald? That seems wrong. But how can we preserve the law of excluded middle? Here is where the second stage of Russell's strategy comes into play. Understanding this stage requires us to understand that the statement "The present king of France is not bald" can be logically analyzed in two ways. In one way, we would have (1)–(3) above, except with the word "not" inserted before "bald" in (3):

(1) There is presently a king of France.
(2) There is presently only one king of France.
(3) For everything whatsoever, if that thing is the king of France, then it is *not* bald.

This analysis would spell trouble for the law of excluded middle, since the conjunction of these three sentences is also false. Fortunately, Russell realized that he could analyze the negation of "The present King of France is bald" another way. Consider the conjunction of the original (1)–(3). We can shorthand that sentence as

(1) and (2) and (3).

What happens if we put "It is not the case that" before that very long conjunction?

It is not the case that [(1) and (2) and (3)].

How does one evaluate the truth of such a complex statement? Logicians tell us that when you negate a long statement composed of conjuncts, you get a new sentence where each conjunct becomes a disjunct, and each disjunct is preceded by "It is not the case that."[42] So translated, what we now have is:

Either: It is not the case that (1) there is presently a king of France, or it is not the case that (2) there is presently only one king of France, or it is not the case that (3) for everything whatsoever, if that thing is the king of France, then it is bald.

Conveniently, for a long sentence made up of shorter sentences connected by "or," only one of the shorter sentences has to be true for the whole thing to be true. After the sentence "Two is a prime number" you can write "or" followed by literally any other statement and your long, two-part sentence remains true. So, since it is not the case that there is presently a king of France, we now have a translation of "The present king of France is not bald" which is true, and so we have preserved the law of excluded middle.

3.3 Substitutional and Objectual Quantification

At this point you may be wondering what Section 3.2, with its laborious logic and complicated analyses of what appear to be straightforward sentences, has to do with existence. So let's focus on just the first of the three statements that Russell thought that "The present King of France is bald" had to be analyzed into: "There is presently a King of France." There has been some controversy regarding what it means to say that this statement is true or false, and the controversy surrounds what Analytic philosophers call the "existential quantifier." Russell favored what is called a "substitutional interpretation" of the existential quantifier; others have favored what is called an "objectual interpretation." Before explaining what those two interpretations amount to, let me tell you a little bit about the existential quantifier itself.

3.3.1 *The Existential Quantifier*

The logical analysis of "The present king of France is bald" that I provided above was written for you in ordinary language, that is, in common English, using the sorts of words that you probably use daily. Indeed, that was largely how Russell himself analyzed it in his 1905 paper. Probably the reason that he did this was because not many people (including the professional philosophers that Russell was writing for) knew the language of symbolic logic in 1905.

Today, philosophers would be more likely to express "There is presently a king of France" differently. To simplify matters a bit, first let's henceforth omit the word "presently." Unless indicated otherwise, assume that the sentences that I tell you about are describing present matters. Temporality can be expressed in symbolic logic, but you don't need it in order to understand the existential quantifier. The way philosophers might express the statement now could look like this:

$\exists x(Kx)$

That backwards E is the existential quantifier. You can read it as "At least one" (and this would be a more-or-less neutral way of reading it, a way offensive to neither those who favor substitutional interpretations nor those who favor objectual interpretations). Given what I said above about statements of existence being statements of number, that is, statements that amount to saying "This is at least one in number," now you can see why this is called existential quantification.

The x in the above statement is called a variable. It serves a similar function as variables in algebra (as I have mentioned, early Analytic philosophers were very interested in mathematics). So, as long as the person who wrote the above statement somehow indicates that K means "is a king of France" we can read "∃x(Kx)" as "There is at least one x such that x is king of France." Before going into more details, however, I need to tell you one more thing about the statement "∃x(Kx)." I need to tell you how it is different from the statement "Kx."

The latter statement just says "x is a king of France." It does not tell us that there is an x that is a King of France. It says nothing about what exists. So there is no way of determining its truth value: Strictly speaking, it has no truth value. Logicians say that the variable x in "Kx" is a *free* variable. It is free because it is not governed by a quantifier, by the logical notions like "some," "none," or "every." This makes the statement "∃x(Kx)" much more interesting because it purports to give us some information; it is the sort of statement that can be true or false. In "∃x(Kx)" philosophers say that the variable x is a *bound* variable. It is bound by the existential quantifier.

3.3.2 Substitutional Quantification

You can safely interpret the existential quantifier to mean "There is at least one ...." But this was not the way Russell would have directed us to interpret it. He favored the substitutional account of quantification. On this account "∃x(Kx)" is a true statement if there is at least one true statement of the form "x is a King of France" where the x is replaced with a name. So, if "Louis is a King of France" is true, then "∃x(Kx)" is as well. But if no name can be substituted for the x such that "x is a King of France," then "∃x(Kx)" is false.

The Rusellian manner of saying what the existential quantifier expresses would be "For some x ...." Notice that this reading is consistent with everything said above about existence not being a property of individuals. It is uninformative to say, for example, "For some x, x is Kovacs." What name can be substituted for the variable in "x is Kovacs" that would be informative? "Kovacs is Kovacs," while true, is trivial.

Substitutional quantification can, however, allow us to answer certain objections that you may try to bring against the claim that existence is not properly predicable of individuals. Consider the case of D.B. Cooper. In 1972 a man hijacked an airplane and told the flight attendant that his name was Dan Cooper. He was almost certainly lying, and a mistake in the press has led to his identity ever since as just being D.B. Cooper. The culprit was never found after he parachuted off the plane in the middle of Washington. Now, you might object to claims that I have been defending regarding existence by noting the sensibility of the question "Does D.B. Cooper still exist?" You are wondering whether the hijacker has since died or if he is still a fugitive. The substitutionalist account of quantification can accommodate your question by rephrasing it as "Is it the case that, for some x, x is D.B. Cooper?"

Suppose that, to my astonishment, the FBI discovered that my grandfather was D.B. Cooper. If my Grandfather were still alive, the statement "For some x, x is D.B. Cooper" would be true since the statement "Eugene Kovacs is D.B. Cooper" would be true. Notice that now we have a sentence that actually is informative because this statement really means "Eugene Kovacs is the man who famously hijacked an airplane in 1972." And notice that, if we understand your question "Does D.B. Cooper still exist?" in this way, an affirmative answer would not be attributing a first-order property called "existence" to a person, it would be merely completing the meaning of "For some x, x is D.B. Cooper" by substituting in a name that produces a true statement.

3.3.3 *Objectual Quantification*

It is difficult to study Analytic philosophy in much depth without coming across the name Willard Van Orman Quine (1908–2000). He coined the phrase "Plato's Beard" discussed earlier. And he summed up his view of existence in the slogan "To be is to be the value of a bound variable." Since I have already explained the difference between bound and unbound variables, I will now try to explain the rest of what Quine meant by saying this.

Let's think about Plato's Beard again for a moment. Suppose I say "Nessie does not exist." This looks like a statement about Nessie. Yet how can it be, if there is no Nessie to be spoken of? Recall that Meinong's solution to this would be to put Nessie on the list of unactualized possible beings. Quine claimed that the error in this solution was to believe that since statements about Nessie can have meanings, then one may therefore infer that the names which such statements contain, names like "Nessie," must therefore name individuals. But this can't be right. From "The average American takes 5.4 showers each week" one cannot infer that there is some object that is called "The average American" or even an object that is 5.4 showers. So the meaningfulness of statements does not derive from the meaningfulness of the names involved.

Quine liked Russell's method of paraphrasing statements and converting names into descriptions. "Nessie does not exist" means "There is no beast living in the Loch Ness in Scotland that has been previously uncategorized by science." If a description is not readily available to us, Quine advises us to just convert the name into a verb, as in "Nothing Nessisizes."

What does Quine admit into his ontology? In other words, what does Quine think that there is? His answer: Everything that can be assigned as a value to a bound variable. So Quine's way of interpreting our example of "∃x(Kx)" would be to say "There exists an x, such that x is the King of France." The point is that it has nothing to do with naming, as it did for Russell, but has to do with what objects are available in the universe which can be assigned as values to bound variables. So Quine warns us to be careful in our speech. If I say "There are prime numbers greater than 2," I have now, according to Quine, admitted that there are numbers, the reality of which is no different than the reality of me or penguins. This is because, according to Quine, the only way to paraphrase such a statement is by saying "There exists an x, such that x is a prime number greater than 2."

You might wonder why Quine favored his interpretation of the existential quantifier over Russell's. Very briefly, Quine was motivated by his desire to deny the existence of universals. A universal is (basically) an entity corresponding to the predicates that we use to signify properties. So, if you are a realist about universals (someone who thinks that universals are real) you will think that in addition to green apples and green vegetables and green traffic lights, there is such a thing as greenness itself. But Quine was not a realist about universals.

And the upside to his theory about existence, thinks Quine, is that it does not commit us to the existence of universals. "Jolly is a green giant" does not entail the reality of greenness, for such a statement is paraphrased "There exists an x, such that x is green and x is a giant and x is called 'Jolly.'" (Note that, if Quine is right, the falsity of such a statement is just the consequence of there being no object in the universe that can be assigned as the value of x.)

There is plenty more that can be said about existence and the existential quantifier. My purpose here has just been to give you a sense of some of the basic facts lurking in some of the debates, should you come across these debates after reading this book. The debates that I have in mind result from the conviction that existence is not a real property of individuals, and that "exist" is akin to statements about number, whose meaning is "There is at least one." Now, let's turn to some Analytic philosophers who have questioned that conclusion.

3.4 Recent Criticisms of Williams on Existence

Analytic philosophers agree about nothing. Some (though not many) Analytic philosophers challenge the view that the only two truth values are True and False. Some Analytic philosophers try to challenge the principle of non-contradiction, the claim that no statement can be both true and false at the same time and in the same respect. So it should come as no surprise that some Analytic philosophers have tried to deny the Fregean thesis and defend the view that existence is a first-order property that every existing individual has. But, I think, those who have the best chance of succeeding are those who try to seriously contend with the defenses of Frege that were put forth by C.J.F. Williams as I have been expounding them.

In this section, I will discuss three people who have criticized Williams on existence: Barry Miller (1923–2006), William Vallicella, and Kris McDaniel. The first two of these have also proposed positive accounts of what existence is, but I cannot report that their positive accounts have gained the sort of popularity that the Fregean analysis put forth by Williams has. Therefore, I will leave it to readers to decide if any of their arguments against Williams are meritorious enough to search out a positive account, resources for which are to be found in the bibliography.

3.4.1 *Barry Miller*

Any attempt to defend a first-order view of existence is going to have to confront the problem of Plato's Beard. Recall that this is the line of thinking according to which, if "exists" is a first-order predicate, someone who utters a statement like "Lincoln does not exist" will have the problem of not being able to say what it is he is denying has the property of existence. So, any statement that denies that an individual exists will be self-contradictory; likewise, any true statement affirming that an individual exists will be a tautology.

Miller considers Plato's Beard to be two separate, but related, problems.[43] The first he calls a paradox: When someone treats existence as a property of individuals and says "Lincoln does not exist," it seems paradoxical since there is no Lincoln for this statement to be about. The second problem he calls an absurdity. Because properties allow us to distinguish things, to sort things out from other things, if existence were a property of things, then we should be able to distinguish existing things from non-existing ones. A sheep farmer may well separate the mature sheep from the young sheep, but imagine a sheep farmer who sets out to separate the existing sheep from the non-existing ones.[44] Such is the purported absurdity, according to Miller, that people like Williams believe occurs when we treat existence as a first-order property.

Here I will show how Miller attempts to respond to both the purported paradox and absurdity that result from considering existence to be a first-order property.

3.4.1.1 *The Paradox: Miller's Response*

Millers devotes only one paragraph responding to the paradox, the claim that "Lincoln does not exist" can supposedly only be true if there is a Lincoln to talk about. Using Williams's example of "Lord Hailsham does not exist," he writes:

> The so-called paradox, however, is illusory, for it arises purely from confusing a name's reference with its bearer. In particular, proponents of the paradox are confusing the reference of "Lord Hailsham" with its bearer .... The truth of "Lord Hailsham does not exist" requires only that "Lord Hailsham" have a reference. To have a reference, however, does not require that the bearer exist *now*, but merely that it does exist or *has existed*. Once that is recognized, there is nothing even odd, let alone paradoxical, about propositions like "Lord Hailsam does not exist."[45]

Miller seems to have in mind a passage from Wittgenstein's *Philosophical Investigations*, where Wittgenstein distinguished between the *meaning* [*bedeutung*] of a word and the reference of a word:[46]

> It is important to note that it is a solecism to use the word "meaning" to signify the thing that "corresponds" to a word. That is to confound the meaning of a name with the bearer of the name. When Mr N.N. dies, one says that the bearer of the name dies, not that the meaning dies. And it would be nonsensical to say this, for if the name ceased to have meaning, it would make no sense to say "Mr N.N. is dead." [*Philosophical Investigations*, § 40][47]

So, once a name has a reference, thinks Miller, it will always have a reference. However, a name stops having a bearer once there is nothing to bear the name. That might seem obvious but Miller thinks that the conflation between bearer and reference is what has led to the purported paradox in sentences like "Lincoln does not exist." I can refer to Lincoln in sentences like "Lincoln was the President of the United States during the American Civil War" even though the name "Lincoln" has no bearer; and so on Miller's view, the statement "Lincoln does not exist" is not saying "There is a man, Lincoln, who does not exist." Rather, Miller thinks it is saying that the name "Lincoln" can still be used to refer to the Lincoln who once existed but no longer does.

3.4.1.2 The Absurdity: Miller's Response

When I say "Lincoln does not exist," it appears that I am predicating non-existence of Lincoln. And if first-order predicates signify first-order properties, it would follow that non-existence is such a property. But if "exists" is admissible as a first-order predicate, then surely "does not exist" must also be; but how then can one escape the absurdity of trying to claim that an individual has the property of non-existence?

Miller responds to this objection by trying to show that non-existence is a mere Cambridge property, even though existence is a real property. A Cambridge property, you may recall from Section 2.1.2, is one which makes no difference to the subject of which it is predicated. When a boy plays a flute, he can be said to have the real property of flute playing; but that he is heard by me makes no difference to him. "Being heard by Kovacs" would be a mere Cambridge property that the flute playing boy has. Likewise, Miller thinks that the statement "Lincoln exists" predicates a real property of Lincoln. "Lincoln does not exist," on this account, predicates a Cambridge property.

Here is a short reconstruction of the argument that Miller will employ to show that non-existence is a Cambridge property. In what follows after this reconstruction, I will provide some further details:

1. In "Lincoln does not exist" either (a) "does not exist" is being predicated of Lincoln, or (b) "It is not the case that _____ exists" is being predicated of Lincoln.
2. If (a), a mere Cambridge property is predicated of Lincoln.
3. If (b), a mere Cambridge property is predicated of Lincoln.
4. Therefore, the statement "Lincoln does not exist" predicates a mere Cambridge property of Lincoln.

To try to build his case that non-existence is a mere Cambridge property, Miller first points out two kinds of negation: sentential negation and predicate negation, or as he calls them, external negation and internal negation. "Lincoln does not exist" can be construed according to either type of negation. It can mean "It is not the case that (Lincoln exists)" or it can mean "Lincoln (does not exist)."[48] In the first of these renderings non-existence is never mentioned.[49] So if Miller can make the case that the two ways of understanding "Lincoln does not exist" do not collapse into the same thing, he thinks we ought to prefer "It is not the case that (Lincoln exists)" for the sake of avoiding the absurdity involved in predicating non-existence.

But what about the negative predicate "It is not the case that ____ exists?" This expression is, after all, what comes about if the name "Lincoln" is removed from "It is not the case that Lincoln exists." Yet this predicate need not signify a real property. Indeed, Miller argues it signifies a mere Cambridge property because it does not occur in what's called the "constructional history" of "It is not the case that (Lincoln exists)." Miller subscribes to the view that we need only admit that a property is a real property if it is mentioned in the constructional history of a proposition.

Elmar Kremer provides an illuminating example of what Miller means when he talks about a constructional history of a proposition.[50] Consider the sentence "Tom is a student and Henry is a student." If true, then being a student is a real property of Tom since "is a student" can be truly predicated of him.

But what of the complex predicate "is a student and Henry is a student"? This surely does not stand for a real property of Tom because if it turns out Henry is not a student it will make no difference to Tom. What we have is the real property expressed by the predicate "Is a student" being said of Tom, and then the resulting statement, "Tom is a student," being inserted into the proposition "____ and Henry is a student." At no point does the complex predicate "Is a student and Henry is a student" come into this constructional history.

Miller thinks something similar happens in the case of "It is not the case that Lincoln exists."[51] Here we have the predicate "____ exists" and we put the name "Lincoln" into the place for a proper name; then we put the resulting expression "Lincoln exists" into the gap which is present in "It is not the case that ____." So, Miller concludes, "It is not the case that ____ exists" plays no logical part in the constructional history of "It is not the case that Lincoln exists" and thus non-existence can be no more than a Cambridge property.

Miller prefers to construe "Lincoln does not exist" as a case of external negation, as "It is not the case that (Lincoln exists)," and to analyze it as I just described, thereby showing that the predicate involved signifies a mere Cambridge property, in order to avoid any purported absurdity. But what if some argument were given to force him to accept "Lincoln does not exist" in terms of internal negation, construed as "Lincoln (does not exist)?" Once again, Miller thinks that the predicate "does not exist" will signify a mere Cambridge property, and once again he argues for this point by making an observation about the proposition's constructional history.

When we negate the predicate "exists" we get "does not exist." And when we insert the name "Lincoln" into the gap in "____ does not exist" we produce "(Lincoln)(Does not exist)."[52] So "does not exist" does enter into the constructional history of "Lincoln does not exist" when this statement is understood in terms of internal negation. The question Miller raises is this: Supposing existence to be a real property, and not a merely Cambridge one, does it follow that non-existence must also be a real property? His strategy for answering that question is to put it in terms of a more general question: Supposing some property *F* is a real property, under what circumstances must non-*F* also be a real property?

Consider a piece of wood that is red. Miller thinks that because it has a property, redness, which precludes other colors, we can say that the wood has a real property that can be expressed, for example, by the predicate "non-green." This entails the awkward conclusion that the piece of wood has an infinite number of real properties (such as non-yellow, non-30 feet long if it is not 30 feet long, and so on). But the situation is different if it is not wood we are speaking of, but glass. Glass can be red, and can be green, but it need not be any color at all. And whereas my statement that "This wood is not red" entails "It is one of the other colors," the same cannot be said if I were to say "This glass is not red." That a piece of glass is not red could mean that it is non-colored; "but," Miller points out, "so too might a pain or a flash of insight, though their being non-colored could hardly be claimed as a real, rather than a Cambridge, property."[53]

With this example in mind, Miller formulates the following principle: Lack of a real property F bespeaks the presence of a correlative real property non-F only if F and non-F are determinates of one determinable property.[54] In the case of a piece of wood, red and non-red are both determinates of a determinable property, namely, color. And so to say that a piece of wood is not red is to attribute a real property to that wood. (Miller prefers to consider properties as determinates related to determinables and not as species related to genera for this reason: Each species in a genus is distinguished according to a specific difference—humans, for example, are animals that are rational, birds are animals that fly, and so on—whereas it is not always the case that one can say what distinguishes determinate properties from the determinables; "One cannot *specify* just what the difference is between color and red").[55]

But, Miller claims, this is not the case with existence. There is no further determinable common to both existence and non-existence such that they could both be considered determinates related in that way. So when I say that something lacks existence, according to Miller, I need not be saying that the thing in question has a real property called non-existence. That is, even if one insists on an internal negation interpretation of "Lincoln does not exist" the predicate "does not exist" would signify a mere Cambridge property, not a real property.

Thus, Miller believes he has dealt with Williams's objections to the claim that existence is a real property of individuals. For, according to Miller, Williams seems to think that statements like "Lincoln does not exist" result in both paradox and absurdity. But, counters Miller, the paradox arises because of confusion of the bearer of a name and the referent. And the absurdity arises only if one thinks that admission of existence as a real property entails that non-existence is a real property. But Miller has tried to show that the statement "Lincoln does not exist," regardless of whether it is interpreted as a case of internal negation or external negation, predicates a mere Cambridge property.

3.4.2 William Vallicella

William Vallicella offers three objections to the traditional Analytic view that existence cannot be predicated of individuals: (1) Frege was mistaken to think that statements of the form "Kovacs exists" are (illegitimately) attaching a second-order predicate to the name of an individual; (2) the Plato's Beard argument is based on what philosophers call a "modal fallacy"; (3) from the fact that non-existence cannot be had by individuals one should not infer that existence cannot.[56]

3.4.2.1 *Attaching Second-Order Predicates to the Names of Individuals*

"Numerous" seems to be an obvious example of a second-order predicate.[57] Attaching it to the name of an individual will not produce an intelligible statement. So, Vallicella notes, there is a fallacy in the following argument:

1. Philosophers are numerous.
2. Socrates is a philosopher.
3. Therefore, Socrates is numerous.

If that argument is fallacious, then is this argument also fallacious?

1. Philosophers exist.
2. Socrates is a philosopher.
3. Therefore, Socrates exists.

Vallicella thinks not. On his view, those who claim that the second argument is as problematic as the first make the mistake of thinking that "exists" must be a univocal term. A term is univocal if it has the exact same meaning in two different utterances, as "animal" has in "The horse is an animal" and "The cat is an animal." Univocal words are opposed to equivocal words, seen in statements like "I would not have won without my *coach*" and "Cinderella was late to the ball because her *coach* broke down." Now if the predicate "exists" in the second argument above were first-order, then the argument would be as unoffensive as:

1. Zebras have stripes;
2. Hamu is a zebra;
3. So, Hamu has stripes.

The reason this argument is valid is because "has stripes" is a first-order predicate. But is it clear that just because "Happy philosophers exist" employs "exist" as second-order that there can be no first-order use of the same predicate?

You may think that if "exists" is not a univocal term, then inferring the existence of Socrates from the existence of philosophers and the fact that Socrates is a philosopher is itself a fallacy, namely the equivocation fallacy. For example, the reason the argument "All banks are FDIC insured; I have walked along the banks of the Mississippi; therefore, I have walked along something FDIC insured" is a bad argument is because the term "banks" is not a univocal term. So if Vallicella is right that "exists" can be both first-order and second-order without being univocal, how can the argument about the existence of Socrates be valid?

The answer, according to Vallicella, is that there is a "systematic connection" between "exist" when it is used in its general, second-order sense, and "exists" when predicated of singular objects.[58] General existential statements tell us that some property is instantiated. But for a property to be instantiated, on Vallicella's way of thinking, it must be instantiated by an existing individual. So Vallicella considers it a necessary truth that "If a property is instantiated, it is instantiated by an existent" and he thinks that this ought to be an available premise in any argument that seeks to deploy "exists" as a first-order predicate. Thus, Vallicella revises the argument about Socrates existing as:

1. The property "being a philosopher" is instantiated.
2. If a property is instantiated, it is instantiated by an existent.
3. Therefore, the property "being a philosopher" is instantiated by an existent.
4. Socrates instantiates the property "being a philosopher."
5. Therefore, Socrates is an existent (=Socrates exists).

According to Vallicella, the upshot of reconstructing the argument this way is that we need not abandon Frege's insight about general statements of existence being statements about number, yet we also need not worry that we are engaged in any fallacy when we argue from the existence of philosophers to the existence of Socrates.[59]

3.4.2.2 Vallicella on Plato's Beard

Vallicella reconstructs the Plato's Beard argument as follows:[60]

1. If' "exists" were a first-order predicate, then affirmative singular existential statements would be necessarily true, and negative singular existential statements would be necessarily false.
2. Some affirmative singular existential statements are contingently true, and some negative singular existential statements are contingently false.
3. Therefore, "exists" is not a first-order predicate.
4. Therefore, existence is not a first-order property.[61]

I explained the reasoning behind the first premise when introducing the problem of Plato's Beard, but it is this premise that Vallicella believes renders the argument unsound. Consider, as an example, the sentence "Kovacs exists." It is certainly the case, Vallicella thinks, that as long as "Kovacs" does name someone, a sentence like this is, at least in some sense, necessarily true. However, Vallicella argues that it does not follow from this that my existence is necessary.[62] In other words, one could consistently hold both of the following sentences to be true: (1) It is possible that Kovacs not exist;[63] (2) if it were to be actually the case that Kovacs never existed, no sentence using the name "Kovacs" could be used to express that state of affairs.

So Vallicella thinks Plato's Beard is entangled in what is called a modal fallacy. This sort of fallacy takes place when one illicitly shifts a modal term, such as "necessarily" or "possibly," in such a way as to alter the truth value of a statement. For example, philosophers generally agree that something can only be known if it is true (see my discussion of Analytic epistemology in the Introduction for details on this claim). So, one might say "Necessarily, if Alvin knows that the Pope is from Argentina, then it is true that the Pope is from Argentina." But notice that from this one cannot infer that "If Alvin knows that the Pope is from Argentina, then it is a necessary truth that the Pope is from

Argentina." After all, one can imagine a scenario where someone from Italy had been elected Pope.

According to Vallicella, the proponents of Plato's Beard have made a similar error. It is fine to say that necessarily, every nonvacuous name (i.e., every name that *does* name) designates something that exists. But from this, Vallicella tells us, we ought not to infer the more dubious claim that every nonvacuous name designates a necessary existent.[64]

And so he urges the rejection of Williams's Plato's Beard argument.

3.4.2.3 *Asymmetry between Existence and Non-Existence*

When I say "Jones does not exist" I cannot mean that there is some individual, Jones, who lacks the property of existence. As we have seen throughout this chapter, it is absurd to talk about non-existence as a property. But can someone infer from this that existence cannot be a property?

Vallicella believes that those who do make such an inference overestimate the symmetry between existence and nonexistence.[65] If I tell you that something exists, you will naturally assume that the thing I am telling you about has some properties. But, according to Vallicella, its instantiation of properties is not identical with its existence; when Descartes proclaimed "I think, therefore I am," he was not trying to tell us "I think, therefore I instantiate properties." On the other hand, statements of non-existence just tell us about properties that are uninstantiated. "Nessie does not exist" is not about an individual, but about a property, and it says something like "The property 'large uncategorized animal living in the Loch Ness' is instantiated by nothing."

So Vallicella's reply to the problem of non-existence is to say that there is no reason to deny that statements about existence can be either specific, as when I say "Kovacs exists," or general, as when I say "Happy philosophers exist." But he says that this does not warrant us to think that statements about non-existence must also be capable of coming in both varieties. "There is," he writes, "only general non-existence, which is a second-order property."[66]

3.4.3 *Kris McDaniel*

Another line of objection to the typical Analytic view of existence comes from Kris McDaniel.[67] Since Williams's arguments rely on the purported claims that statements about existence are statements about number, and that they therefore ascribe second-order properties (i.e., they tell us about concepts or other first-order properties, but not individuals), McDaniel tries to show that attributions of number can be first-order.[68] And he does this by drawing a distinction between what he calls distributive and non-distributive predicates. Suppose I said "Pints of beer sold during happy hour are cold." The predicate "cold" tells you something about each and every pint of beer sold during happy hour. If I point to any pint of beer sold during happy hour, you will know something about it. This sort of predicate, which tells you "whenever some things are F, each one of them is F," is called distributive.[69]

On the other hand, consider the statement "Pints of beer are lined up along the bar." Here, the predicate "lined up along the bar" is not a distributive predicate. I cannot point to any pint of beer and say that it is lined up along the bar. So any predicate that is not distributive is non-distributive.

With this in mind, McDaniel's argument might be reconstructed as follows:

1. All predicates are either first-order or higher-order.
2. Higher-order predicates are about concepts, not individuals.
3. First-order predicates are about individuals, not concepts.
4. Some non-distributive predicates (such as "lined up along the bar") are not about concepts.
5. Therefore, such predicates are about individuals.
6. Therefore, such non-distributive predicates are first-order.

A striking feature of McDaniel's claim is that non-distributive predicates "say something of some *things* not of some particular thing" but that, nonetheless, these predicates attribute a property to individuals.[70] So, on his account, the following argument is flawed not because it treats a second-order predicate as first-order, but because it treats a non-distributive predicate as distributive:

1. The students are numerous.
2. Theresa is a student.
3. Therefore, Theresa is numerous.

According to McDaniel, a similar mistake is committed by the argument:

1. Those students have surrounded the building.
2. Theresa is one of those students.
3. Therefore, Theresa has surrounded the building.

McDaniel thinks that neither "Numerous" nor "Surrounded the building" is predicate telling us about concepts, and thus must be about individuals.

So McDaniel believes that he can attribute predicates like "at least three in number" and "at least one in number" to, for example, the people at a dinner party.[71] And he thinks Frege thought numerical predicates could not be applied to individuals because of a purported mistake Frege made concerning examples involving composition.[72] Frege asks us to consider a standard deck of fifty-two playing cards divided among the four suits. If it is possible to predicate numbers of individuals, then Frege thinks we will have a problem deciding which number to predicate of the deck: One, because (as has been a popular saying since Aristotle) everything is one? Four, because of the four suits? Fifty-two, for each of the cards? Since these cannot all be the right answer, Frege thought it best to abandon any hope of predicating number of individuals and to instead say something like "being a suit in this deck is exemplified four times," "being a card in this deck is exemplified fifty-two times," and so on.

McDaniel responds that Frege missed a simpler answer: The deck of cards is one, but is *composed* of fifty-two cards, and is *composed* of four suits. And he denies that composition is the same as identity. So the answer to Frege's question "What number is to be predicated of the deck of cards?" is, on McDaniel's way of thinking, "One." Likewise, when Frege writes that he can conceive of the *Iliad* as one poem, or as twenty-four books, or as a large number of verses, McDaniel replies that he can conceive of the *Iliad* only as one poem. Yes, McDaniel agrees, he can understand what it means to say that the *Iliad* is composed of twenty-four books, but he thinks this does not warrant predicating the number twenty-four of *Iliad*.

To sum up: McDaniel is willing to grant the claim made by Frege and Williams that statements of existence are statements of number (or at least they are sufficiently similar), but he denies that number statements are ordinarily second-order statements. In fact, they are first-order predicates that tell us about individuals, albeit non-distributively. So, if existence is itself an answer to "How many?" type questions, it too is a non-distributive, first-order property.

§4 Conclusion

In this chapter, I have aimed to give you some sense of what contemporary Analytic philosophers are saying about existence. In short, they are debating whether or not it is a real property of individuals that can be expressed by a first-order predicate. And, if I have succeeded in what I set out to do, you now have a sense of what that last sentence means. While the view that existence is only a higher-order property, one that tells us something about properties or concepts, is still widely held, it has its critics. It is unlikely that this debate will be definitively resolved any time soon. Nevertheless, that should not stop you from now engaging the debate yourself, as I hope this chapter has given you the resources to begin doing so.

I now invite you to turn to the concluding chapter of this book, where I will say something about why I think that Williams's view is the correct one regarding existence. There I will also say something about what I believe to be the strengths and weaknesses of the Continental and Thomistic philosophies of being (as laid out in previous chapters).

5

Conclusion: Being in Three Traditions

Joseph P. Li Vecchi, Frank Scalambrino,
and David K. Kovacs

§1 Opening Remarks

We have constructed this final chapter to place our traditions into dialogue, indicating how our respective traditions diverge from one another. Each of us comments on the other two traditions from the point of view of the tradition we represent. Each of us will say what we find problematic about the theory of being proposed in the other two traditions, as well as what we find valuable, and we will each make some effort to defend our tradition from criticisms.

§2 Thomistic Philosophy of Being and the Continental and Analytic Traditions
Joseph P. Li Vecchi

Aquinas never explicitly defends our knowledge of being from what I have characterized in Chapter 2 as "hyperbolic subjectivism" and "hyperbolic objectivism."[1] Now that this book has addressed some of the principal doctrines of the three traditions concerning being, the present section will provide explicit rebuttals to Continental and Analytic doctrines that contrast with those of the Thomistic philosophy of being. Generally, these rebuttals concern the tension between the objective and subjective poles of knowledge, and the middle path that the Thomistic Tradition steers between these extremes.

2.1 The Thomistic Tradition Regarding Continental Philosophy of Being

Chapter 3 presents a wide range of doctrines and interpretations that constitute developments in continental philosophy of being. The present section focuses its criticisms on what it takes to be the fundamental tenet of Kant and the Continental Tradition that most directly contrasts with Thomistic philosophy of being: the derivation of ontology from an investigation of the conditions of the possibility of knowledge.

2.1.1 *The Fundamental Thomistic Critique of the Continental Tradition*

Kant famously follows Hume in holding that sensory experience directly yields only knowledge of phenomena, and not of reality.[2] Unlike Hume, however, Kant claims that investigation into the conditions of the possibility of knowledge yields an ontology. Kant articulates a complex ontology within the bounds of the knowing subject's possible experience that by no means is limited to justifying the phenomenal. Within that ontology, Kant is able to distinguish the knowing subject from the object known, to cast space and time as *a priori* forms of sensibility, and to justify judgments about reality and being, all within the bounds of possible subjective experience. From the Thomistic perspective, the derivation of this ontology from his investigation of the conditions of the possibility of knowledge is the fundamental tenet of Kantian philosophy and of continental philosophy of being.

2.1.2 *Criticizing Continental Philosophy of Being*

The ontology that Kant derives from his investigation of the conditions of the possibility of knowledge is fundamentally at odds with Thomistic philosophy of being. In particular, his ontology is limited to the bounds of the knowing subject's possible experience, and thus, necessarily excludes knowledge of what he calls "the noumenon," or reality in itself.[3] All psychological processes transpire exclusively based on sensation as conceived within the architecture of the understanding. Kant presents logical principles, such as the principle of non-contradiction, as laws of understanding that apply to phenomena because of the *a priori* origin of space and time in sensible experience. These laws, according to Kant, have no necessary relation to reality in itself.

The Thomistic section of Chapter 2 characterizes Kant's philosophy as a form of hyperbolic subjectivism because it exemplifies the perennial tendency in the history of thought to blur the distinction between reality and the knowing subject's knowledge. In so doing, it overestimates the creative role of the intellect in knowing reality. Kant's subjectivism, pushed to its logical extremes, dissolves the distinction between thought and reality in itself, denies all knowledge of reality in itself, and denies that the fundamental actuality of appearance is subject to the laws of logic.

The Scholastic tradition's criticism of this Kantian tenet derives from the Thomistic doctrine of cognition's ontological import. The Continental Tradition, by prioritizing the subjective conditions of knowledge to the logic of the subject-object relation, ignores that phenomena themselves are a kind of being. They are subject to the fundamental logical and metaphysical requirements of rational inquiry because, whatever the intellect grasps, it grasps as being.

2.1.3 *The Being of Cognition as Ontological Evidence*

Thomistic philosophy of being agrees with the Continental Tradition that phenomena are the spring point of our knowledge of reality. It disagrees, however, with the Kantian claim that phenomena provide no evidence of being in itself. Chapter 2 presents Aquinas's doctrine that cognition is the foundation of knowledge. It is the foundation of the knowledge of an object's nature, which is subjective to the extent that the intellect receives this nature according to the intellect's mode of receiving. It is also the foundation of the irrefutable evidence of being in itself. For Aquinas, being is not an aspect of reality that the intellect receives as a representation. It is an aspect of reality in itself that the object directly presents to the intellect in the form of the actuality of a phantasm, to which the intellect must turn if it is to produce any knowledge at all.

On the one hand, knowledge of an object's essence is a representation rather than a presentation of that essence to the intellect.[4] This knowledge is subjective to the extent that it results from the intellect's mode of receiving species in sensation. On the other hand, knowledge of an object's existential independence from the knowing subject is not a representation of an ontological status. The actuality of the phantasm confronting the intellect, and in particular its logical distinction from the knowing subject, is the foundation of the intellect's objective knowledge of being in itself. Whether a phantasm derives directly from simple apprehension, or indirectly from memory and imagination, in either case, the intelligible species that constitute the phantasm derive from an existentially independent object.[5] We can be wrong about an object's nature or essence, and even about what does or does not exist. We cannot be wrong, however, about the ultimate derivation of the intellect's knowledge from its simple apprehension of individual objects that are existentially independent of the knowing subject.

Since whatever we conceive, we conceive of as a being of some sort,[6] the knowledge of being is prior to any other knowledge, in both the logical and psychological orders.[7] Thus, the undeniable being of cognition provides irrefutable evidence for our knowledge of being itself.[8] In Kantian terms, for Aquinas, we have knowledge of noumenal being. Objectivity, reality, and being are noumenal aspects of ontology. They are not ontologically posterior to a critical evaluation of phenomena, but are aspects of the intellect's act of cognition.[9]

The Thomist Tradition holds that through phenomena the intellect is able to know being in itself, and not as a representation. From the perspective of the Scholastic tradition, Kant's error is fundamental: to have ignored that the process of cognition is itself an instance of being, and to have thought that cognition testifies only to the nature of the object and to being as constituted within the bounds of subjective experience.

This flaw does not prevent Kant from extending his philosophy of being beyond the bounds of phenomena considered within the bounds of the subject's possible experience. To the contrary, from the basis of phenomena Kant elaborates a highly complex theory of reality and objectivity, as understood within the bounds of possible experience. Having taken phenomena as his foundation without having appreciated its full ontological import, however, Kant fails to recognize that being in itself is the foundation of all knowledge.

While nothing is in the intellect that is not first in the senses, knowledge derived from the senses is not completely subjective. Not everything that the intellect comes to know through simple apprehension is conceptual content, affected by the subjectivity of the intellect's mode of receiving. Aquinas recognizes the reciprocal impact exercised by the knowing subject and object known. Both knowledge and phenomena necessarily have an objective and a subjective pole.

2.1.4 *Corollaries, Criticisms, and Conclusions*

The present section will now examine and criticize four corollaries of what the Thomistic perspective considers the fundamental tenet of continental philosophy of being that Chapter 3 highlights, and draw some conclusions.

First Corollary

Both Chapters 1 and 3 highlight the incommensurability of the Continental Tradition with other traditions because of a "Copernican shift" in perspective that gives rise to a revolutionary methodology. The Scholastic perspective on Thomism adopted in this book rejects this incommensurability and methodological shift, because it rejects the fundamental tenet upon which they rest concerning the ontological import of cognition.[10] Since cognition provides evidence not only of the nature of phenomena, but also of its own being, the intellect knows being in itself directly. It has no grounds for demanding a critique of sensation before acknowledging being in itself as its ontological and epistemological foundation. For the same reason Scholastic Thomism rejects the claim that the Continental Tradition is the only tradition to properly contextualize being in the philosophy of being.

Second corollary

A second corollary of what the Thomistic perspective considers the fundamental tenet of continental philosophy of being concerns the rules of inference admitted by its methodology. Kant's philosophy of being takes cognition as its starting point, employing what Chapter 3 refers to as the "human-existential rules of inference." It claims that inference from cognition of reality, however, is insufficient to warrant the knowledge of being in itself, but only the meaning of the term *being*. It makes this claim based on the observation that a judgment based on the data of cognition concerns a predicate whose meaning derives from its relation to the judgment's subject. From the Kantian perspective, *being* is not such a predicate because there is nothing in cognition corresponding to the predicate *being* in a judgment about being that relates to the judgment's subject. The Kantian philosophy thus concludes that *being* is not a real predicate.

Here two responses are in order. First, Aquinas takes pains to observe that the term *being* cannot signify a thing's ontological status. He does so most clearly in the quotation presented in Chapter 2 above.[11] That the use of the term *being* as a predicate cannot signify that a thing exists is no news to Aquinas or to the Thomistic Tradition, for as Aquinas notes: "No verb signifies that a thing exists or does not exist, since 'is' said by itself does not signify that a thing exists, although it signifies existence."[12] As will be discussed below,[13] however, this observation does not imply that *being* or *existence* fails to be a logical predicate.

A second response of Thomistic philosophy of being to the observation that *being* is not a real predicate concerns the relation of the logical predicate *being* to any possible subject of judgment. In a judgment of being the logical predicate *being* not only indicates the meaning (*ratio*) of the term *being*, which Aquinas notes in the passage just cited, but also relates to the judgment's subject, if knowledge of the subject's being is founded upon the indubitable being of the cognition. Not only does the predicate *being* indicate the meaning of *being*, but the property referred to by the predicate also provides the real foundation of all being in the form of the being of cognition. Kant overlooks that cognition itself is a kind of being, and that the indubitable being of cognition is the foundation of the knowledge of the being of everything referred to in a judgment of being.

Third corollary

A third corollary of what the Thomistic perspective considers the fundamental tenet of continental philosophy of being concerns what Chapter 3 calls "the principle of actuality." As presented in that chapter, Kant bases his philosophy of being on the assumption that the actuality of cognition is prior to the knowledge of being. While the ultimate principle determining the rules of inference for other philosophical traditions is the principle of non-contradiction, the principle determining the rules of inference for the Continental Tradition is the principle of actuality. To claim to reason about cognition by means of the principle of actuality, before acknowledging the principle of non-contradiction, however, is to deny that the principle of non-contradiction is a first principle of reason, and that the first principles of reason are derived from the intellect's knowledge of being, as discussed in Chapter 2.[14] Prioritizing the principle of actuality to the principle of non-contradiction ignores that actuality, like all objects of the intellect, is a kind of being. To the contrary, in the Thomistic Tradition the knowledge of being precedes the distinction of being from its two fundamental modes, actuality and potentiality.

Fourth corollary

A fourth corollary of what the Thomistic perspective considers the fundamental tenet of continental philosophy of being concerns what Chapter 3 calls the "Peripatetic Axiom."[15] As presented in that chapter, this doctrine states that the Aristotelian and Thomistic Traditions take induction to be the origin of all knowledge. This doctrine belies the same misunderstanding about the ontological import of cognition as previously noted in rejecting the Continental Tradition's incommensurability, Copernican shift, and transcendental methodology. Strictly speaking, in the Aristotelian and Thomistic Traditions all knowledge begins with the senses.[16] This sensory foundation gives rise to both inductive and deductive knowledge. Kant overlooks that cognition provides not only inductive data concerning the nature of phenomena, but also deductive knowledge of its own being, which is indubitable on pain of self-contradiction, and which provides the ontological evidence of the being of all possible objects of knowledge.

Conclusion

The intellect cannot know and measure reality without receiving notification of reality according to its subjective mode of receiving. Thus, knowledge of reality is always in part subjective. The neglect of this subjective aspect of knowledge presents the occasion for the rise of the hyperbolic subjectivism of Modern Philosophy in general and of the Continental Tradition in particular. To the extent that the Analytic philosophy of being denies this subjective aspect, and to the extent that the Thomistic Tradition at times in its history neglects this aspect, the Continental Tradition serves as a needed reminder.

The focus on the subjective pole of knowledge generated by the Continental Tradition, however, is hyperbolic. To know that something is a being is not merely to know that it has an ontological status within the bounds of subjective experience. Rather, it is to know that as a being, whether a real being or a being of reason, it is rooted ultimately in the being of cognition, which we cannot deny on pain of contradiction, and the knowledge of being in itself that cognition provides. To accept phenomena as a basis of investigation and then to deny that on that basis we can know real being in itself is to ignore that phenomena, whose being cannot be denied on pain of self-contradiction, are real beings.

2.2 The Thomistic Tradition Regarding Analytic Philosophy of Being

This section does not attempt to review and evaluate the full range of doctrines and developments in Analytic philosophy of being that Chapter 4 treats. Rather, it criticizes what it considers to be two fundamental tenets of this tradition that contrast directly with Thomistic philosophy of being.[17]

2.2.1 *The Fundamental Thomistic Critique of the Analytic Tradition*

Analytic philosophy of being typically admits as a fundamental tenet, the rejection of the distinction between being and existence. In the introduction of the present book, for example, Kovacs states, "The ordinary words with which this book is concerned are 'existence' and 'being' (which appear, to my eye, roughly synonymous; I see no reason, as opposed to some thinkers in other traditions, to distinguish between the two)."

The rejection of this distinction is rife throughout the literature and aims at deflating a purportedly "bloated" ontology.[18] In contrast, the Thomistic section of this concluding chapter presents a defense of this distinction, and argues that the conflation of being and existence is the basis of the common and erroneous view that "existence is not a real predicate."

Analytic philosophy of being also typically admits as a fundamental tenet, the rejection of subjective influences in matters of logic, truth, and knowledge. It proposes a purely objective ontology established in complete isolation from the psychological processes of the knower, and denies that the knowing subject contributes in any way to the reality known. This ontology eschews all psychological processes, and applies logical laws such as the principle of non-contradiction to objects that in no way are determined by the knowing subject.[19] The present section of this chapter provides a defense of the subjective aspect of knowledge.

Conclusion: Being in Three Traditions   133

2.2.2 *Criticizing Analytic Philosophy of Being*

The two tenets of the Analytic Tradition criticized in this section are fundamentally at odds with Thomistic philosophy of being. The Thomistic section of Chapter 2 characterizes Analytic philosophy as a form of hyperbolic objectivism because it exemplifies the perennial tendency in the history of thought to exaggerate the distinction between reality and the knowing subject's knowledge. In so doing, it denies the creative role of the intellect in knowing reality. This exaggerated objectivism, pushed to its logical extremes, ends with the incoherent claim that reference to reality involves no necessary role for the knowing subject. The Thomistic Tradition's criticism of these Analytic tenets depends respectively on the ontological import of cognition's actuality in founding various modes of being, and the ontological import of the intellect's subjective receptivity.

2.2.3 *The Ontological Import of Cognition's Actuality*

Chapter 2 of the present book presents Thomistic doctrine about various modes of being that is the basis of the distinction of being and existence. It notes that, for Aquinas, the term *being* applies most broadly to whatever signifies the truth of a sentence, which is to say that we say "is" of it, and can form true sentences about it.[20] It also describes how the term *being* applies most properly to real being (*ens reale*) because only real beings constitute something in reality independently of the mind.[21] Real being (*ens reale*) includes substances first, because they possess their own act of being, but also accidents, which depend on substances for their being. It notes that being is not part of the essence of natural objects, so that they must participate in being, which is to say that they "exist." Chapter 2 also describes how real being has two modes: the actual and the possible.[22] Finally, it describes how the term *being* applies to being of reason (*ens rationis*), or what does not constitute something in reality. This mode of being neither possesses its own act of being, nor depends as a material accident on the being of a material substance.[23]

For Thomistic philosophy of being, existence and being are distinct since saying that something makes a sentence true is different from saying that it participates in being. Existence is the real property of participating in being that characterizes substances, that real accidents have derivatively from substances, and that beings of reason lack because they do not participate in being.

The Analytic Tradition sometimes casts attempts to distinguish being and existence unfavorably by comparing them to the highly unusual ontology of Alexius Meinong (1853–1920). Chapter 4, for example, notes that "for Meinong, whatever can be thought of should be admitted into the philosopher's ontology." The reader will recall from Chapter 2 that this equally well describes Thomistic philosophy of being.[24] On this point, the two ontologies agree since Meinong borrows some distinctions from Thomistic scholasticism through his mentor Franz Brentano (1838–1917).

Meinong's ontology, however, differs greatly from that of the Thomistic Tradition in at least one important way. In addition to subsistence and existence, Meinong's theory of objects posits a third ontological category, "absistence" (*ausserseiend*), for objects that stand entirely outside of being.[25] Chapter 4 does not attempt to expose the paradoxical nature of absistence. It merely observes that "Meinong's ontology includes not only you, this book, and penguins, but also ghosts, Sherlock Holmes, golden mountains, and, famously, a present king of France. The former objects, according to Meinong, exist, and the latter subsist."[26]

Without admitting the category of absistence, Thomistic philosophy of being recognizes you, this book, penguins, Sherlock Holmes, golden mountains, and the present king of France as beings because we can make true sentences about them. We can just as truly say, "David Kovacs is a being that exists" as we can say, "Sherlock Holmes is a being that does not exists." Neither of these enunciations is gibberish. They both are meaningful and true. Of course, they are true in different ways, but that is precisely the point of distinguishing existence from being. Every existent thing is a being, but not every being, is an existent being.

Another way to see this distinction is to note that we can be wrong about the nature and existence of particular beings, but not wrong that what we might be mistaken about are beings of some type. On the one hand, the judgment that existentially independent objects are necessary to actualize cognition can never be wrong. On the other hand, the judgment that a particular object before the mind is such an object can be wrong. As stated in Chapter 2, Section 3.6, the intellect may perceive its object by means of a phantasm deriving directly from the simple apprehension of an existentially independent object, or by means of a phantasm deriving from memory and imagination. In both cases, however, the indubitable evidence of a phantasm's actual presence to the intellect ensures the ultimate foundation of our knowledge of reality in itself.[27]

What grounds the knowledge of the existential independence of an object is the actual presence of a phantasm to the intellect, and not what the intellect receives according to its subjective mode of receiving. On the other hand, knowledge claims about the existential independence of a particular object can be wrong, as common experience bares out, since a single act of cognition cannot certify that the phantasm activated by the intellect derives directly from an act of simple apprehension rather than from the memory or imagination.[28]

2.2.4 *The Ontological Import of Subjective Receptivity*

Thomistic philosophy of being agrees with the Analytic Tradition that we have objective knowledge, but disagrees that we can have knowledge apart from the psychological processes of the knowing subject, and, therefore, disagrees that knowledge can be purely objective. In focusing on the objective conditions of knowledge and ignoring the necessary relation between object known and knowing subject, the Analytic Tradition fails to recognize the ontological impact of the psychological process of the knowing subject on the object known. The Thomistic Tradition affirms the mutual epistemic determination of knowing subject and object known. What I have called the "reception dictum," that "whatever is received is received according to the mode of the receiver" implies not only that the object known epistemically determines the knowing subject, but also that the knowing subject, in virtue of its mode of receiving, and only to that extent, epistemically determines the object known.[29]

The Thomistic Tradition avoids the hyperbolic objectivism of thematizing being that is unrelated to the knowing subject. We cannot refer to objects that are entirely independent of the mind, but only to objects as the mind knows their natures and their being. Given the ontological import of the psychological process of simple apprehension, and the multifaceted structure of reality that it reveals, Thomistic philosophy of being avoids the hyperbolic objectivism that characterizes the logico-mathematical methodology of the Analytic Tradition. By looking to models that exaggerate the distinction of the object known from the knowing subject, the Analytic Tradition fails to recognize the psychological requirements of rational inquiry. The mind can apprehend and measure reality only if it has a relation to reality. The nature of this relation is determined not only by the nature and being of reality, but also by the psychological nature of the mind.

Knowledge of reality is always partially subjective. To ignore this is the error of the Analytic school. This error fosters a hyperbolically objective conception of existence that conflates being with existence, leading to the erroneous conclusion that *exists* is not a real predicate. We can form true sentences about objects other than those having the act of being through participation.

2.2.5 Corollaries, Criticisms, and Conclusions

The present chapter will now examine and criticize two corollaries of what the Thomistic perspective considers the fundamental tenets of Analytic philosophy of being that Chapter 4 presents, and draw some conclusions about them. These corollaries concern the claim of Analytic philosophy of being that "existence is not a real predicate," and the purported logical difficulties that arise in treating it as one.

According to Chapter 4, Analytic philosophy of being considers it naive to think that *exists* is like other predicates. For example, the statement, "Pope Francis exists" is not on par with the statement, "Pope Francis is from Argentina." Both statements have an individual for their subject and purport to tell you something about that individual by means of attaching a predicate to the subject term. According to the Analytic Tradition, however, the statement about existence does not tell you something about that individual subject by means of the predicate. Rather, when existence statements are true, they are tautologous since they provide no new information. If names are proper only to existing things, then sentences like "Pope Francis exists" or "Kovacs exists" tell us nothing about the individual that the name did not already tell us.

Some analytic philosophers, however, have questioned whether names are proper only to existing things. Saul Kripke (1940–) has claimed at least that the coherence of existence statements cannot depend on the accuracy of their associated descriptions. An inaccurate description would otherwise seem to disqualify a named subject from existing. Surely if Moses had not parted the sea, he would nonetheless have existed.[30]

The theory of names as "rigid designators," moreover, seems to have a progenitor in Aquinas's doctrine that nouns in the nominative case have the property of being "rectus" or standing firm in relation to a different sense they could have, such as other grammatical noun cases (*casus*), which fall (*cadunt*) from the nominative.[31]

John Knasas (1948–) holds that names do not presuppose existence or the mind-independence of their referents, so that predicating existence of named things is not tautologous. Names are existentially neutral, but not ontologically neutral. The ontological question of why named things have being, for Aquinas, leads to the conclusion that they received their being from outside their essence by participating in being through their act of being (*actus essendi*). This is what Aquinas means by *existence*.[32]

The Thomistic doctrine presented in Chapter 2 permits an explanation of the Analytic Tradition's error in claiming that statements like "Pope Francis exists" or "Kovacs exists" are tautologous. Saying that a thing is named is tantamount to saying that it is a being, whether a real being or a being of reason. This means that we can apply the verb *to be* to it, and can form true sentences about it. Saying that a being exists, on the other hand, conveys the additional information that the being has the act of being, and the property of participating in being, since being is not part of its essence. Therefore, an existence statement about a named individual conveys something about the subject by means of the predicate *exists*, and is not tautologous. Saying "Kovacs exists" says that the named being, here a substance since it has its own being independently of the mind, has the act of being, and the property of participating in being, or existing, since being is not part of its essence.

Given the distinction between being and existence drawn above, it becomes possible to recognize that *exists* is a real predicate. *Exists* is a real predicate because it signifies a property that any being can possess or lack, the property of receiving the act of being by participation, which is not a property that all beings possess. *Real being* and *being of reason* are real predicates for similar reasons.

That the use of the term *being* as a predicate cannot signify that a thing exists is no news to Aquinas or to the Thomistic Tradition, for as Aquinas notes: "No verb signifies that a thing exists or does not exist, since 'is' said by itself does not signify that a thing exists, although it signifies existence."[33] This observation, however, does not imply that *being* or *existence* fails to be logical predicates.

Finally, we may attempt to predicate *exists* in a variety of ways. We may predicate it of some real thing, as in "A westward passage to India exists." We may predicate it of beings of reason, whether falsely as in "Santa does exist after all!," or truthfully as in "A proof of Fermat's last theorem does exist after all!," or even by analogy, as in "God exists."

Second Corollary

According to Chapter 4, Analytic philosophy of being considers negative existential statements such as "The Loch Ness Monster does not exist" and "The Library of Alexandria no longer exists" to be self-contradictory. As with affirmative existential statements, the purported problem arises because of the nature of naming. In negative existential statements, while the name of the subject indicates the subject's existence, the predicate indicates its non-existence.

The Thomistic doctrine presented in Chapter 2 permits an explanation of the error of the Analytic Tradition in claiming that negative existential statements are self-contradictory. Saying that a thing is named is saying that it is a being of some sort, whether a real being or a being of reason. This means that we can say "is" of it, and can form true sentences about it. Saying that a being does not exist says that the being does not have the property of participating in being in order to have the act of being. Therefore, in a negative existential statement about a named individual, the meaning of the subject does not contradict the meaning of the predicate. Saying "The Loch Ness Monster does not exist" says that a named being, here a being of reason since, having never existed, it depends on the mind for its being, lacks the property of participating in being in order to have the act of being, or exist. Similarly, saying "The Library of Alexandria no longer exists" says that a named being, here a being of reason since, no longer being in existence, it depends on the mind for its being, lacks the property of participating in being in order to have the act of being, or exist.

Conclusion

From the Thomistic point of view, it is meaningful, and not gibberish, to say that some things exist, and some things do not. *Existence* is a real predicate, since not everything that the mind can conceive of as being has the property of existence. Because the Analytic Tradition fails to recognize the subjective aspect of knowledge, that the intellect's mode of receiving its object conditions knowledge,[34] it fails also to admit that whatever the intellect apprehends is a kind of being. Thus, Analytic philosophy of being ends by denying the coherence of even the deeply intuited claim: "I exist." Defending such deeply intuited claims, based on the distinction of the myriad modes of being that shoot through a manifold of the actual, the possible, and the conceptual, is a profound contribution of Aquinas to the philosophy of being, and a distinctive mark of philosophy in the Thomistic Tradition.

§3 The Continental Tradition Investigates the Be-ing of Beings, Other Traditions Merely Investigate Beings
Frank Scalambrino

I believe that the Continental Tradition chapter of this book sufficiently distinguishes the Continental Tradition from all other traditions; I believe it sufficiently shows how the Continental Tradition approaches philosophy, in general, and answers the two ultimate questions in the philosophy of being, in particular. Moreover, I believe Kant accomplished what he—and some of the greatest philosophers in the history of Western philosophy, who came after him—believed he had accomplished. Namely, Kant successfully formulated a method with which to make metaphysics a science. Thus, I sincerely believe that "You can philosophize with Kant or against Kant, but you cannot philosophize without him" (Beck, 1950: 1).

As a result, toward concluding remarks addressing the other traditions, there are three points I would like to make here. First, as noted in the Continental Tradition chapter and as stated in the title of this subsection, only the Continental Tradition methodologically and systematically investigates the be-ing of beings; all other traditions approach metaphysics as if it were a patchwork, or they simply investigate beings. Second, academic philosophy has failed to rise to the level of philosophy as a science. Rather than approach philosophy as a science, academic philosophy, today, approaches philosophy as if it were merely a democratic endeavor. Philosophy as a language game of "what if," within the confines of the political-correctness of the university's culture, beyond a mockery of genuine philosophy, is really a fraudulent bill of goods.[35]

On the one hand, failing to rise to the level of a science, academic philosophy encourages pluralism and diversity of thought, *rather than truth*. On the other hand, it is why philosophy at the universities articulates its mission in terms of cultural politics. In other words, the agenda is set for philosophy departments based on their university's political affiliations and funding expectations. Thus, the business of "philosophy" at the universities is not genuine philosophy. Of course, the Continental Tradition is in favor of liberty and freedom; however, the "freedom" on which academic philosophy bases its "pluralism, diversity, and equality" is—to put it euphemistically—merely a fantasy, and, as has been clear to the Continental Tradition for over a century now: Academic philosophy's supposed adherence to the principles of "pluralism, diversity, and equality" is, inwardly facing, ultimately a convenient way to justify vainly placing whims on pedestals, and, outwardly facing, it is ultimately a marketing strategy in the service of avaricious money-making.

This leads directly to the third point. The difference between the Continental Tradition and continental philosophy is important, because many of the political activists who want to invoke high-flown sounding philosophy make use of concepts, for example, from Nietzsche, Foucault, or Derrida, without understanding the context of the Continental Tradition regarding which these concepts emerged. Thus, the third point is that many—what amounts to (both conservative and liberal) politicians—misuse the genuine concepts of the Continental Tradition; that is, they produce phony articulations of genuinely philosophical concepts, illustrating that they see truth as in the service of political preference, and not the other way around.

In sum, there is a distinction between a methodologically and systematically scientific approach to philosophy and a patchwork, willy-nilly, whatever-we-would-like-to-talk-about approach. Likewise, there is a distinction between genuine philosophy and phony philosophy, and that distinction—though it, generally, echoes Plato's distinction between philosophers and sophists—was originally formulated by Schopenhauer to defend the Continental Tradition from the very "Hegelry" that, as Schopenhauer predicted, has become mainstream philosophy at the universities.[36]

It is tempting to rail against phony academic philosophy and the haphazard use of genuine philosophical concepts for political ends; however, to do so would be to assume that the *academic* audience is persuaded by truth. And, the truth is that academic philosophy is merely a pawn in the service of a university system that effectively functions as a cartel. Academic philosophy, that is, philosophy at the universities, today amounts to a Ponzi scheme. The only real value in learning all the possible positions one could take in the "Trolley Problem" is to perpetrate the same sleight-of-hand, for your own livelihood, against others betting on education with their loan money, that is, of course, if you could find a group of "academics," aka, "a philosophy department," whose politics finds your presence acceptable enough for them to recommend their university hire you.

3.1 Be-ing, Becoming, and Non-Being: Being in Itself as Becoming for Us

In his *Critique of Pure Reason* at A 370, Kant clarifies that "The transcendental idealist … can be an empirical realist." It is helpful to point this out for philosophers outside the Continental Tradition because, among other things, it distinguishes Kant from Hume.[37] That is to say, for Hume, it is impossible "for us so much as to conceive or form an idea of any thing specifically different from ideas and impressions."[38] One way to characterize the difference, then, is that whereas Hume's thorough-going skepticism stops at ideas and impressions, Kant is not opposed to us having "objective knowledge" of a thing in reality. Thus, Kant allows for empirical realism, where Hume does not; however, Kant does not allow us to have knowledge of the thing-in-itself.

Though it is beyond the scope of the present conclusion to exhaustively explain the difference between objective knowledge of a thing and knowledge of a thing as it is in itself, the distinction has been standardized in the Continental Tradition as between how something is for beings with our species-specific conditions for the possibility of experiencing objects and how something is in itself; in other words, *for us* versus *in itself*. Whereas Hume stops at for us and does not allow for realism, Kant allows the for us to accurately characterize the thing in reality; however, Kant does not maintain that how the thing in reality is for us is how the thing in reality is for itself.[39]

Recognizing the limitations to our cognitive capacities allows us to use a "placeholder" concept to refer to whatever "exceeds" those capacities and, therefore, cannot be *experienced* as a cognitive object *for us*, that is, for humans.

In nature, the parameters of these capacities are species specific. Thus, on the one hand, again we can see that dealing merely with objectivity and subjectivity is insufficient for the philosophy of being. And, on the other hand, things *in themselves* function in time registers different from, and including, the natural human capacities to experience time. Mathematics can help us think about this; however, beyond staring into the abyss, beyond contemplating the fractal depths of reality, these aspects of things in themselves that exceed our capacity to experience and these time registers—the chunking, frequency, and speed of which we cannot intuit—indicate the grandeur of the eternal flux that is metaphysical becoming. For Kant has given us the method with which to look into the river of Heraclitus.

Lastly, this line of thought gives us access to a question in metaphysics that it seems appropriate to call "very deep," if we consider all the layers of thought we have traversed to be able to ask this question in an envisioning way. The question can be formulated by placing emphasis on the term "eternal" in the phrase "eternal flux," when we consider this in the context of transcendental philosophy. In other words, what is the relation between be-ing, becoming, and non-being? Or, for simplicity sake, here, what is the relation between be-ing and becoming?

On the one hand, it seems to follow be-ing is a part of a whole that is becoming. Of course, that is the idea of eternal *flux*. However, on the other hand, when we consider that we are confined to the experiential capacities of mere mortals, then we can also notice that our experience of be-ing is always already in time. Thus, it may be the case that the bandwidth, so to speak, of the temporality of becoming to which we have access as change, as flux, may simply *be* from a different temporal point of view. Of course, this problem could be formulated either in terms of mereology or temporality; however, the fact that both formulations amount to cases of antinomy should give us pause to be astounded and, yet again, thank Kant.[40]

3.2 A Post-Modern Perplexity? Romantic Irony versus Insincerity

Because the thing-in-itself actually exceeds its objectification (even its "objectivation," for Husserlians) and its subjectification, then the dynamic dimension of things-in-themselves may be characterized in terms of what (out of that dimension) we *do* experience—the phenomenal—and what out of it *exceeds* our experience—the noumenal.

This insight provides another essential way to highlight the incommensurability between the Continental and other traditions. Credit for getting at the heart of this insight and deeply developing it should go to the German Romantics. In other words, despite our natural objectification and subjectification of existence,[41] existence always exceeds our experience of it. The following response to the question "What is romanticism?" may be helpful.

> [T]here is among us a fierce struggle between two fundamental human traits ... There is a struggle between Heart and Head. It is in every domain: whether we turn to science or literature or art or history or religion or education or philosophy or society—everywhere we find two parties warring against each other, one representing the intellect, the other the heart ... by gradual, steady increase, the world of reality has opened its fascinating realm to us, has taught us its truths, and has led us to respect the value and sternness of "facts." Yet, these facts are forcing themselves upon us in ever increasing legions, with such persistency, and such downright crudity that many thoughtful minds have become weary of them.[42]

What this means for us is that when our "transcendental eyes and ears," so to speak, have been opened, we cannot help but relate to objects as if with a kind of irony.

That is to say, we realize that the human manifestation of the experience of this object is existence expressing itself ironically. It is expressing itself ironically because it is more than the truth it reveals to us—the truth it reveals notwithstanding. Perhaps the value of this insight to distinguish the Continental Tradition cannot be overstated. Yet, importantly, the thing is *not* expressing itself insincerely. It *is* what it "says" it is, so to speak; however, what it says it is it says ironically. The abyss smirks; Dionysus laughs.[43]

Thus, how to understand irony is perhaps the most significant issue with which the general public and academics alike struggle to recognize the Continental Tradition, and appreciate its depth and value.[44] Moreover, the reason it is relevant to emphasize here is that it seems to function as one of the major points of resistance between the other traditions and the

Continental. In other words, it may refer to the greatest stumbling block or obstacle for individuals interested in philosophy who might adopt the Continental Tradition's method. For, in truth, the depth of the philosophical coherency that the Continental Tradition brings to experience is philosophy itself. So, getting clear on the role irony plays in the domain of experience should help the Continental Tradition regain its prior stature over the tyranny of the "cult of objectivity."

To be clear, it is—both philosophically and in terms of transcendental logic—a mistake to determine the relation between object and thing or between subject and thing in terms of insincerity. Romantic irony is the proper context for understanding the excessiveness of the thing-in-itself. For, it is in the context of irony that the noumenal dimension can be both what it is transcendentally and what it is in terms of objectification/subjectification. Otherwise, philosophers end up suggesting that the thing-in-itself is somehow *not* its objective expression, which is a mistake. Logically, notice that the mistake stems from applying the principle of non-contradiction-centric "either/or" to a dimension of reality that belongs to the scope of a more primordial principle, that is, the principle of actuality. And, yet, again, this is both/and logic, so it is not *either* the principle of actuality *or* the principle of non-contradiction (which is merely an attempt to reassert the principle of non-contradiction as primordial). It is both: the principle of actuality and, *then*, the principle of non-contradiction. Transcendental logic and, *then*, general logic.[45]

3.3 Concluding Comments Regarding the Other Traditions

What I have to say here is directed exclusively at the traditions of philosophy in question, and absolutely not at my co-authors. In other words, the following is in no way a personal critique or attack; rather, it is my attempt and hope to be as open and honest as possible about the other traditions, from the point of view of the Continental Tradition. I believe deeply in the use of the concept of "incommensurability" to organize and make essential distinctions regarding one's theorizing. In that sense, I think the greatest value *for students of the philosophy of being* is to learn how to see these traditions as incommensurable.

Of course, the real value of pluralism amounts to (and, therefore, could be simply replaced by) professional courtesy; however, speaking from the point of view of the Continental Tradition, which is, in fact, an under-privileged philosophical tradition nowadays, terms like "pluralism" have afforded other traditions un-merited privilege in our current historical situation.

Thus, it seems to me that those who adhere to Thomistic philosophy do so out of religious reverence. As if, to ask rhetorically: How could one be a Catholic and not be a Thomist? However, that is most likely sufficient for Catholic students of the philosophy of being, since what will be most important for them is following a religious characterization of reality—not philosophically investigating the truth of reality.[46] That being said, in praise of Thomism, Aquinas's ability to link morality with natural function is uncanny. It is most likely unsurpassed in the history of philosophy. However, in regard to *the science of being*, I think Kant bested him.[47]

In praise of the Analytic Tradition, there is no doubt it attracts people with very high IQs, and, in terms of pure thinking and pure reason, they will most likely never be surpassed as a tradition. In a deep sense, they have an answer for the question: How many kings of France can dance on the tip of pin? The way in which they have taken to talking about possible worlds is—in my opinion—every bit a continuation and perfection of the exercises in pure reason carried on by Scholastic monks. The major difference now being that, by definition, the Analytics tend more toward atheism, specifically of the David Hume type.[48] Moreover, they continue to dominate English-speaking academic departments. However, again, I think they have not, and by definition cannot, surpass Kant's philosophical accomplishment.

On the one hand, the above comments, in this section, directed at the Thomistic and Analytic Traditions may be understood, ultimately, as re-acknowledging that academic philosophy is guided by cultural politics. On the other hand, if the distinction between continental philosophy and the Continental Tradition were to become "mainstream" in the popular academic portrayals of Western philosophy, then perhaps a sufficient amount of "continental philosophers" would wake from the dogmatic slumber of the blind obedience with which they allow cultural politics to determine their understanding of reality.

§4 The Analytic Tradition regarding the Other Traditions
David Kovacs

4.1 Williams's "Master Argument"

I cannot, in this book, provide detailed evaluations of the arguments from Miller, Vallicella, and McDaniel against the standard Analytic claim that there is no first-order property called "existence." My concern in this final chapter is to say something about the arguments presented in previous chapters that are influenced by the Continental and Thomistic Traditions. But, before I do so, I want to mention one final argument from C.J.F. Williams that defends the Fregean thesis. I mention it here because I think that it gives us strong reason to be suspicious of any claim that "exists" can be legitimately used as a first-order predicate. This might be thought of as Williams's "Master Reply" to anyone, whether Analytic or Continental or Thomist or otherwise, who claims that the Fregean analysis is incorrect.

Williams realizes, of course, that there is nothing to prevent a word from having a use both as a first-order predicate and as second-order. He thinks "disappearing" is such a word. I can say "Reasonable Senators are disappearing" and I can say "At David Copperfield's magic show I saw the Statue of Liberty disappearing before my eyes" and I can say of some ice cream on a hot summer day "That ice cream is disappearing too quickly to eat." In the first statement, "disappearing" functions as a second-order predicate but it functions as a first-order predicate in the other sentences. Nevertheless, it cannot be the case that the word is being used univocally in all three sentences. From "Reasonable Senators are disappearing" one cannot then infer "Since my Senator is reasonable, she must be disappearing." Whatever sense can be made of a statement about my Senator disappearing (perhaps David Copperfield can make her disappear, too), it just cannot be the same sense in which reasonable Senators are disappearing.

But the two uses of the word are not entirely equivocal, either. When an ordinary English speaker hears the sentences "The team lost because of a bad coach" and "In spite of his wealth the miser would only pay for a coach seat," the native English speaker is unlikely to perceive any connection between the two uses of the word "coach."[49] However, this is not the case with our examples involving the word "disappear." So Williams tells us that when a predicable has both a first-order and second-order use, we can expect to find that the two uses are "in between," so to speak, equivocation and univocation. This "in-between" use he calls "analogical."[50]

"It is not difficult," Williams writes, "to show connections between these different uses" of a word like "disappears" when it has both first-order and second-order uses. The connection here is that in each instance an ordinary English speaker might get in mind something of the phenomenon of becoming "less and less." If I hear someone say "Reasonable Senators are disappearing" I understand that person to mean that it seems that every year there are fewer and fewer of them in number (and, as a statement about a number, "disappearing" is here a second-order predicate); a cup of ice cream left outside on a hot summer day becomes less and less bound together as it becomes more and more melted cream until it is no longer ice cream proper at all; a magician makes something disappear by making it less and less a part of the world we can perceive, by making it shrink from visibility (even if only by sleight of hand).

So when a word can be used as either a first- or second-order predicate, the two uses are called analogous and it should be possible to point to some connection between them, just as it is when we point to "less and less" in the above example.[51] What could be the point of connection between "exists" as a second-order predicate and any conceivable first-order use it might have? Williams reminds us of what he takes himself to have established regarding the relation between "exists" and "some." Since, Williams argues, the negation of "Happy philosophers exist" is no different from "No philosophers are happy," and since the negation of "No philosophers are happy" is no different from "Some philosophers are happy," Williams takes "exist" and "some" to do the same logical work (see Chapter 4, Section 2.1.9 above).

Thus, Williams's Master Reply to any possible objection to his view will be this:

> We cannot then in principle rule out the possibility that "exist" can have different senses, one in which it is first-level and in another of which it is a second-level predicable. But if it is held to be used analogically, now as a

first-level, now as a second-level predicate, the person who holds this owes us an account of the connection between the two senses.⁵²

And such an account, Williams goes on to say, will have to turn on how the word "some" or "something" can do the work of "exists" when used as a first-order predicate.

Neither Miller, nor Vallicella, nor McDaniel, nor anyone that I have read makes an effort to show how their accounts of the word "exists" when said of individuals can do the logical work that "some" does. "Something is blue" is informative; it tells us blue things exist, that there are things that are colored (and so are extended in space) in a certain way. But "Something is qipf" is not informative since you have no idea what qipf is: It could be a person, an economic system, a school of literary criticism, and so on. Thus, "some" just can't do any work as a first-order predicate and neither can "exists." And if you agree with what I have called Williams's Master Reply you might consider this pretty damning evidence against Miller, Vallicella, and McDaniel. Nevertheless, you might think that something ought to be said for the Continental or Thomistic views provided in this book; or perhaps you think that Williams's Master Reply does not pertain to those views about being. I now turn, then, to those other philosophical traditions.

4.2 Thomism and the Analytic Tradition

I should say upfront that I think Aquinas is on to something important when he writes about *esse*. What I deny is that this Latin word, and what Aquinas intends by it, can be adequately captured by English words like "existence" or "being." I do not think that Aquinas could have intended *esse* to refer to some first-order property that individuals have. Since it is not my task to provide exegesis of Aquinas's texts, I will simply say that I think what Aquinas meant to do was to point us toward, to borrow the words of another noted Thomist, "the gratuitousness of things."⁵³ Aquinas, on my view, wanted to show how, in created things, essence alone was not sufficient to actualize any entity, and so something else has to be posited, which he calls *esse*.⁵⁴

Some Analytic philosophers do not even admit the legitimacy of talking about essences. But even among those who do, I can agree with the Thomists that far too few realize that essences are not sufficient to account for things

(Miller, Vallicella, and McDaniel are exceptions). You might know everything that there is to know about the essence *humanity*: You might understand human psychology, physiology, and what is involved in our rationality. But suppose I then started asking you questions about Dale. "Who?" you ask. "Dale," I reply, "He lives in Greensburg, PA." And after you inform me you never knew about Dale, I would surely be wrong to respond, "Oh, then why did you assure me that you know everything that there is to know about humanity?" The point is this: The essence *humanity* is not enough to explain why there is a Dale in Greensburg. So, I think that Analytic metaphysicians would do well to consider something along the lines of Aquinas's *esse* in order to complete their theories.

Analytic philosophers can (and, I think, should) read and evaluate Aquinas on Aquinas's own terms. His arguments are usually carefully constructed and merit the same level of evaluation that Analytic philosophers afford to arguments made in the English-speaking world over the past hundred years.[55] But are there ways in which the Analytic Tradition, as inherited from Frege, overlaps with what Aquinas thought? In this section, I wish to suggest that there are, and that this overlap lies in Aquinas's distinction between the two ways that he identified for using the word *est*, translated neatly into English as "is."[56]

Bertrand Russell often drew attention to an ambiguity in how English speakers use the word "is." In particular, he identified three ways this word could be used:[57] People sometimes use it to indicate existence, and this is what Russell thought that the existential quantifier was about; and people sometimes use it to make a predication, as when I say "Russell is a philosopher"; lastly, people use "is" to signify identity, as when someone says "Clark Kent is Superman." Russell's concern was to make sure that the symbolic logic he was developing, which was supposed to be a perfect language free from all ambiguity, would have clear ways of distinguishing each of these three senses of "is." If you have read the chapter on Analytic philosophy earlier, you have already encountered two of these: "Russell is a philosopher" can be written P(b) where the predicate "is a philosopher" is signified by P, and where it is stipulated that *b* names Bertrand Russell. The "is" of existence is indicated by the backwards E. In Russell's system, identity is signified, naturally enough, by an equal sign (=).

Is this tripartite division of meanings compatible with Aquinas's dichotomy? I think that it is. Aquinas, recall, echoed Aristotle in noting that we sometimes speak of something as *being* just in case it falls into one of the ten Aristotelian categories, that is, if it has an essence. There are cats and colors and hearings and so on just because there are things with the essences corresponding to catness and (the accidental essences) colorness and hearing-nesses. But, as you will also recall, Aquinas notes that we also use the verb "to be" (and its derivations) in lots of true statements that refer to things that lack real essences. "Ron is blind," like the statements "Lawyers like money" and "Capitalism is responsible for Taco Bell" may all be true statements. Nevertheless, there is no essence corresponding to blindness (a privation) or lawyers (a social function) or money (a conventional sign), capitalism (an economic system), or Taco Bell (a corporation). Medieval philosophers produced many commentaries on the ten categories, dividing and sub-diving each one, yet none of their analyses that I know of could locate privations, social functions, conventional signs, economic systems, or corporations. So, if you had not read the chapter about Thomism in this book, you might wonder what it is in virtue of which these statements are true. If, however, you had read the relevant chapter, you may recall Aquinas's theory about beings of reason. We can, thinks Aquinas, refer to beings that do not have essences falling into the ten categories just in case we can talk about those beings in true statements.

The two ways of using the verb "to be" that Aquinas identifies, and the three that Russell and others have exploited, may not be incompatible. I mean to suggest that there may be a way of mapping one onto the other. Consider Aquinas's so-called "actuality" sense of being with regard to things with real essences. Here, one might say "Socrates is." But why not understand this to mean "Socrates is a living human being"?[58] And thus we see the word "is" being used in the predication sense that Russell specified. This is even more obviously so in the case of accidental predications, such as "Socrates is happy." As for Aquinas's beings of reason, many statements can be understood in terms of what I described above as the "is of predication." When Aquinas says "Blindness is," we can understand him to mean "Some things are blind," and this is easily conveyed using existential quantification (or as "There is at least one blind thing"). Aquinas, as far as I know, has little to say about the "is" that appears in statements of identity, as it does when I say "Clark Kent is Superman." But I think that both the Thomist and the Analytic philosopher can easily accommodate it, perhaps by understanding such a statement to mean "The thing that is called 'Clark Kent' is also called 'Superman,'" thus reducing that use of "is" to the "is" of predication.

So I believe that the Analytic philosopher and the Thomist can learn from each other. The former ought to consider Aquinas's arguments surrounding *esse*, because if Aquinas is getting at something true, then this will have profound implications for metaphysics and (especially) for philosophy of religion. Likewise, I think that a follower of Aquinas ought to seriously reconsider the tendency to think of *esse* as something reducible to what the English words "being" or "existence" express or else risk illegitimately treating existence as a first-order property.

4.3 The Continental and Analytic Tradition

This book traces the Continental Tradition (which is related to, but not co-extensive with, continental philosophy) back to the work of Immanuel Kant. Any serious student of the history of philosophy should read Kant's *Critique of Pure Reason*, not to mention his subsequent ethical works. One who reads the first Critique will find that Kant is very concerned with the distinction between analytic statements and synthetic statements, a distinction sometimes just called the "analytic/synthetic distinction." Moreover, one who reads Kant will see why the chapter on the Continental Tradition in this book stakes out the claim that time is the "ground of being." Analytic philosophers have also had things to say about both the analytic/synthetic distinction and the nature of time. Since I think that a philosopher in the Continental Tradition would do well to consider what Analytic philosophers have written about these two issues, in this section I will summarize some noteworthy arguments pertaining to them.

In Chapter 4 I said that it is difficult to get far in Analytic philosophy without encountering the thought of W.V.O. Quine. And this is especially true when it comes to the history of the analytic/synthetic distinction, for Quine proposed a famous argument that was intended to show that the distinction itself was bogus.[59] According to Quine, a statement is analytic if "it is true by virtue of meanings and independently of fact."[60] Quine, presumably, had in mind here analytic statements that express something that is true: "Humans are animals" is true, but it is true in virtue of what the words "human" and "animal" mean, just as "Squares are triangular" is false just in virtue of what the words "square" and "triangular" mean; you don't have to investigate the world to see that these statements are true or false, as you would if, for example, you wanted to know whether "The Statue of Liberty is taller than The Liberty Bell" is true. Anyone who knows the meanings of the words in any analytic statement will know, as a result of those meanings, whether or not the statement is true. But what does the word "meaning" mean? An investigation of this question, according to Quine, will lead us to reject the whole idea that a statement can be analytic at all. To put Quine's point bluntly: If we cannot get ourselves clear on what "meaning" amounts to when we say that analytic statements are true or false in virtue of their meanings, then we don't really understand what an analytic statement is or, for that matter, how it is different from a synthetic one.

The question "What is meaning?" is not a new one in philosophy. Plato, on at least one interpretation, was attempting to answer this question when he proposed his so-called "Theory of Forms." According to Plato, on this interpretation, meanings reside in their own imperceptible realm, independently of any particular item which we might encounter in our own perceptible world. Quine rejects this way of thinking, however, and such a rejection is characteristic of his way of treating philosophical problems. To simplify Quine's argument, meanings have to be understood in terms of synonymy. Consider the statement "All bachelors are unmarried." This looks like a paradigmatic case of an analytic statement: Anyone who knows the meaning of "bachelor" will recognize that the meaning contains "unmarried" within it. On Quine's view, when I say that I *know* that "bachelor" means "unmarried man," I mean that I know that the two terms are synonymous. Thus, Quine goes on to say that we can replace the notion of meaning with that of synonymy.

But what is synonymy? How can one "check," so to speak, whether or not two terms are synonymous? Quine considers various options (some of which are quite technical). Perhaps you believe that two terms are synonymous just in case they are always interchangeable. On such a view, "bachelor" and "unmarried man" are synonymous since, given any true statement where someone uses the word "bachelor," I could substitute in "unmarried man" and still have a true statement. But consider the analytic statement we began with: "All bachelors are unmarried." Substitute out "bachelor" for "unmarried man" and you have "All unmarried men are unmarried." Such a statement is true, surely, but it is true analytically! Thus, attempting to define synonymy in terms of substitutability, according to Quine, presupposes some notion of analyticity, and we are thus no closer to understanding analyticity. Nor does it do any good to appeal to definitions: Who coined the definition of "bachelor"? On what authority? And how could anyone have done so without already having a prior understanding of synonymy and analyticity?

I have here glossed over Quine's arguments regarding analyticity much too briefly. To be sure, Analytic philosophers have certainly not given up on the distinction. But they have, for the past half century, recognized a need to contend with his arguments in order to offer a more precise understanding of the distinction. My suggestion here is that, insofar as the Continental Tradition traces its heritage back to Kant and his work involving the distinction, philosophers in that tradition would do well to concern themselves with Quine's arguments.

When someone working in the Continental Tradition says "Time is the ground of being," what sense is to be made of the word "time?" One might think that time is so intuitive, or maybe even (speaking loosely) so "intimate," that it escapes definition. Augustine dedicated a whole book of his *Confessions* to the issue of time, and his puzzles are sometimes summed up "If no one asks me, I know what time is; if you ask me to explain it, I do not."[61] And Augustine is surely tracking something true when he says this: What higher genus can time be placed in such that we can talk about it or distinguish it from something else? Nevertheless, it seems that we can talk about time. Physicists take themselves to have insights about it, and so do Analytic philosophers. So, to conclude my dialogue with the Continental Tradition, I will tell you about one famous debate regarding the nature of time, and I will leave it to you to decide whether it might be a threat to the Continental Tradition or something with which continental philosophers ought to contend.

In 1908 J.M.E. McTaggart (1866–1925) proposed a now-famous argument that time cannot be real.[62] He does this by noting two ways one might think of a temporal ordering of events. The first way, which philosophers now call "the A-series," conceives of moments in time as characterized by properties like "being five days into the future" or "being seven minutes in the past." In other words, the A-series represents time as past, present, and future. On the other hand, there is the B-series, where time is represented in terms of "prior to," "simultaneous with," and "later than." My death will be later than my birth, but (hopefully) prior to the extinction of humanity. The key difference between these two conceptions of time is that the A-series is wholly transitory: As I write this, my death is an event in the future; sadly, some day it will be an event of the past. Moreover, with each passing moment the distance it is in the future changes. On the other hand, my birth was prior to my death, and it always will be the case that it is prior to my death. The B-series is permanent.

McTaggart urges us to abandon any hope of conceiving of time in terms of the B-series for the simple reason that time involves change. As philosophers since Aristotle have said, "Time is the measure of change." The A-series is essential to time since if time is real, then there must be such a thing as a past (how things were), a present (the way that things have changed), and a future (how things will change). Moreover, to admit the reality of change is to admit that, in at least some cases, what is true at one time will not be true at another: To say that my temperature has changed is just to say "There was a moment when 'I was 98.6 degree Fahrenheit' was true but now it is not." So, given the necessity of the A-series for time to be real, it is also necessary that something true at one point in time will not be true at another.

The problem, according to McTaggart, is that the A-series is self-contradictory. Consider some event such as the American Civil War. It is marked, on the A-series conception, with the property *past*. Every event is marked with one of three properties: Past, present, or future. For any event to have one of those three properties entails it having none of the others. But, of course, for the Civil War to be past means that it *was* present, and even that it *was* future. In other words, this one event has three incompatible properties. It does not do, thinks McTaggart, to respond "Well, the Civil War was present in the past," because any moment you try to invoke as that moment when the Civil War was present is itself a moment characterized as *past* by the A-series; and so that moment could not have the property *present*. It is a moment that will have all three incompatible properties: past, present, and future. If you say of that moment, "It *was* present but now is past," you get yourself into an infinite regress: When was it present? In the past?

McTaggart's rejection of the reality of time has had a similar legacy as Quine's rejection of the analytic-synthetic distinction: Fewer philosophers accept the conclusion, but many see the importance of the argument. So influential has McTaggart been that Analytic philosophers who discuss time today describe themselves as A-theorists or B-theorists, depending on which conception of time they put priority on. And McTaggart's arguments raise questions that I think continental philosophers could benefit by asking, for if time is (as such philosophers say) "the ground of being," then I think that we owe it to ourselves to say what time is and how it is possibly real.

Notes

Chapter 1

1. It is our belief that readers will become familiar with different philosophical traditions by exploring how each tradition approaches the philosophy of being. On the one hand, we recognize that these traditions may be incommensurable. On the other hand, it is our hope that this project will contribute to a renewed sense of philosophical "pluralism" and "ecumenism."
2. Whereas this section was constructed through a collaborative effort on our parts, the remaining portions of the book were constructed by each of us independently. That is to say, each of us bears the responsibility for representing our respective traditions: Joseph P. Li Vecchi for the Thomistic, Frank Scalambrino for the Continental, and David Kovacs for the Analytic.
3. Quoted from *A Presocratics Reader*, edited by Patricia Curd and translated by Richard McKirahan (Indianapolis, IN: Hackett Publishing, 1995): 46.
4. For an overview of the main interpretive schools about Parmenides, see the Stanford Encyclopedia of Philosophy article "Parmenides," by John Palmer, available as of May 2019 at https://plato.stanford.edu/entries/parmenides/.
5. For an introduction to Aristotle's thought that pays special attention to the influence of Parmenides, see Jonathan Lear's *Aristotle: The Desire to Understand* (Cambridge and New York: Cambridge University Press, 1988).
6. Cf. *Parmenides* (163c5-8), *Republic* (479b-e), *Sophist* (237a-239e), and *Timaeus* (27d5-28a3).
7. Are the terms "being" and "existence" ever interchangeable, from a philosophical point of view, in English? The present authors have different opinions. Each will speak for himself in the text that follows.
8. Cf. *Metaphysics*, Book IV, §1 (1003a21-23) and Bk VI, §2 (1026a33-1026b4).
9. See John F. Wippel, *The Metaphysical Thought of Thomas Aquinas* (Washington, DC: Catholics University of America Press, 2000).
10. See Etienne Gilson, *Being and Some Philosophers* (Toronto: Pontifical Institute of Medieval Studies, 1952).

11 According to the Continental Tradition, the fact that "science" was understood differently between the Ancient and Modern periods of Western philosophy does not diminish the thrust of this truth.
12 The Analytic Tradition was widely considered the dominant tradition in English-speaking countries for most of the twentieth century.

Chapter 2

1 Aquinas, *Truth* (*De ver.*), 1, 1, co.: *Illud autem quod primo intellectus concipit … est ens …*; *Scriptum super Sententiis* (*Sup. Sent.*), I, 8, 1, 3, co.; *Summa theologiae* (*S. th.*), I–II, 94, 2, resp.
2 *S. th.*, I, 4, 2, co.: *Deus est ipsum esse per se subsistens ….*
3 For a good overview of Aquinas's works, see Jean-Pierre Torrell, *Saint Thomas Aquinas*, Vol. 1, *The Person and His Works*, translated by Robert Royal (Washington, DC: The Catholic University of America Press, 1996).
4 A comprehensive history of Thomism has yet to be written. For the earliest Thomists, see Frederick J. Roenisch, *Early Thomistic School* (Dubuque, Iowa: The Priory Press, 1964). Some surveys of comparatively recent Thomism include: Fergus Kerr, *After Aquinas: Versions of Thomism* (Oxford: Blackwell, 2002); Robert J. Henle, "The American Thomistic Revival" in the *Philosophical Papers of R. J. Henle, S.J.* (St. Louis, MO: St. Louis University Press, 2000); Battista Mondin, *La Metafisica di san Tommaso d'Aquino e i suoi interpreti* (Bologna: Edizioni Studio Domenicano, 2002); John F. X. Knasas, *Being and Some 20th Century Thomists* (Fordham University Press, 2003); Edward Fezer, "The Thomistic Tradition," 2009, http://edwardfeser.blogspot.com/2009/10/thomistic-tradition-part-i.html (accessed October 17, 2017).
5 *S. th.*, I, 85, 1, resp.: *Proprium eius est cognoscere formam in materia….*
6 Aquinas, *Commentary on Boethius's The Trinity* (*In Boeth. De Trin.*), V, 2–3; VI, 1.
7 Aquinas, *Commentary on Aristotle's On the Soul* (*In De an.*), III; *S. th.*, I, 75–86.
8 Aquinas, *Commentary on Aristotle's Metaphysics* (*Sup. Metaph.*), IV, 4, n. 5; *S. th.*, I, 28, 1, ad 2.
9 Aquinas, *Commentary on the Book of the Ethics* (*Sup. Ethic.*), I, 1, 2.
10 Aquinas, *Commentary on Aristotle's Politics* (*Sup. Pol.*); *Summa contra gentiles* (*S.c.G.*), III, Vol. 2; *S. th.*, I–II, 94. 2 and 3, and generally 90–114.
11 *S. th.*, I, 39, 8, resp.; *Commentary on the Divine Names* (*In div. nom.*), IV, 5.

12　*In div. nom.*, V, 1, 1: *Omnia autem alia … habent esse receptum.*
13　*Sup. Metaph.*, I, 2, 1: *… omnia ista conveniunt universali scientiae, quae considerat causas primas et universales ….*; *Sup. Metaph.*, Prooemium: *… oportet quod ad eamdem scientiam pertineat considerare … ens commune*; *In Boeth. De Trin.*, V, 4; Aquinas, *On Being and Essence* (*De ente*), V.
14　*S. th.*, I, 4, 2, co.: *… ipsum esse per se subsistens*; *In Boeth. De Trin.*, V, a. 3.
15　For such an account see, for example, John Wipple. *The Metaphysical Thought of Thomas Aquinas: From Finite Being to Uncreated Being* (Wipple) (Washington, D.C.: Catholic University of America Press, 2000).
16　*S. th.* I, 2, 3, co.: *… Deum esse quinque viis probari potest*. For a discussion of Aquinas's proofs of God, see among others, Wipple, Chapters X, "Argumentation for God's Existence," XI, "Argumentation for God's Existence in Earlier Writings," and XII, "The Five Ways."
17　*S. th.*, I, 13, 5, co.: *Neque enim in his quae analogice dicuntur, est una ratio, sicut est in univocis; nec totaliter diversa, sicut in aequivocis; sed nomen quod sic multipliciter dicitur, significat diversas proportiones ad aliquid unum; sicut sanum, de urina dictum, significat signum sanitatis animalis, de medicina vero dictum, significat causam eiusdem sanitatis.* For a discussion of Aquinas on analogy, see Wipple, chapter 3, "The Problem of Parmenides and Analogy of Being"; Ralph McInerny, *Aquinas and Analogy* (Washington: Catholic University of America Press, 1996), Bernard Montagnes, *The Doctrine of the Analogy of Being According to Thomas Aquinas, Marquette Studies in Philosophy*, translated by Edward M. Macierowski (Milwaukee: Marquette University Press, 2004).
18　See Section 4 below. For an in depth summary of Aquinas's view of participation and its retrieval from the Platonic tradition, despite Aristotle's rejection of Plato's doctrine of participation, see, among others, Wipple, Chapter 4, "Participation and the Problem of the One and the Many," Cornelio Fabro, *La nozione metafisica di partecipazione secondo S. Tommaso d'Aquino*, Vita e Pensiero, Milano, 1939. Louis-Bertrand Geiger, *La participation dans la philosophie de s. Thomas d'Aquin* (Paris: Librairie Philosophique J. Vrin, 1942).
19　See note 4 for some sources.
20　Leo XIII, "Aeterni Patris," August 4, 1879, http://www.vatican.va/content/leo-xiii/en/encyclicals/documents/hf_l-xiii_enc_04081879_aeterni-patris.html (accessed June 6, 2020).
21　Sacred Congregation on Study, *Acts of the Holy See*, "The 24 Theses" Year 6—Vol. 6, July 27, 1914, Rome: Vatican Polyglot Publishing, 1914, 383–6. http://www.vatican.va/archive/aas/documents/AAS-06-1914-ocr.pdf (accessed June 6, 2020).
22　See note 4 above.

23 Salvatore Roselli, *Summa Philosophica ad mentem angelici doctoris s. Thomae Aquinatis, I. Pars prima logicam complectens*, q. XXIV, a. 2, *De criterio veritatis*. Ex typographia Octavii Puccinelli, Rome, 1777.

24 For a discussion of this doctrine and its impact of the objectivity of knowledge, see Joseph Li Vecchi, "Logical Objectivity and Second Intentions" (Li Vecchi 2014), *Angelicum* 91, no. 4, December 2014: 795–812.

25 Willard Van Orman Quine, "On What There Is," *Review of Metaphysics* 2, no. 5, September 1948: 21. Cf. Li Vecchi, Joseph. "Quine and Aquinas: On What There Is" (Li Vecchi 2008), *The Modern Schoolman* 85, no. 3, 2008: 207–23.

26 Immanuel Kant, *Critique of Pure Reason*. Translated by P. Guyer and A. W. Wood. (Cambridge, England: University of Cambridge Press, 1998).

27 This Medieval Latin 3rd declension neuter noun derives from the would-be present active participle of the verb *to be* used as an adjective. Its singular/plural forms are: nominative: *ens/entia*; genitive: *entis/entium*; dative: *enti/entibus*; accusative: *ens/entia*; ablative: *ente/entibus*.

28 *De ente*, I: ... *quod significat propositionum ueritatem*. Here the reader may take proposition to be roughly equivalent to sentence or statement.

29 *Expositio libri Peryermenias* (*Sup. Pery.*), I, 11, 7: ... *verum nihil aliud est, nisi quando dicitur esse quod est, aut non esse quod non est; falsum autem, quando dicitur esse quod non est, aut non esse quod est*.

30 *S.c.G.*, I, 22. *Omnis res est per hoc, quod habet esse*; *De ver.* 1, 1 co.: ... *ens sumitur ab actu essendi*. *Sup. Pery.* I, 5, 20. Fabro, 1939, and Gilson, 1941, first recognize the doctrine of *actus essendi* in Aquinas. See Mondin.

31 *S.c.G.*, I, 29, 9: *Substantia est ens per se*.

32 Aquinas, *On Spiritual Creatures* (*De spirit. creat.*), 1, 25: *Primus actus est causa omnis entis in actu*.

33 Aquinas, *On the Virtues* (*De virtut.*) I, 2, 2: *Bonum, quod convertitur cum ente, est commune omni enti*.

34 Aquinas, *On the Power of God* (*De pot.*) VII, 7, co.: *Omne quod est in potentia, reducitur ad actum per ens actu*.

35 *De ente*, I: ... *aliqua enim hoc modo dicuntur entia que essentiam non habent*.

36 The forms of this Medieval 2nd declension neuter singular-only verbal noun or gerund are: nominative: *esse*; genitive: *essendi*; dative *essendo*; accusative: *esse*; ablative: *essendo*.

37 *S. th.* I, 54, 1, co.: *Esse est actualitas substantiae vel essentiae*. Ibid., I, 75, 5. Cf. I, 75, 5, ad 4: *Ipsum enim esse est, quo aliquid est*; *S.c.G.*, I, 22, 5: ... *unumquodque est per suum esse*; I, 22, no. 7: *esse actum quendam nominat*.

38 Aquinas, *Commentary on Aristotle's Physics* (*Sup. Phys.*) I, 12, 10: *Fieri importat initium essendi.* Cf. *S. th.* I 89, 1, co.
39 *De ente*, IV: *Omnis essentia potest intelligi sine hoc quod aliquid intelligatur de esse suo.*
40 *De ver.*, IV, 1 ad 7: *Causa est prius quam effectus in essendo.*
41 *S. th.*, I, 104, 4 ad 2: *Potentia creaturae ad essendum est receptiva tantum.*
42 *De ente*, I, a: *Ens per se dupliciter dicitur: uno modo quod diuiditur per decem genera, alio modo quod significat propositionum ueritatem. ... Potest dici ens omne illud de quo affirmatiua propositio formari potest, etiam si illud in re nichil ponat; per quem modum priuationes et negationes entia dicuntur.*
43 *De ente*, I: *... dicimus enim quod affirmatio est opposita negationi, et quod cecitas est in oculo*; *Sup. Metaph.*, VII, 1: *... ens dicitur multipliciter*; *Sup. Phys.*, I, 3, 2; I, 6, 2. Cf. Aristotle, *Metaphysics* (*Metaph.*), IV, 2, 1003a33.
44 *Sup. Phys.*, III, l. 5 n. 15: *Praedicando enim aliquid de aliquo altero, dicimus hoc esse illud.*
45 *Loc. cit.*: *Modi autem essendi proportionales sunt modis praedicandi.*
46 *S. th.*, I, 5, 2: *Ratio enim significata per nomen, est id quod concipit intellectus de re, et significat illud per vocem.*
47 *S. th.*, I, 2, a. 1 resp.: *Aliqua propositio est per se nota, quod praedicatum includitur in ratione subiecti.*
48 *Metaph.*, XI, 7, 1064a23ff.
49 *S. th.*, I, 2, 1 co.
50 *S. th.*, I, II, 55, a. 4, ad 1: *Unicuique apprehenso a nobis attribuimus quod sit ens.*
51 *De ver.*, 1, a. 1, ad 3: *Ratio autem entis ab actu essendi sumitur.*
52 See note 4 above.
53 *Sup. Pery.*, I, 5, 18–22. Cf. Aristotle, *On Interpretation* (*Interp.*), 3, 16b, 21–6.
54 *De ver.*, I, 1, co.: *Illud autem quod primo intellectus concipit quasi notissimum ... est ens*; *S. th.*, I, II, 94, 2, co.: *... illud quod primo cadit in apprehensione, est ens, cuius intellectus includitur in omnibus quaecumque quis apprehendit*; *Sup. Sent.*, I, 19, 5, 1 ad 2: *... nunquam potest intelligi intelligibile, secundum hanc rationem, nisi intelligatur ens.*
55 *De ver.*, I, 1, co.: *... sicut in demonstrabilibus oportet fieri reductionem in aliqua principia per se intellectui nota, ita investigando quid est unumquodque; alias utrobique in infinitum iretur, et sic periret omnino scientia et cognitio rerum. Illud autem quod primo intellectus concipit quasi notissimum, et in quod conceptiones omnes resolvit, est ens. ... Unde oportet quod omnes aliae conceptiones intellectus accipiantur ex additione ad ens.*

56 *S. th.*, I, II, 55, 4, ad 1: ... *unicuique apprehenso a nobis attribuimus quod sit ens.*
57 *S. th.*, I, 5, 2, co.: *Secundum hoc unumquodque cognoscibile est, inquantum est actu. Sup. Sent.* I, 8, 1, 3 co. and ad 3: ... *ens, sine quo nihil potest apprehendi ab intellectu*; *S. th.*, I, 85, 3.
58 Michael Tavuzzi, "Aquinas on the Preliminary Grasp of Being," (Tavuzzi 1987), *The Thomist* 51, no. 4, 1987, 555–4.; *Cf.* Li Vecchi 2014.
59 *S. th.*, I, 33, 1, co.: ... *principium nihil aliud significat, quam id, a quo aliquid procedit; omne enim, a quo aliquid procedit quocumque modo, dicimus esse principium, et e converso.*
60 *S. th.*, I–II, 94, 2, co.: ... *primum principium indemonstrabile est quod non est simul affirmare et negare, quod fundatur supra rationem entis et non entis, et super hoc principio omnia alia fundantur. S.c.G.*, II, c. 83: ... *ens ... in qua cognitione fundatur primorum principiorum notitia, ut non esse simul affirmare et negare, et alia huiusmodi.*
61 *S. th.*, I, 2, 1, resp.: ... *in primis demonstrationum principiis, quorum termini sunt quaedam communia quae nullus ignorat, ut ens et non ens.*
62 *S.c.G.*, II, 83: *Haec igitur sola principia intellectus noster naturaliter cognoscit, conclusiones autem per ipsa: sicut per colorem cognoscit visus tam communia quam sensibilia per accidens.*
63 *S. th.*, I, 1, 7 co.: *Se habet subiectum ad scientiam, sicut obiectum ad potentiam vel habitum.*
64 *In Boet. de Trin.*, I, 1, 2, 3: *Cognoscentis et cognoscibilis oportet esse aliquam proportionem, sicut et potentiae cuiuslibet ad suum obiectum.*
65 *S. th.*, I, 1, 7 co.: *Proprie autem illud assignatur obiectum alicuius potentiae vel habitus, sub cuius ratione omnia referuntur ad potentiam vel habitum.*
66 See Sections 2.2 and 2.3 above. *S. th.*, I, 5, a. 2 co.: *Primo autem in conceptione intellectus cadit ens, quia secundum hoc unumquodque cognoscibile est, inquantum est actu, ut dicitur in IX Metaphys. Unde ens est proprium obiectum intellectus, et sic est primum intelligibile. S.c.G.*, II, 98, 9: *Comprehendit omnes differentias et species entis possibiles; quicquid enim esse potest, intelligi potest. S. th.*, I–II, 57, a. 1, ad 2: *Obiectum intellectus est quod quid est.*
67 *S. th.*, I, 5, a. 2 co.: *Unde ens est proprium obiectum intellectus, et sic est primum intelligibile.* For being as the first intelligible object in the logical and psychological orders, see Sections 2.2 and 2.3 above.
68 *S. th.*, I, 78, 4, 4: *Intellectus nihil cognoscit nisi accipiendo a sensu*; *S. th.*, I, 84, 3, co.: *Deficiente aliquo sensu, deficit scientia eorum.*; *De ver.*, q. 2 a. 3, 19: *Nihil est in intellectu quod non sit prius in sensu.*

69 *S. th.*, I, 87, 3, ad 1: ... *primum obiectum intellectus nostri secundum praesentem statum est ... ens et verum consideratum in rebus materialibus.* Cf. *In Boet. de Trin.*, I, 3. *S. th.* I, 84, 7, co.: *Intellectus autem humani, qui est coniunctus corpori, proprium obiectum est quidditas sive natura in materia corporali existens.*

70 *S. th.*, I, 76, 5, co.: *Anima intellectiva ... oportet quod ... colligat ex rebus divisibilibus per viam sensus.*

71 *De ente*, I: *Et quia illud per quod res constituitur in proprio genere uel specie est hoc quod significatur per diffinitionem indicantem quid est res.*

72 *In De an.*, III, 7, 690: *Hic homo intelligit.* Cf. Aristotle, *Aristotle's De Anima. (De an.)*, III, 5, 429a24–25.

73 *S. th.*, I, 78, 4, co.: *Animal per animam sensitivam ... recipiat species sensibilium, cum praesentialiter immutatur ab eis.* For the senses and their proper objects, see *S. th.*, I, 78, 3 and *In De an.*, II, 14.

74 *S. th.*, I, 79, 3–4; 85, 6–7. *De spirit. creat.*, 10.

75 *S. th.*, I, 2, 3.

76 *S. th.*, I, 78, 4, 4: *Intellectus nihil cognoscit nisi accipiendo a sensu.*

77 *S. th.*, I, 85, 3, co.

78 *In Boet. de Trin.*, V, 3; *Sup. Pery.*, I, 3, 3.

79 *S. th.*, I, 79, 2–4.; I, 86, 1, co.: *Quod autem a materia individuali abstrahitur, est universale. Unde intellectus noster directe non est cognoscitivus nisi universalium.*

80 *S. th.*, I, 86, 1, co.: *Indirecte autem, et quasi per quandam reflexionem, potest cognoscere singulare.*

81 *Sup. Sent.*, II, 17, q. 2, a. 1, 3: *Omne quod recipitur in aliquo, recipitur in eo per modum recipientis.*; *De pot.*, III, a. 11, 14; *S. th.*, 84, 1, co. Cf. Li Vecchi 2014.

82 *De ver.*, VIII, 8 co.: *Omnis cognitio est per assimilationem; similitudo autem inter aliqua duo est secundum convenientiam in forma.* Ibid., II, 5 ad 7: ... *applicatio cogniti ad cognoscentem, quae cognitionem facit, non est intelligenda per modum identitatis, sed per modum cuiusdam repraesentationis; unde non oportet quod sit idem modus cognoscentis et cogniti.*

83 Cf. Tavuzzi 1987, 568.

84 *Sup. Sent.*, I, 23, 1, 1, co: ... *materia demonstrata determinatis accidentibus substante, in qua individuatur forma.*; *De ente*, II, 371a, 73–7: ... *materia non quolibet modo accepta est indiuiduationis principium, sed solum materia signata; et dico materiam signatam que sub determinatis dimensionibus consideratur.*

85 *De ente*, II.

86 *De ver.*, II, 6, ad 3: *Homo praecognoscit singularia per imaginationem et sensum, et ideo potest applicare cognitionem universalem quae est in intellectu, ad particulare.*

87 *De ver.*, 2, 6, ad 3: *Non enim, proprie loquendo, sensus aut intellectus cognoscunt, sed homo per utrumque, ut patet in I de anima.*

88 *S. th.*, I, 86, 1, co.: *Indirecte autem, et quasi per quandam reflexionem, potest cognoscere singulare, quia ... etiam postquam species intelligibiles abstraxit, non potest secundum eas actu intelligere nisi convertendo se ad phantasmata, in quibus species intelligibiles intelligit.* Cf. *De ver.*, 10, 5, co.

89 *S. th.*, I, 86, a. 1–4: *Singulare in rebus materialibus intellectus noster directe et primo cognoscere non potest ... quia principium singularitatis in rebus materialibus est materia individualis .... Quod autem a materia individuali abstrahitur, est universale. Unde intellectus noster directe non est cognoscitivus nisi universalium.*

90 *S. th.*, I, 84, 1, co.: *... cum nihil operetur nisi inquantum est actu, modus operandi uniuscuiusque rei sequitur modum essendi ipsius.*

91 See Section 3.6.2 concerning the *formal value* of the universal concept.

92 See Section 3.6.2 concerning the passage of the actually present potentially intelligible phantasm to actual intelligibility.

93 See Section 3.6.1

94 See Section 2 for real being versus being of reason.

95 See Section 3.6.2–3.6.4.

96 *S. th.*, I, 85, 2, co.: *Species intellectiva secundario est id quod intelligitur. Sed id quod intelligitur primo, est res cuius species intelligibilis est similitudo.*

97 *S. th.*, I, 5, 2, co.: *Secundum hoc unumquodque cognoscibile est, inquantum est actu.*

98 *De ver.*, I. 1, co.: *Hoc autem est anima, quae quodammodo est omnia, ut dicitur in III de anima.*; *S. th.*, I, 85, 2, 1: *Intellectum enim in actu est in intelligente: quia intellectum in actu est ipse intellectus in actu: Ibid. ad 1: Intellectum est in intelligente per suam similitudinem. Et per hunc modum dicitur quod intellectum in actu est intellectus in actu, inquantum similitudo rei intellectae est forma intellectus.*

99 *In Boeth. De Trin.*, V, a. 3, 121–32. *In De an.*, III, 1, 11, 19: *Scientia secundum actum est idem rei scitae secundum actum ... quia omnia quae sunt in actu, fiunt ex ente in actu.*

100 See Section 2.1.

101 *Sup. Sent.*, II, 34. 1. 1 co.: *Uno modo dicitur ens quod per decem genera dividitur: et sic ens significat aliquid in natura existens.*

102 *Sup. Phys.*, I, 9, 3: *Quae igitur naturaliter fiunt, non fiunt ex simpliciter non ente, sed ex ente in potentia; non autem ex ente in actu, ut ipsi opinabantur. Unde quae fiunt non oportet praeexistere actu, ut ipsi dicebant, sed potentia tantum.*

103 *Sup. Metaph.*, V, 14, 594: *Ens dividitur per actum et potentiam*; V, 14: *Prima [divisio] est, quod ens dividitur per potentiam et actum*; Aquinas, *Disputed Questions on Evil (De malo)*, 1. 2 co.; *Sup. Metaph.*, V, 9, 889.
104 *Sup. Phys.*, I, 15, no. 3; I, 3, no. 6: *Actus et potentia dividunt quodlibet genus entium; Sicut potentia ad qualitatem non est aliquid extra genus qualitatis, ita potentia ad esse substantiale non est aliquid extra genus substantiae.*
105 *Sup. Phys.*, III, 2, 3.
106 *S. th.*, I, 77, 1; *Metaph.* VII, 1; IX, 1 and 9.
107 *Sup. Phys.*, I, 9, 3: *Ens enim in potentia est quasi medium inter purum non ens et ens in actu.*
108 *S. th.*, I, 50, a.2 ad 3.
109 *S.c.G.*, I. 15: *Omne, quod incipit esse vel desinit, per motum vel mutationem hoc patitur.*
110 *Sup. Sent.*, IV, 1, 1, 4, 2 c: *... motus autem non est ens completum, sed est via in ens sc. completum.*
111 *Sup. Metaph.*, I, n. 541: *... proximum in debilitate est ... enim aliquid admixtum de privatione et negatione.*
112 *Sup. Phys.*, I, 1, 7: *Magis autem entia sunt, quae sunt magis in actu.*
113 *S. th.*, I, 7, 1–2; *S.c.G.*, I, c. 43.
114 *S. th.*, I, 3, 4; I, 7, 2.
115 See Section 3.6.2 above.
116 *Sup. Pery.*, I, pr.: *In iis, quae possunt esse et non esse, prius est non esse, quam esse.*
117 *Sup.Phys.*, I, 1, 7; *Sup. Metaph.* IX, 7.1846. Cf. *De an.* 412a22-7.
118 *Sup. Sent.*, II, 34. 1. 1 co.: *Uno modo dicitur ens quod per decem genera dividitur: et sic ens significat aliquid in natura existens*; *Sup. Metaph.*, V, 14, 594: *Secunda divisio est, prout ens dividitur secundum decem genera. S. th.*, I, 48, 2 ad 2: *dividitur per decem praedicamenta.* Cf. Aristotle, *Categories*, (*Categ.*) 4, 1b25-2a4.
119 *Sup. Sent.*, 3, 23. 2. 1 ad 1: *Substantia est fundamentum et basis omnium aliorum entium.* Cf. *Categ.*, 5, 2a34-b6.
120 See Section 3.5.
121 *S. th.* I. 3. 6; *S.c.G.*, II. 21; *De pot.*, III. 6, 5.
122 *S. th.*, I. 104, 4 ad 3; *S.c.G.*, II. 58; *Sup. Sent.*, 1, 19. 5, 1 co.;.
123 *S. th.*, I. 76. 4 ad 4: *Esse substantiale cuiuslibet rei in indivisibili consistit.*; *Sup. Sent.*, III, d. 6 q. 1 a. 1 qc. 1 co.: *... per se subsistat*; *De pot.*, IX. 1, co.: *... non praedicatur de alio*; *S. th.*, I, 11, 1, co.: *... esse cuiuslibet rei consistit in indivisione*; *Sup. Metaph.*, IV, 4, 543: *... est perfectissimum, quod scilicet habet esse in natura absque admixtione privationis, et habet esse firmum et solidum, quasi per se existens.*

124 *De ver.*, 1, 1 co.: ... *imponitur hoc nomen res, quod in hoc differt ab ente ... quod ens sumitur ab actu essendi, sed nomen rei exprimit quidditatem vel essentiam entis.*
125 *Categ.*, 5, 2a11.
126 *Categ.* 4, 1b25-27.
127 *Sup. Metaph.*, IV, 4, 542: *Nihil habet de non ente admixtum, habet tamen esse debile, quia non per se, sed in alio, sicut sunt qualitates, quantitates et substantiae proprietates.*
128 *S. th.*, I. 3. 6; *S.c.G.*, II. 21.
129 *De pot.*, III. 6, 5: ... *quod est per accidens, est ut in paucioribus.*
130 *S.c.G.*, III. 11: *Omne, quod est per accidens, reducitur ad id, quod est per se.*; *S.c.G.* III. 15: *Quod est per accidens, est posterius eo, quod est per se.*
131 See Sections 2.1 for being as the principle of entity, and 3.3 and 3.5 for being as the principle of intelligibility.
132 See Section 3.6.1. Cf. *De ente*, I and III.
133 *S. th.*, I, 28, 1 and following. Cf. Aristotle, *De an.* II, 1, 412a22-7 and II, 5, 417a22-9.
134 Aristotle, Categ. 4, 1b25-27; *De pot.*, VII, a.2, ad 9: *Esse est actualitas omnium actuum, et propter hoc perfectio omnium perfectionum.*
135 *S. th.* Ia. q.3, a.6; *S.c.G.*, I, c.23; II, c.52; *De ente*, V.
136 *In Boeth De Trin.*, V, 3: *Sunt enim quedam partes ex quibus ratio totius dependet, quando scilicet hoc est esse tali toti quod ex talibus partibus componi, sicut se habet sillaba ad litteras, et mixtum ad elementa; et tales partes dicuntur partes speciei et forme, sine quibus totum intelligi non potest, cum ponatur in eius diffinitione.*
137 See Section 3.6.1. Cf. *De ente*, I and III.
138 *D ente*, IV. There is controversy among scholars about whether, and at what point, Aquinas establishes the distinction between being and essence, and about whether it is metaphysical or conceptual in nature. An overview of the debate is provided by Walter Patt, "Aquinas's Real Distinction and Some Interpretations," *The New Scholasticism* 62, no. 1, 1988: 1–29. See also Wipple, Chapters IV, "Participation and the Problem of the One and the Many," and V, "Essence-*Esse* Composition and the One and the Many." See also Steven A. Long, "On the Natural Knowledge of the Real Distinction of Essence and Existence," *Nova et Vetera* English edition, Vol. 1, no. 1, 2003: 75–108, David Twetten's "How Save Aquinas's 'Intellectus essentiae Argument' for the Real Distinction between Essence and Esse?" *Roczniki Filozoficzne* 67, no. 4, 2019: 129–43.
139 Immediately following the cited passage from *De ente*, IV, Aquinas discusses the exceptional case of a substance whose essence is identical to its being, God.

140 See Section 2.1.

141 For Aquinas on *quid est* and *an est* see *Sup. Sent.* lib. II, 34, 1, 1, co.; II, 37, 1, 2 ad 1 and ad 3. Cf. *Sup. Boet. De Trin.*, V, 3, 87–95: ... *duplex est operatio intellectus: una que dicitur intelligentia indiuisibilium, qua cognoscit de unumquodque quid est.*

142 *In div. nom.*, V, 1, 1: *Omnia autem alia ... habent esse receptum.* Wipple, Chapter 4, "Participation and the Problem of the One and the Many" provides a thorough and enlightening discussion of the participation of finite beings to *esse commune*, and how *esse commune* relates to being that subsists in itself, or God.

143 See Section 4.3.1 and 4.3.3.

144 See Section 3.1.

145 See Section 4.3.1.

146 *In div. nom.*, V, 1, 1: *Omnia autem alia ... habent esse receptum.*

147 *S. th.*, I. 75. 5 ad 4: *Omne participatum comparatur ad participans ut actus eius. Quaecumque autem forma creata per se subsistens ponatur, oportet quod participet esse.*

148 *De ente*, V: *Esse autem commune sicut in intellectu suo non includit aliquam additionem, ita non includit in intellectu suo precisionem additionis.* Wipple, Chapter 4, "Participation and the Problem of the One and the Many" provides a thorough and enlightening discussion of the participation of finite beings to *esse commune*, and how they relate to God.

149 For a discussion of this original feature of Aquinas's metaphysics see, for example, Wipple, Chapter 4, "Participation and the Problem of the One and the Many." For a discussion of the discovery of this originality see Mondin, *La Metafisica di san Tommaso d'Aquino e i suoi interpreti* 2002, Part One, especially his chapters entitled "Cornelio Fabro (1911–1995) and "Etienne Gilson (1884–1990).

150 See Section 2.1.

151 *Sup. Pery.*, I, 5, n. 20: *Et sic videtur et rem significare, per hoc quod dico quod et esse, per hoc quod dico est.*

152 *S.c.G.*, I 22. *Omnis res est per hoc, quod habet esse.*

153 *S. th.* I, 4, 1 ad 3: *Unde ipsum esse est actualitas omnium rerum et etiam ipsarum formarum; unde non comparatur ad alia sicut recipiens ad receptum, sed magis ut receptum ad recipiens.* Cf. *S. th.*, I, 3, 4 co.; I, 50, 2 ad 3.

154 See Section 4.4.1.

155 *Sup. Sent.*, II. 37, 1, 2 co.: ... *cujus esse est ipsum quod est, quia esse ejus non est receptum, sed per se subsistens* .... *S. th.*, I, 6, 4 co.

156 *S. th.*, I. 75. 5 ad 1; *Sup. Sent.*, II, 34. 1. 1 co.: ... *et sic ens significat aliquid in natura existens.*

157 *Sup. Sent.* II, 34. 1. 1 co.: ... *et sic ens significat aliquid in natura existens.*; *S. th.*, I, 75, 5, ad 4: *Omne participatum comparatur ad participans ut actus eius. Quaecumque autem forma creata per se subsistens ponatur, oportet quod participet esse.* Cf. Section 4.1 above.

158 *Sup. Sent.*, II. 37, 1, 2 co.: ... *per se dictum, est causa ejus quod per participationem dicitur.*

159 *De pot.*, VII, a. 2 ad 9: *Hoc quod habet esse, efficitur actu existens.* ... *est actualitas omnium actuum, et propter hoc est perfectio omnium perfectionum*; *S.c.G.*, 1, 22, n. 208: *Esse actum quaendam nominat: non enim dicitur esse aliquid ex hoc quod est in potentia, sed ex eo quod est in actu.*; *De ver.*, XXI. 5 co.

160 *In div. nom.* V, 1, 1: *Omnia autem alia ... habent esse receptum.* Cf. *S. th.*, I, 4. 2 co.; *De ente*, V.

161 *De pot.*, X, 1, arg. 6: *Divina dignitas, quod est prima causa essendi*; Aquinas, *Compendium of Theology, (Compend.)*, 68: *Primus autem effectus Dei in rebus est ipsum esse, quod omnes alii effectus praesupponunt, et supra quod fundantur. Necesse est autem omne quod aliquo modo est, a Deo esse. In omnibus autem ordinatis hoc communiter invenitur, quod id quod est primum et perfectissimum in aliquo ordine, est causa eorum quae sunt post in ordine illo .... Deus est primum et perfectissimum ens: unde oportet quod sit causa essendi omnibus quae esse habent. Adhuc. Omne quod habet aliquid per participationem, reducitur in id quod habet illud per essentiam, sicut in principium et causam.*

162 *In Boeth. De Trin.*, V, 1–3; VI, 1. For a discussion of Aquinas's doctrine concerning the distinction between finite being and infinite see Wipple. "Part Three, From Finite Being to Uncreated Being."

163 See Sections 2 and 4.

164 *Sup. Sent.*, II, 34. 1. 1 co.: *Uno modo dicitur ens quod per decem genera dividitur: et sic ens significat aliquid in natura existens.* Cf. *Sup. Sent.*, I, 19, 5, 1 co.

165 *S.c.G.*, I, 68, 2: ... *in anima ... in voluntate vel cogitatione.*

166 *Sup. Metaph.*, IV, 1, n. 540: *negociatur quasi de quibusdam entibus, dum de eis affirmat vel negat aliquid.*

167 Sup. Metaph., IV, 2, 540: ... *quod est debilissimum.*; Ibid., IV, 4, 574: ... *considerationem rationis consequuntur*; Cf. *Sup. Phys.*, III 1 c.

168 For a summary of types of being of reason, see the division of being in Bernard Wuellner, *Summary of Scholastic Principles* (Chicago: Loyola University Press, 1956): 32–3.

169 *De ente*, I; *Sup. Sent.*, II, d. 34, 11, 2; *S.c.G.*, III, 9.

170 *S.c.G.*, I, 84, 5.

171 *S. th.*, I–II, 8, 1 ad 3; I, 78, 4 co.; *Sup. Sent.*, II, d. 1 q. 1 a. 5, 5.
172 *Sup. Metaph.*, IV, 4: … *intentio generis, speciei et similium … proprie subiectum logicae.*
173 See Section 3.6.2.
174 *Sup. Sent.*, II, 17, q. 2, a. 1, 3: *Omne quod recipitur in aliquo, recipitur in eo per modum recipientis. Cf. De pot.*, III, 11, 14; *S. th.*, I, 84, 1, co. See Li Vecchi 2014, in which I refer to this doctrine as the *recipitur dictum*.
175 The knowing subject does not determine, for example, the being of the object known, as is shown above in Section 3.
176 *De ver.*, q. 1, a. 1, co.: *Veritas est adaequatio rei et intellectus.*
177 See Section 3. Nature's foundation in being is warranted by cognition's insusceptibility to error regarding the actual presence and intelligibility of the phantasm to the intellect, since a given nature is intelligible only to the extent that it is in act. *Cf. In Boet. De Trin.*, V, 3, 121–32; *In De an.*, III, 1, 11, n. 19.
178 *Sup. Sent.*, I, 23, 1, a. 3 co; *De ver.*, 21, 3 ad 5. In discussing logic's subject matter Aquinas describes second intentions as: … *illis intentionibus, quas ratio adinvenit in rebus consideratis … quae quidem non inveniuntur in rerum natura, sed considerationem rationis consequuntur.*
179 See Michael Tavuzzi, "Hervaeus Natalis and the Philosophical Logic of the Thomism of the Renaissance," *Doctor Communis* 45, (1992): 137.
180 See Section 2.1.

Chapter 3

1 The Continental Tradition portion of the concluding chapter of this book is dedicated to clarifying and emphasizing ways—which will have already been presented in this chapter—in which the philosophy of being in the Continental Tradition is distinguished from the philosophy of being in the Thomistic Tradition and the Analytic Tradition.
2 This is a stumbling block for many who approach the Continental Tradition: They equate Descartes and Kant. Though Kant was, of course, versed in Descartes's philosophy, and even phrased some of his own philosophy with Cartesian-inspired terms, Descartes did not ascend to Kant's vision of ontology, as evidenced, for example, by the different ways they understood: space, time, subjectivity, and God. Moreover, ultimately, Descartes's famous "method of doubt" pales in comparison to Kant's Transcendental Method.

3   In the history of philosophy, incommensurability can be traced back, at least, to Aristotle and Scholastic philosophy (*c.* 1100–*c.* 1700) where it was understood in terms of "essential distinction." Moreover, I am using the precise senses of the terms "distinguish" and "differentiate" throughout this chapter: distinguish meaning *uniquely* differentiated.

4   Recall, this means treating the Transcendental Method as a set of rules with which to validate inferences made in transcendental philosophy.

5   I would like to thank the anonymous reviewer who suggested I add further clarification around my use of Aristotle and the history of philosophy to emphasize the methodological incommensurability between Kant and, especially, the philosophers in the Thomistic Tradition.

6   Later, in order to signify the difference between other kinds of being and "being as being" or the "being of a being," we will adopt the convention of writing transcendental being as "be-ing."

7   To see Aristotle's famous statement of this truism, go to *Metaphysics* Bk VI §2 1026a33-1026b4.

8   For, it is insufficient to characterize Kant's Copernican Revolution—as Li Vecchi does in his Introduction to the Thomistic Tradition—as merely an investigation of the question "What appears?"

9   Per the helpful suggestion of an anonymous reviewer, readers should note that I am providing an articulation of Kant's philosophy here, not from an absolute point of view; rather, I am articulating Kant's philosophy in terms which will help readers compare the Continental Tradition with the other traditions; thus, I refer herein to the "Peripatetic Axiom" and "Thomistic Abstraction." In other words, in this chapter I am not arguing for an interpretation of Aquinas; I am borrowing Scholastic terms to help formulate Kant's philosophy in a way that may be easier for those not versed in the Continental Tradition to understand and digest. Yet, at the same time, I do heuristically endorse the idea that Kant was "the last Scholastic."

10 Though the term "epistemology" may be the present academic standard, I prefer the—more accurate—older term: "criteriology."

11 In this way, commentators emphasizing Kant's critical philosophy have erroneously concluded that Kant renders *all* metaphysics impossible. Kant still considered metaphysics possible through the Transcendental Method.

12 It may be beneficial to mention here that the subtitle of this section "Being Is Not a Real Predicate" speaks directly to what the Aristotelian-Scholastic Tradition calls "Predication and Modes of Being."

13 Aquinas, *De Veritate*, q. 2 a. 3 arg. 19.
14 Cf. Moltke S. Gram, "Things in Themselves: The Historical Lessons," *Journal of the History of Philosophy* 18, no. 4, 1980: 407–31.
15 For a discussion of these distinctions as they pertain to the history of Western psychology, see Scalambrino (2018). *Philosophical Principles of the History and Systems of Psychology* (London: Palgrave).
16 Importantly, this means that the products of the intellect are ordered—placed into, and considered as, an orderly whole—*by the intellect*.
17 In the *Critique of Pure Reason* Kant calls this the "Transcendental Deduction."
18 Think of the "first intention" as a concept with which an aggregate of the five senses are "grasped."
19 I usually paraphrase this by saying: "Substance is not its definition." That is to say, a sandwich "in reality" has caloric content, yet the definition of "sandwich" is calorie free, since it is merely an intellectual "predication." For example, to be a sandwich is (insert predication here) to have two slices of bread with a filling in between. Thus, the judgment "a sandwich is two slices of bread with filling in between" *is* two concepts combined through predication. As obvious as this next point may seem its critical value for metaphysics and the Continental Tradition cannot be overstated. Concepts and acts of predication are "in the soul," not "in reality." Hence, whereas sandwiches have calories, neither concepts nor acts of judgment have calories.
20 Aristotle's reason for eliminating the third possibility will be especially relevant below.
21 Cf. Polansky, 2007: 40, ftn 14. Furthermore, notice that—from Kant's point of view—Aquinas's move here treats all judgments as if they were determining judgments.
22 Moreover, this is a fundamental tenet of Kant's "Transcendental Idealism."
23 This is the "Mind/Body" problem in Descartes.
24 Recall regarding the methodological use of "pure reason," it is possible for an argument to be simultaneously valid and not sound. Thus, on purely rational grounds, an argument cannot guarantee the *existence* of that to which its terms are supposed to refer. In contrast to the way formal logic may provide such a false justification when applying the method of pure reason, the TUA—evidenced by both cognition and judgment and justified by transcendental logic, when applying the Transcendental Method—provides a revelation of metaphysical being.
25 Here is an example of why we needed to introduce the value of the term "order" when discussing the difference between the order of the intellect and the order of nature.

26 cf. Kant's *Critique of Pure Reason* (B 134) and Heidegger's *Being and Time* (H. 428) the end of §81.
27 Cf. Kant's *Reflexionen*, No. 5297: "a subject to which no predicate is attached ... because it is ... substratum of other subjects."
28 I put the word "immediately" here because some readers may point out that being in reality, in the order of nature, is also in the order of the cosmos, so why is it not "in the world"? What "immediately" indicates, then, is that the psychological order is invoked, here, methodologically. In other words, we arrived at *the truth of being* through the Transcendental Method in relation to the psychological order. The result of that application of the method is immediate. In other words, on the one hand, what is revealed here is the be-ing of beings, it is primordial being. To characterize the identity of the transcendental be-ing revealed as either psychological or cosmological would be a further step. On the other hand, regarding the characterization of this as merely subjective or psychological, I cannot emphasize enough that Descartes is not even in Kant's league. The similarities regarding their philosophies are superficial and terminological. Hume, not Descartes, woke Kant from his "dogmatic slumbers," to think Kant simply reiterated Descartes's philosophy in the wake of Hume's criticisms of it would be silly.
29 A popular way to criticize Kant regarding "things-in-themselves" is to attempt to put the burden on Kant by asking: How could things-in-themselves be any way other than how we experience them as cognitive objects (Thomistic Tradition) or how a general logic of quantification considers them (Analytic Tradition)? One possible way to envision an example of how we may not know how the "things" in mind-external reality are, beyond our capacity to experience them, is to consider "anamorphic art," or simply the idea of "anamorphosis."
30 I considered whether this should read "through" time or "as" time, and I decided to use "through" because it retains—by implication—the idea that there is not simply one "structure of time" through which being expresses itself; in other words, "as time" seems to suggest that the human experience of time is sufficient to understand the expressions of being, and that conclusion would be thoroughly *not Kantian*. Moreover, this same clarification may be understood as a feature of the motor force for the, existential, "primacy of becoming" in the Continental Tradition, which I consider in the Conclusion of this book.
31 Think "diachronic unity" in Kant. Thus, across time, for Kant, not "the categories."
32 The term "poetic," here, should, absolutely, be taken in the context of *nous poiētikos* discussed previously in this chapter.

33 Think: Transcendental *Unity* of Apperception.
34 Notice that in this way being is not the predicate of the judgment; the object may be the predicate of the judgment; however, being is that which the action of the judgment reveals. It is as if there is simultaneously a dual function to judgment—one logical and one transcendental.
35 Taking into consideration that Hegel called his Idealism "speculative" to differentiate it from the "reflective" Idealism of Kant, by focusing one their philosophies of the relation between the noetic process and the TUA, it is possible to produce a list of the different interpretations of Transcendental Idealism: Kant's "Reflective" Transcendental Idealism (TI), Fichte's "Absolute" TI, Hölderlin's "Logos-Presencing" TI, Novalis's "Magical" TI, and Schelling's "Nature" TI.
36 Novalis' reading of Kant's transcendental philosophy is also sometimes referred to as "magical idealism."
37 Notice, whereas Hölderlin characterized *being* as a whole with parts, Hegel characterized *the system* as a whole with parts.
38 As I always try to point out when discussing Hegel, it is my belief that Kant would have accused him of relying on Transcendental Illusion to complete the system, and, therefore, we may take issue with what Hegel means by "Logic." However, for the sake of focusing on the Homeric Contest and the Continental Tradition, rather than simply Kant and Hegel, I am not going to take issue with what Hegel means by Logic here. In other words, it is in terms of Hegel's next move that we can clearly see his style for characterization the TUA.
39 This insight and distinction came, originally, from Nietzsche.
40 The sense in which this aspect of Schelling's late philosophy anticipates Carl Jung's understanding of archetypes is remarkable. Cf. F.W.J. Schelling (2019), *On the Divinities of Samothrace*.
41 Cf. Gilles Deleuze's *Difference & Repetition*.
42 Notice, Novalis was the first to explicitly state this insight regarding transcendental philosophy.
43 In his defense of the Thomistic Tradition in the Conclusion of this book, Dr. Li Vecchi treats the domain of the science of transcendental philosophy as more primordial than its method. His concern for "the being of cognition as ontological evidence" misses the profundity of Kant's *method*. For, it is not the cognition, but the relation to cognition, which (reflectively and apperceptively) provides "evidence" of—though I prefer the term "awareness of" (Kant said "extends our cognition" into)—the transcendental dimension. Therefore, transcendental being is neither cognition nor subjectivity or objectivity.

44 Moreover, rational here even refers to the rationality in terms of which some commentators talk about the irrationality of the unconscious. This is why I used "canonical," which is, in fact, the better term. That is to say, any form of subjectivity determined through *inference* will provide a conceptual understanding of a subject (even a "non-discursive" subject) based on some method. Kant's higher ground is needed on which to see the higher distinction between—canon and organon—the applications of a method. In this way, *organic*-transcendental reflection reveals that which is the condition for the possibility of be-ing-conceptualized-as-a-subject. Such subjectivity represents a significant reduction of the profundity of transcendental philosophy and a confusion with early modern substance ontology.

45 This question may also be formulated as: "What is being *qua* being?"; "What is being as being?"; "What is being in terms of being?"; or "What is the be-ing of beings?"

46 For example, recall the brief clarification regarding these terms in the Introduction chapter of this book.

Chapter 4

1 I cannot here go into details for why someone would accept what appears to be a very counter-intuitive view. For a classical defense of idealism, see George Berkeley's *Principles and Three Dialogues*, edited by Howard Robinson (Oxford: Oxford University Press, 1996). Howard Robinson is one of the most rigorous contemporary defenders of idealism from an analytic perspective, and anyone looking for a formidable statement of the position would do well to start with his *Matter and Sense: A Critique of Contemporary Materialism* (Cambridge: Cambridge University Press, 1982).

2 For a much more thorough overview of British Idealism than I can provide here, see W. J. Mander's *British Idealism: A History* (Oxford: Oxford University Press, 2011).

3 G. E. Moore, "Proof of an External World," *Proceedings of the British Academy* 25 (1939): 273–300.

4 See, for example, G. E. Moore, "A Defense of Common Sense," in *Contemporary British Philosophy*, 2nd Series, edited by J. H. Muirhead (New York: Macmillan Company, 1925): 191–223, reprinted in G. E. Moore, *Philosophical Papers* (London: Collier Books, 1962): 32–59.

5   Bertrand Russell, *The Philosophy of Logical Atomism* (London and New York: Routledge, 2010).

6   I say "for the most part" because there were exceptions to this rule, such as mathematical statements like "Two plus two equals four." Such a statement cannot, of course, be confirmed nor disproven by observation.

7   A. J. Ayer, *Language, Truth, and Logic* (New York: Dover Publications, 1952): 36.

8   Logical Positivism is one of the rare schools of thought in the history of philosophy that is considered to have been definitively defeated.

9   I note that this is how we use the word "know" in English because epistemology is sometimes complicated by translation issues. For the Ancient Greeks, the word "episteme," which is usually translated "knowledge," pertained to necessary truths; there could be no knowledge, in that sense, of "the cat is on the mat" since the cat may well go off somewhere else. A similar problem presents itself in the Latin of Thomas Aquinas, with no single word that he uses lining up neatly with the English verb "to know." For some details, see Martin Pickavé "Human Knowledge," *in The Oxford Handbook of Aquinas*, edited by Brian Davies and Eleonore Stump (Oxford: Oxford University Press, 2012): 311–26.

10 There are at least two other ways we use the word "know" in English. I can know individuals ("I know the other co-authors of this book") and I can know how ("I know how to ride a bike"). These senses of "know" are outside of the scope of the present discussion.

11 The classic statement of the problem is found in Edmund Gettier's very short paper, "Is Justified True Belief Knowledge?" in *Analysis* 23 (1963): 121–3.

12 Readers interested in epistemology might begin their studies with Richard Fumerton's *Epistemology* (Malden, MA: Blackwell Publishing, 2006).

13 Jacques Maritain, *An Introduction to Philosophy* (New York: Sheed and Ward, 1962): 129. Maritain takes himself here to be reporting the view, correct in his eye, of Aquinas and Aristotle.

14 In fact, I think that it does. For an Analytic philosopher who ably parses out at least a few of the insights hidden within the proposed statement (or ones like it), see Anthony Kenny, *Aquinas on Mind* (New York: Routledge, 1993).

15 Socrates was often engaged in inquiry in a way that strikes me as decidedly analytic.

16 Frege's system of symbolic logic was not the first, but it was arguably the most rigorous. However, it is not the system that most philosophers who learn symbolic logic today find themselves using; the most popular system today is better credited to Bertrand Russell, who modeled his efforts on Frege's.

17 For Frege's own writings on these matters, see "On Sense and Reference," "On Concept and Object," and "Function and Concept," all available in Translations from *The Philosophical Writings of Gottlob Frege*, edited by Peter Geach and Max Black (Oxford: Basil Blackwell, 1960). For a clear summary of these papers, as well as an introduction to Frege generally, see Anthony Kenny's *Frege* (London: Penguin Books, 1995).

18 This tendency is not new. Plato is at times very influenced by his thinking about mathematics. Plato was probably influenced by the mathematician-philosopher Pythagoras.

19 You should bear in mind while reading this chapter that I make no distinction between the noun "existence" and the verbal-noun "being."

20 Williams often implies in his writings that his thoughts on existence are entirely derived from Frege. However, I am not interested in whether Williams correctly interprets Frege or not and will stick as closely as possible to Williams's own text. Williams also offers reasons to think that the advances made by Russell and Quine (as well as Kant, who anticipated Frege's thesis) run into obstacles; his arguments on this matter are outside the scope of this chapter. See *What Is Existence,* chapters 2 and 8. Moreover, Analytic philosophers who wish to show that existence is a property of individuals recognize that Frege's arguments otherwise were brief and in need of further development. Williams made such developments and so opponents to the Fregean view invariably confront Williams's arguments more than Frege's. For this reason I, too, make more use of Williams than of Frege.

21 I am personally critical of the tendency to lump a property like "humanity" (what medieval philosophers would call a "substantial form") in with other properties (so-called "accidental forms"). But I am in the minority on this issue.

22 Philosophers approaching this chapter from other philosophical traditions may wish that I could offer a more technical explanation of what I mean by "thing." But Analytic philosophy often favors the ordinary, everyday meanings of words. You, me, my cell phone, and mountains are all things. Here I distinguish things from their properties.

23 It is possible to have *conjunctive properties* which, because of the constituents of the conjunction, cannot be repeated. For example, plenty of people have been president of the United States. Moreover, plenty of people have been the first to do something or other (Neil Armstrong was the first to walk on the moon, Ishmael was the first son of Abraham, and so on). But when you combine the properties "first" and "president of the United States," you have a

conjunctive property which cannot be true of more than one person. But the notion of property as something able to be exemplified by more than one thing provides a rough and ready understanding of the difference between properties and individuals. If this seems problematic, consider that someone other than George Washington could have been the first president, but no one but George Washington can be George Washington.

24 I am offering here but one simplified way of thinking about properties that, I think, suffices for understanding what I have to say regarding existence. For a good anthology that explores how different Analytic philosophers have thought about the notion of a property, see *Properties*, edited by D. H. Mellor and Alex Oliver (Oxford: Oxford University Press, 1997).

25 If this is a controversial claim, I can only remind the reader of Michael Dummett's saying that "Language may be a distorting mirror, but it is the only mirror we have." *Origins of Analytical Philosophy* (Harvard, MA: Harvard University Press, 1993): 7.

26 Williams, *What Is Existence*, ix, ff.

27 This distinction can be found in P. T. Geach, *Reference and Generality* (Ithaca, New York: Cornell University Press, 1980): 50, § 18. Geach loosely based this distinction on a similar distinction made in Medieval logic; however, its meaning here is not the same as it would have been for, say, Thomas Aquinas.

28 In contemporary symbolic logic, this operation is accomplished by placing the tilde, "~," in front of the statement that one wishes to negate.

29 Williams, *What Is Existence?* 79.

30 The argument, and its associated name, comes from Quine's "On What There Is," in *From a Logical Point of View* (Harvard University Press, 1963): 2.

31 Cf. Williams, *What Is Existence*, 37–41.

32 I do not mean to imply that Analytic philosophers were the first to notice the logical problems inherent with so-called "negative existential" statements. Late Medieval philosophers were also aware of this problem, and some of them like Buridan developed their own sophisticated responses. For details on Buridan's take, see Gyula Klima's John Buridan (New York: Oxford University Press, 2009).

33 Williams, *What Is Existence,* 42–73.

34 *The Foundations of Arithmetic*, translated by J. L. Austin (1980): 59.

35 Ibid.

36 There is disagreement about how to understand "instantiation" here, but it doesn't concern us. I just mean by the word something like "can be found" or "occurs in reality."

37 Frege preferred to err on the side of caution and say existence statements are analogous to statements of number; Williams makes the stronger claim that statements of existence *are* statements of number. *What Is Existence*, 54.
38 Williams at times does write this way, suggesting that "Happy" is a subject-term while "some" a predicate; however, he prefers to replace the whole subject-predicate language of grammarians with the language of "wrapping around." See *Being, Identity, and Truth*, 14.
39 A. N. Prior, "Is the Concept of Referential Opacity Really Necessary?" *Acta Philosophica Fennica* 16 (1963): 95–6.
40 *Being, Identity, and Truth*, 18.
41 Given the rapidly changing world and its political landscape, I should perhaps mention that as I write this France has no King, nor did it when Russell and Meinong were writing.
42 This is known as "DeMorgan's Principle."
43 *Fullness of Being*, 31.
44 Miller takes this example of the sheep farmer from D. G. Londey, "Existence," *Philosophia Arhusiensis* 1 (1970): 3. The objection is echoed by Williams, who asks what he could do if he were told that blue buttercups do not exist: "Would I have felt obliged to examine several specimens of *blue buttercup* before concluding that none of them exist, that as a variety blue buttercup lacks existence?" *Being, Identity, and Truth*, 1.
45 *Fullness of Being*, 32.
46 *Bedeutung* is the German word that appears in Frege's "*Über Sinn und Bedeutung*," which is typically rendered in English as "On Sense and Reference." In the passage quoted, Anscombe has translated the same word as "meaning."
47 Wittgenstein, Ludwig, *Philosophical Investigations*, Revised 4th edition, edited by P. M. S. Hacker and Joachim Schulte (Malden, MA: Blackwell Publishing, 2009): 24.
48 Miller never says what he intends to convey by his use of parentheses. Presumably he wants to draw the reader's attention to what exactly is being predicated. "Lincoln (does not exist)" predicates non-existence of Lincoln; "It is not the case that (Lincoln exists)" predicates existence of him, but *asserts* the denial of that predication. Cf., *Fullness of Being*, 34.
49 Miller never, to my knowledge, says why the negation of "Lincoln exists" would not produce a new predicate, namely, "does not exist," as we have seen that it does in every other instance of negating first-order predications.

50 Elmar Kremer, *Analysis of Existing, Barry Miller's Approach to God* (New York: Bloomsbury, 2014): 27–30.
51 *Fullness of Being*, 35.
52 I am, again, following Miller's own convention regarding the use of parentheses.
53 *Fullness of Being*, 36.
54 Ibid.
55 Ibid., 37, n. 27. Miller traces this distinction to A. N. Prior, "Determinables, Determinates, and Determinants (I, II)," *Mind* 58 (1949): 1–20 and 178–94.
56 Vallicella is unique among critics of the traditional analytic view in that he does not call existence a property. Rather, he thinks existence is the precondition for anything having properties (in contrast to, say, Barry Miller, who is content to say that existence is a unique property in that it does not presuppose something's existence). Instead Vallicella prefers to say something "has existence." In this section, I will attempt to follow his conventions.
57 I say it *seems* to be because, as we will see below, Kris McDaniel has denied that it is.
58 *A Paradigm Theory of Existence*, 110.
59 A similar argument was put forth by Geach in "Form and Existence."
60 Vallicella, 112.
61 Again, Vallicella does not call existence a property. Rather, he claims that the Plato's Beard argument ought to be rejected insofar as it establishes that existence is only a second-order property or insofar as it shows that individuals cannot have existence. Ibid., 114.
62 Aquinas was also aware of such a distinction. He writes, "It is not necessary that Socrates is sitting; but that he is sitting while he is sitting is necessary." *ST* 1a2ae,14,6.
63 Williams too considers this kind of sentence unoffensive, for reasons he explains in *What Is Existence?* 101–4.
64 Ibid., 113.
65 Ibid., 114–15.
66 Ibid.
67 Kris McDaniel, "Existence and Number," *Analytic Philosophy* 54 (2013): 209–28.
68 McDaniel agrees that "the most promising version of this argument [i.e., that existence is only a second-order property] is by C. J. F. Williams." Ibid., 209. McDaniel expressed skepticism that the connection between existence and number is as close as Williams maintains, but contents himself merely with attacking the premise that number statements must be second-order.

69 Ibid., 212.
70 Ibid., 213.
71 This is his example. Ibid., 215.
72 Ibid., 216.

Chapter 5

1 See Chapter 2, sections 1.4, 1.6 and 1.7.
2 David Hume, *Treatise of Human Nature,* 1739, Book I, "Of the Understanding" 1.2.6: "Since nothing is ever present to the mind but perceptions, and since all ideas are deriv'd from something antecedently present to the mind; it follows that 'tis impossible for us so much as to conceive or form an idea of any thing specifically different from ideas and impressions. ... The farthest we can go towards a conception of external objects, when suppos'd *specifically* different from our perceptions, is to form a relative idea of them, without pretending to comprehend the related objects."
3 Kant. *Critique of Pure Reason,* 1998. Chapter II. "The Deduction of the Pure Concepts of the Understanding," Second Section. "On the a priori grounds for the possibility of experience." 3. "On the synthesis of recognition in the concept," p. 233, A108, 26–109, 4: "Appearances are the only objects that can be given to us immediately, and that in them which is immediately related to the object is called intuition. However, these appearances are not things in themselves, but themselves only representations, which in turn have their object, which therefore cannot be further intuited by us, and that may therefore be called the non-empirical, i.e., transcendentally object = X."
4 *De ver.*, 8, 8 co. See Chapter 2, Section 3.6.2.
5 See Chapter 2, Sections 3.6.2 and 3.6.3.
6 *S. th.* I–II, 55, a. 4, ad 1: ... *unicuique apprehenso a nobis attribuimus quod sit ens.*
7 See Chapter 2, Sections 3.1 and 3.2.
8 See Chapter 2, Section 3.6.4
9 See Chapter 2, Section 3.
10 Adherents to the Transcendental school of Thomism mentioned in Chapter 1, include Joseph Maréchal (1878–1944) and Bernard Lonergan (1904–1984), who attempt to harmonize Kant's methodological shift with a roughly Thomistic framework. See Maréchal's *Le point de départ de la métaphysique. Leçons sur le développement historique et théorique du problème de la connaissance.* 5 vols. Vols.

I, II, III, Bruges and Paris, 1922–1923; Vol. IV, Brussels, 1947; Vol. V, Louvain and Paris, 1926, and Lonergan's *Insight: A Study of Human Understanding*. Vol. 3 of the *Collected Works of Bernard Lonergan* (Toronto: University of Toronto Press, 1997).

11 See Chapter 2, Section 3.4.
12 *Sup. Pery.*, I, 5, 18–22. Cf. Aristotle, *Interp.* 3, 16b, 21–6.
13 See Chapter 2, Section 2.2.1.
14 See Chapter 2, Section 3.4
15 See Chapter 2, Section 1.1
16 *S. th.*, I, 78, 4, 4: *Intellectus nihil cognoscit nisi accipiendo a sensu.* Cf. Aristotle, *Posterior Analytics*, II, 19, 99b20-35.
17 In chapter 4, Section 1.1, "There is no central doctrine that everyone who is grouped under the label *Analytic Philosophy* adheres to." To the contrary, few, if any, analytic philosophers reject the two tenets chosen here for criticism.
18 One example of this tendency is part of Quine's ontological "clearance program," that brands the distinction between existence and being as one of "pure lexicography," "On What There Is" 23.
19 Gottlob Frege's anti-psychologism is expressed in *The Basic Laws of Arithmetic*, [1893], Preface, Introduction, §§1–52, translated by, M. Furth (Berkeley, CA: University of California Press, 1964). See p. 14: "One could scarcely falsify the sense of the word 'true' more mischievously than by including in it a reference to the subjects who judge" and pp. 15–16: "I understand by 'laws of logic' not psychological laws of takings-to-be-true, but laws of truth. ... If being true is thus independent of being acknowledged by somebody or other, then the laws of truth are not psychological laws."
20 See Chapter 2, Section 2.1
21 See Chapter 2, Section 2.2. *Sup. Sent.*, II, 34. 1. 1 co.: *Uno modo dicitur ens quod per decem genera dividitur: et sic ens significat aliquid in natura existens.* Cf. *S. th.*, I. 16. 3 ad 2; I–II, 8, 1 ad 3; *S. c. g.*, I. 68; *Sup. Sent.*, I, 19, 5, 1 co.; II, 2, 2, 2 ad 4; *Sup Metaph.*, IV, 4b; VI, 4c; XI, 8 f.
22 See Chapter 2, Section 4.1.
23 See Chapter 2, Section 4.5.
24 See Chapter 2, Section 1: "For Aquinas, being shoots through a manifold that contains all things actual, possible, and conceptual."
25 Alexius Meinong, *On Emotional Presentation*, 1917, English Translation by M.-L. Schubert Kalsi (Evanston, IL: Northwestern University Press, 1972), §11:103.
26 Quine seems to have a similar strategy in "On What There Is."

27 Chapter 2, Section 3.6.1.
28 See Chapter 2, Sections 3.6.2 and 3.6.3 above.
29 Aquinas, *Sup. Sent.* II, d. 17, q. 2, a. 1, 3: *Omne quod recipitur in aliquo, recipitur in eo per modum recipientis*; See also *De pot.* III, 11, 14. Cf. Pseudo-Dionysius, *De divinis nominibus*. IV, 1 and *De caelesti hierarchia*, XII, 2; Boethius, *De consolatione philosophiae*, V, proem. 4. The *recipitur dictum* is discussed in Li Vecchi, "Logical Objectivity and Second Intentions" (2014): 795–812, 807.
30 Saul Kripke, *Naming and Necessity* (Cambridge, MA: Harvard University Press, 1972): 58–9.
31 *Sup. Pery.*, I, 1, 4, 14.
32 John Knasas, *Being and Some Twentieth-Century Thomists* (New York: Fordham University Press, 2003): 202–3: "The judgmental grasp of the thing's real existence enables Aquinas to treat the logic of positive and negative existential propositions as subject-attribute without incurring … problems.… For Aquinas 'martyrs exist' is subject-attribute but translates to 'the existentially neutral martyrs exist.' This is not a tautology."
33 *Sup. Pery.*, I, 5, 18–22. Cf. Aristotle, *Interp.* 3, 16b, 21–6.
34 See Chapter 2, Section 3.6.2 and Chapter 5, Section 2.2.
35 My experience is that philosophy departments use "pluralism" and "diversity" to justify nepotism. At least in industry either you perform or you don't and eventually those who can't perform are removed by the very process of not being able to perform; however, in academia, if they stand something to gain from you, then they'll justify your non-performance in terms of supporting diversity and pluralism. In other words, they're so "philosophical" that they—on purpose—have people on the payroll who don't understand philosophy.
36 Cf. Arthur Schopenhauer, 2020, *On Philosophy at the Universities*. Translated by F. Scalambrino.
37 Cf. Josef, Pieper, 1957, *The Silence of St. Thomas*. Translated by D. O'Connor, 56–9.
38 David Hume, 1739, *Treatise of Human Nature*, Book I, "Of the Understanding," 1.2.6.
39 When discussing this, I often invoke William James's idea of the "specious now," and point out that just as non-human-species observers of things, such as humming birds, experience time differently from humans, so too they experience the thing *as in time differently*. Moreover, think of how some species experience flowers in ultraviolet light. The bee's experience of the *thing* that is the flower is quite different from the human's, so what is the flower-thing in itself? Notice that

the thing in itself can be *both* what it objectively is for humans and bees, even though the experience of the thing is different for a bee from its experience for a human.

40   Notice that just because this is as far as *the science* of metaphysics can go, that is not a reason to reject the Transcendental Method that got us there or to think that one could not move *beyond the science* in another way. In other words, the science, in this case, provides the correct point of departure. Moreover, there is no reason here that one cannot take the next step, which we might characterize—with Kierkegaard—as a kind of "leap," and resolve a methodologically-clarified philosophical antinomy with, for example, myth or religion or personal experience.

41   This is to say: how we can experience some "thing" both subjectively and objectively.

42   Robert M. Wernaer, *Romanticism and the Romantic School in Germany* (London: D. Appleton & Company, 1910): 3.

43   Cf. Frank Scalambrino, 2019, *Full Throttle Heart: The Rapture and Ecstasy of Nietzsche's Dionysian Worldview*.

44   This is philosophically, for example, what is at the heart of the philosophy of gender—whether those philosophers realize it or not—and, based on the sense in which those discussions misunderstand the Continental Tradition, it seems they do not realize it. Too many "continental philosophers," parrot-like, condescend "binary opposition," while still treating the principle of non-contradiction as more primordial than the principle of actuality.

45   I'm italicizing "then" to emphasize its *ontological* characterization as *temporal*, not merely formal. Moreover, the use of the term "merely" may help us keep in mind the both/and aspect of transcendental logic regarding the principle of actuality beyond the either/or aspect of general logic regarding the principle of non-contradiction.

46   It is, obviously, not lost on me that many Thomists would claim these are one and the same. In either case, I sincerely assert the truth of this statement here. By far the majority of my former students who are Catholic are spending their time raising families and participating in Catholic culture; that is, they are not spending their time reading Aristotle's *Metaphysics* or contemplating the possible relation between transcendental properties of being and divinity. And, that is not intended to be a critique of their activities; it is merely intended to accurately characterize them.

47 Briefly, two points: Kant allows for a "visualization" of being that surpasses traditional Thomism; second, Thomists can only say "transubstantiation" is a "miracle." And, students may nod faithfully; however, Kant can say: The bread as a cognitive object of experience remains the same, while the *spirit* of the bread, that is, the bread as the thing-in-itself, changes.
48 Hume, of course, being the one who "woke Kant from his dogmatic slumber" *and* whose philosophy the Kantian project ultimately overcame.
49 I use this example because I think an English speaker unlikely to perceive a connection, even though there is such a connection: The coach carriage was invented in the Hungarian town Kocs (pronounced "coach"). Wealthy young boys receiving lessons from tutors in coach carriages were thus said to be "coached." Despite the etymology, the two sentences in the main text clearly use the word equivocally. Equivocation does not depend on etymology.
50 Aquinas, of course, also has something to say about analogical uses of words that are neither entirely equivocal nor univocal. It is best not to treat Williams's and Aquinas's accounts of analogy at the same time. It is probable that their uses of the same word are not univocal.
51 It seems possible that a word can be used as a first-order predicate and have a completely unrelated, completely equivocal use as a second-order predicate.
52 *What Is Existence*, 72–3. Recall that Williams typically uses the older "level" where I have used the more fashionable "order."
53 See Herbert McCabe's "The Logic of Mysticism" in *God Matters* (New York: Bloomsbury, 1987).
54 For more details on my view of Aquinas and *esse*, see my *The Coherence of Aquinas's Account of Divine Simplicity* (PhD diss., Fordham University, 2018), especially Chapter 4.
55 There has been, in fact, a growing effort to do this, resulting in a school of philosophers sometimes now called "Analytic Thomists." In 1997 John Haldane edited a special edition of *The Monist* devoted to Analytic Thomism. See *The Monist* 80 (4): 1997.
56 My analysis in what follows is influenced by Herman Weidemann's "The Logic of Being in Thomas Aquinas," in *Thomas* Aquinas: *Contemporary Philosophical Perspectives*, edited by Brian Davies (Oxford: Oxford University Press, 2002), 77–96.
57 For some history on this, see Jaakko Hintikka's "'Is', Seminatical Games, and Semantical Relativity" in *Journal of Philosophical Logic* 8 (1979): 433–68.

58 *Vivere viventibus est esse* is a slogan Aquinas sometimes invokes: "To live is what it is for living things to be."
59 His now-classic statement of this argument is in "Two Dogmas of Empiricism," *The Philosophical Review* 60 (1951): 20–43. Notably, Quine had been struggling with what he thought regarding the distinction for at least twenty years before he published "Two Dogmas."
60 Ibid., 21.
61 *Confessions*, Book XI.
62 "The Unreality of Time," *Mind: A Quarterly Review of Psychology and Philosophy* 17 (1908): 456–73. McTaggart was a British Idealist in the tradition of Bradley, whom I discussed in Chapter 4 of this volume. Nevertheless, his arguments about time have been taken seriously by Analytic philosophers and continue to be influential.

Bibliography & Further Reading

Anderson, James F. *The Bond of Being*. St. Louis: Herder, 1949.

Aristotle. *Categories*. Translated by J. L. Ackrill. In *Aristotle's Categories and De interpretatione*. Oxford: The Clarendon Press, 1963.

Aristotle. *Metaphysics*. Translated by W. D. Ross. In *The Complete Works of Aristotle*: Vol. 2. Edited by J. Barnes. New Jersey: Princeton University Press, 1995a.

Aristotle. *On the Soul*. Translated by J. A. Smith. In *The Complete Works of Aristotle*: Vol. 1. Edited by J. Barnes. New Jersey: Princeton University Press, 1995b.

Aristotle. *Posterior Analytics*. Translated by J. Barnes. In *The Complete Works of Aristotle*: Vol. 1. Edited by J. Barnes. New Jersey: Princeton University Press, 1995c.

Arnauld, Antoine, and Pierre Nicole. *The Port Royal Logic*. Translated by T. Spencer Baynes. London: Hamilton, Adams, and Co, 1861.

Aquinas, St. Thomas. *On the Power of God*. [*Quaestiones disputatae De potentia*]. Translated by The English Dominican Fathers and Fr. Lawrence Shapcote, O.P. London: Burns Oates & Washbourne, 1932–1934.

Aquinas, St. Thomas. *The Summa contra gentiles of Saint Thomas Aquinas*. [*Summa contra Gentiles*]. Translated by The English Dominican Fathers. London: Burns, Oats and Washbourne, 1934.

Aquinas, St. Thomas. *On Spiritual Creatures*. [*Questio disputata De spiritualibus creaturis*]. Translated by M. C. Fitzpatrick and J. J. Wellmuth. Milwaukee, WI: Marquette University Press, 1949.

Aquinas, St. Thomas. *On the Virtues (in general)*. [*Quaestiones disputatae de virtutibus*]. Translated by J. P. Reid. Providence, RI: Providence College Press, 1951.

Aquinas, St. Thomas. *Aristotle's on Interpretation: Commentary by St. Thomas and Cajetan*. [*Expositio libri Peryermenias*]. Translated by J. T. Osterle. Milwaukee, WI: Marquette University Press, 1962.

Aquinas, St. Thomas. *Commentary on Aristotle's Physics*. [*Sententia super Physicam*]. Translated by R. J. Blackwell et al. New Haven: Yale University Press, 1963.

Aquinas, St. Thomas. *The Summa Theologica of St. Thomas Aquinas*. [*Summa theologiae*]. Translated by Fathers of the English Dominican Province. New York: Benzinger Brothers, 1947; McGraw Hill, 1964.

Aquinas, St. Thomas. *Saint Thomas Aquinas, The Division of the Sciences. Questions V and VI of His Commentary of the De Trinitate on Boethius*. Translated by A. Maurer. In *Medieval Sources in Translation*, Vol. 32. Toronto: Pontifical Institute of Mediaeval Studies, 1986.

Aquinas, St. Thomas. *On the Divine Names*. [*In librum Dionysii De divinis nominibus*]. Turin: Marietti, 1950]. Translated by Harry C. Marsh in H.C. Marsh, "In Cosmic Structure and the Knowledge of God: Thomas Aquinas' *In librum Dionysii De divinis nominibus expositio*. Nashville, TN: Vanderbilt University PhD Thesis, 1994.

Aquinas, St. Thomas. *Truth*. [*Quaestiones disputatae de veritate*]. Translated by R. W. Mulligan, J. V. McGlynn, and R. W. Schmidt. Indianapolis, IN: Hackett, 1994.

Aquinas, St. Thomas, *On Being and Essence* (De ente et essentia), Translated by Robert T. Miller, 1997. https://sourcebooks.fordham.edu/basis/aquinas-esse.asp#f2

Aquinas, St. Thomas. *Compendium theologiae [Compendium of Theology]*, Opera Omnia, www.corpusthomisticum.org

Aquinas, St. Thomas. *Expositio libri Posteriorum [Commentary on Aristotle's Posterior Analytics]*, Opera Omnia, www.corpusthomisticum.org

Aquinas, St. Thomas. *In librum Dionysii De divinis nominibus* [Commentary on the Divine Names], Opera Omnia, www.corpusthomisticum.org

Aquinas, St. Thomas. *Quaestiones disputatae De malo [Disputed Questions on Evil]*, Opera Omnia, www.corpusthomisticum.org

Aquinas, St. Thomas. *Scriptum super libros Sententiarum* [Commentary on Peter Lombard's *Sentences*], *Opera Omnia*, www.corpusthomisticum.org

Aquinas, St. Thomas. *Sentencia libri De anima* [Commentary on Aristotle's *On the Soul*], *Opera Omnia*, www.corpusthomisticum.org.

Aquinas, St. Thomas. *Sententia libri Ethicorum* [Commentary on Aristotle's *Nicomachean Ethics*], *Opera Omnia*, www.corpusthomisticum.org

Aquinas, St. Thomas. *Sententia libri Politicorum* [Commentary on Aristotle's *Politics*], *Opera Omnia*, www.corpusthomisticum.org

Aquinas, St. Thomas. *Sententia super libros De generatione et corruptione* [Commentary on Aristotle's *On Generation and Corruption*], *Opera Omnia*, www.corpusthomisticum.org

Aquinas, St. Thomas. *Sententia super Metaphysicam [Commentary on Aristotle's Metaphysics]*, *Opera Omnia*, www.corpusthomisticum.org

Aquinas, St. Thomas. *Super Boetium De Trinitate* [Commentary of the De Trinitate of Boethius] *Opera Omnia*, www.corpusthomisticum.org

Baugh, Bruce. *French Hegel: From Surrealism to Postmodernism*. New York, NY: Routledge, 2003.

Beiser, Frederick C. *The Romantic Imperative: The Concept of Early German Romanticism*. Cambridge, MA: Harvard University Press, 2003.

Boethius, Opuscula Sacra, and De consolatione Philosophiae, C. Moreschini (ed.), revised edition, Munich/Leipzig: K.G. Saur, 2005.

Brandom, Robert B. *A Spirit of Trust: A Reading of Hegel's Phenomenology*. Cambridge, MA: Harvard University Press, 2019.

Breazeale, Daniel. "Between Kant and Fichte: Karl Leonhard Reinhold's 'Elementary Philosophy'," *The Review of Metaphysics* 35, no. 4 (1982): 785–821.

Carnap, Rudolf. "The Elimination of Metaphysics through Logical Analysis of Language." In *Logical Positivism*. Edited by A. J. Ayer Translated by Arthur Pap. New York: Free Press, 1959.

Coxon, A. H. "Parmenides on Thinking and Being," *Mnemosyne* 56, no. 2 (2003): 210–12.

Dejnožka, Jan. *The Ontology of the Analytic Tradition and Its Origins: Realism and Identity in Frege, Russell, Wittgenstein, and Quine*. New York, NY: Rowman & Littlefield, 2003.

Deleuze, Gilles. *Kant's Critical Philosophy*. Translated by H. Tomlinson and B. Habberjam. Minneapolis: University of Minnesota Press, 1984.

Deleuze, Gilles. *Difference & Repetition*. Translated by P. Patton. New York: Columbia University, 1994.

Deleuze, Gilles. *Francis Bacon: The Logic of Sensation*. Translated by D. W. Smith. Minneapolis: University of Minnesota Press, 2002.

Derrida, Jacques. "Structure, Sign, and Play." In *Writing and Difference*. Translated by A. Bass. 278–94. Chicago: University of Chicago, 1978.

Derrida, Jacques. "Différance." In *Margins of Philosophy*. Translated by A. Bass, 1–28. Chicago: University of Chicago. 1982.

Dummett, Michael. *Frege: Philosophy of Language*. London: Duckworth Press, 1973.

Dummett, Michael. *Origins of Analytical Philosophy*. Harvard, MA: Harvard University Press, 1993.

Fabro, Cornelio. *La nozione metafisica di partecipazione secondo S. Tommaso d'Aquino*. Milan: Vita e Pensiero, 1939.

Fabro, Cornelio. "The Intensive Hermeneutics of Thomistic Philosophy. The Notion of Participation," *The Review of Metaphysics* 27, no. 3 (1974): 449–91.

Fezer, Edward. *The Thomistic Tradition*. http://edwardfeser.blogspot.com/2009/10/thomistic-tradition-part-i.html, 2009.

Fichte, Johann Gottlieb. *Attempt at a Critique of all Revelation*. Translated by G. Green. Cambridge: University of Cambridge Press, 1978.

Fichte, Johann Gottlieb. *Foundations of the Entire Science of Knowledge*. In *The Science of Knowledge*. Edited and translated by P. Heath and J. Lachs. Cambridge: University of Cambridge Press, 1982.

Foucault, Michel. *Discipline and Punish: The Birth of the Prison*. Translated by A. Sheridan. New York: Vintage Books, 1995.

Foucault, Michel. *Madness and Civilization: A History of Insanity in the Age of Reason*. Translated by R. Howard. London: Routledge, 2001.

Frege, Gottlob. *The Basic Laws of Arithmetic*. Translated by M. Furth. Berkeley: University of California, 1964.

Frege, Gottlob. *Foundations of Arithmetic*. Translated by J. L. Austin. Evanston, IL: Northwestern University Press, 1980.

Frege, Gottlob. *Translations from the Philosophical Writings*. Edited by P. T. Geach and Max Black. Oxford: Blackwell, 1980.

Garrigou-Lagrange, Reginald. *Reality. A Synthesis of Thomistic Thought*. Translated by P. Cummins. O.S. St. Louis: Herder, 1950.

Geach, Peter. "Form and Existence." *Proceedings of the Aristotelian Society* 55 (1954): 251–72.

Geach, Peter. *God and Soul*. New York: Schoken Books, 1969.

Geach, Peter. "Names and Identity." In *Mind and Language*. Edited by Samuel Gutterplan. 139–58. Oxford: Oxford University Press, 1975.

Geach, Peter, and Max Black. *The Philosophical Writings of Gottlob Frege*. London: Blackwell, 1970.

Geach, Peter, and Robert Stoothoff. "Symposium: What Actually Exists," *Aristotelian Society Supplementary* 42 (1968): 7–30.

Geiger, Louis-Bertrand. *La participation dans la philosophie de s. Thomas d'Aquin*. Paris: Librairie Philosophique J. Vrin, 1942.

Giladi, Paul. "Hegel, Analytic Philosophy's Pharmakon," *The European Legacy* 22, no. 2 (2017): 185–98.

Gilson, Etienne. *Le Thomisme*, 4th edition. Paris: Vrin, 1941.

Gilson, Etienne. *Being and Some Philosophers*. Toronto: Pontifical Institute of Medieval Studies, 1952.

Glenn, Paul J. *Ontology: A Class Manual in Fundamental Metaphysics*. London: B. Herder, 1949.

Gram, Moltke S. "Things in Themselves: The Historical Lessons," *Journal of the History of Philosophy* 18, no. 4 (1980): 407–31.

Haldane, John. *Mind, Metaphysics, and Value in the Thomistic and Analytical Traditions*. Notre Dame, IN: University of Notre Dame Press, 2002.

Hamann, Johann Georg. "Metacritique on the Purism of Reason." In *Writings on Philosophy and Language*. Edited by K. Ameriks and D. M. Clarke. Translated by K. Haynes. Cambridge: University of Cambridge Press, 2007.

Hegel, G. W. F. *Hegel's Logic: Being Part One of the Encyclopedia of the Philosophical Sciences*. Translated by W. Wallace. 3rd edition. Oxford: Clarendon, 1975.

Hegel, G. W. F. *Phenomenology of Spirit*. Translated by A. V. Miller. Oxford: Oxford University Press, 1977.

Hegel, G. W. F. *The Difference between Fichte's and Schelling's System of Philosophy*. Translated by W. Cerf and H. S. Harris. Albany, NY: SUNY Press, 1988.

Heidegger, Martin. *Being and Time*. Translated by J. Macquarrie and E. Robinson. New York: Harper & Row, 1962.

Heidegger, Martin. *Hegel's Phenomenology of Spirit*. Translated by Parvis Emad and Kenneth Maly. Bloomington: Indiana University Press, 1988.

Heidegger, Martin. "What Is Metaphysics?" Translated by David Farrell Krell. In *Basic Writings: From Being and Time (1927) to The Task of Thinking (1964)*. San Francisco: HarperCollins, 1993.

Heidegger, Martin. *Kant and the Problem of Metaphysics*. Translated by R. Taft. Bloomington: Indiana University Press, 1997.

Heidegger, Martin. *Phenomenological Interpretation of Kant's* Critique of Pure Reason. Translated by P. Emad and K. Maly. Indiana: Bloomington, 1997.

Heidegger, Martin. "Husserl's Mangling of Phenomenological Findings [sic] through the Care, Derived from Descartes, about Certainty." Translated by D. O. Dahlstrom. In *Introduction to Phenomenological Research*. Indiana: Bloomington, 2005.

Heidegger, Martin. *The History of Beyng*. Translated by W. McNeill. Bloomington: Indiana University Press, 2015.

Henle, Robert J. "The American Thomistic Revival." In the *Philosophical Papers of R. J. Henle, S. J*. St. Louis: St. Louis University Press, 2000.

Hölderlin, Friedrich. "Oldest Programme for a System of German Idealism." In *Classic and Romantic German Aesthetics*. Edited by J. M. Bernstein. 185–7. Cambridge: University of Cambridge Press, 2003.

Hume, David. *A Treatise of Human Nature*. Edited by D. F. Norton and M. J. Norton. Oxford: Oxford University Press, 2000.

Hüntelmann, Rafael, and Johannes Hattler, editors. *New Scholasticism Meets Analytic Philosophy*. Germany: Editiones Scholasticae, 2014.

Husserl, Edmund. *Ideas: A General Introduction to Pure Phenomenology*. Translated by W. R. B. Gibson. The Hague: HarperCollins, 1931.

Husserl, Edmund. *Cartesian Meditations. An Introduction to Phenomenology*. Translated by D. Cairns. The Hague: Martinus Nijhoff Publishers, 1960.

Hyppolite, Jean. *Logic and Existence*. Translated by Leonard Lawlor and Amit Sen. Albany: SUNY Press, 1997.

Kant, Immanuel. *Religion within the Limits of Reason Alone*. Translated by T. M. Greene and H. H. Hudson. New York: Harper & Row, 1960.

Kant, Immanuel. *Critique of Pure Reason*. Translated by P. Guyer and A. W. Wood. Cambridge, England: University of Cambridge Press, 1998.

Kant, Immanuel. *Prolegomena to Any Future Metaphysics*: and the "Letter to Marcus Herz," February 1772. Translated by J. W. Ellington. Indianapolis, IN: Hackett, 2001.

Kant, Immanuel. *Critique of the Power of Judgment*. Translated by P. Guyer and E. Matthews. Cambridge, England: University of Cambridge Press, 2006.

Kenny, Anthony. *Frege*. London: Penguin Books, 1995.

Kenny, Anthony. *Aquinas on Being*. Oxford: University of Oxford Press, 2002.

Kerr, Fergus G. *After Aquinas: Versions of Thomism*. Blackwell, 2002.

Kerr, Gaven. *Aquinas's Way to God: The Proof in* De Ente et Essentia. Oxford: Oxford University Press, 2015.

Kierkegaard, Søren. *Concluding Unscientific Postscript to Philosophical Fragments, Vol. I*. Translated by H. V. Hong and E. H. Hong. Princeton, NJ: Princeton University Press, 1982.

Kierkegaard, Søren. *Either/Or, Vol. I*. Translated by Howard V. Hong and Edna H. Hong. Princeton, NJ: Princeton University Press, 1987.

Kierkegaard, Søren. *The Concept of Irony/Schelling Lecture Notes*. Translated by H. V. Hong and E. H. Hong. Bloomington: Indiana University Press, 1992.

Klima, Gyula. *John Buridan*. New York: Oxford University Press, 2009.

Knasas, John F. X. *Being and Some Twentieth Century Thomists*. New York: Fordham University Press, 2003.

Kremer, Elmar. *Analysis of Existing: Barry Miller's Approach to God*. New York: Bloomsbury Academic, 2014.

Kripke, Saul. *Naming and Necessity*. Cambridge, MA: Harvard University Press, 1972.

Kuhn, Thomas S. *The Structure of Scientific Revolutions*. Chicago: University of Chicago, 1962.

Leo XIII, *Aeterni Patris*, August 4, 1879. http://w2.vatican.va/content/leo-xiii/en/encyclicals/documents/hf_l-xiii_enc_04081879_aeterni-patris.html

Lewis White Beck. "Introduction: Kant and His Predecessors." In *Critique of Practical Reason and Other Writings in Moral Philosophy*. Chicago: University of Chicago Press, 1950.

Li Vecchi, Joseph. "Quine and Aquinas: On What There Is," *The Modern Schoolman* 85, no. 3 (2008): 207–23.

Li Vecchi, Joseph. "Logical Objectivity and Second Intentions," *Angelicum* 91, no. 4 (2014): 795–812.

Londey, D. G. "Existence," *Philosophia Arhusiensis* 1 (1970): 3–6.

Lonergan, Bernard. *Insight: A Study of Human Understanding*. Volume 3 of the *Collected Works of Bernard Lonergan*. Toronto: University of Toronto Press, 1997.

Long, Steven A. "On the Natural Knowledge of the Real Distinction of Essence and Existence," *Nova et Vetera*, English edition, 1, no. 1 (2003): 75–108.

Losee, John. *A Historical Introduction to the Philosophy of Science*. Oxford: Oxford University Press, 2001.

MacBride, Fraser. *On the Genealogy of Universals: The Metaphysical Origins of Analytic Philosophy*. Oxford: Oxford University Press, 2018.

Maréchal, Joseph. *Le point de départ de la métaphysique. Leçons sur le développement historique et théorique du problème de la connaissance*. 5 vols. Vols. I, II, III, Bruges and Paris, 1922–1923; Vol. IV, Brussels, 1947; Vol. V, Louvain and Paris, 1926.

Maritain, Jacques. *A Maritain Reader: Selected Writings*. Edited and translated by Donald and Idella Gallagher. Garden City, NJ: Image Books, 1966.

Maritain, Jacques. *Being in the World: A Quotable Maritain Reader*. Edited by Mario O. D'Souza and Jonathan R. Seiling. Notre Dame, IN: Notre Dame University Press, 2016.

Marmion, Declan. "Transcendental Thomisms." In *The Oxford Handbook of Catholic Theology*. Edited by L. Ayres and M. A. Volpe. Oxford: Oxford University Press, 2019.

Marx, Karl. *Capital: A Critique of Political Economy*. Translated by D. Fernbach. New York: Vintage Books, 1977.

Maurer, Armand. "Thomists and Thomas Aquinas on the Foundation of Mathematics," *Review of Metaphysics* 47 (1993): 43–61.

McCabe, Herbert. "The Logic of Mysticism." In *Religion and Philosophy*. Edited by M. Warner, 45–60. Cambridge: Cambridge University Press, 1992.

McCabe, Herbert. *God Matters*. New York: Bloomsbury, 2000.

McDaniel, Kris. "Existence and Number," *Analytic Philosophy* 54 (June 2013): 209–28.

McGinn, Colin. *Logical Properties: Identity, Existence, Predication, Necessity, Truth*. Oxford and New York: Oxford University Press, 2000.

McInerny, Ralph. *Aquinas and Analogy*. Washington: Catholic University of America Press, 1996.

Meinong, Alexius. *On Emotional Presentation*. Translated by M.-L. Schubert Kalsi. Evanston, IL: Northwestern University Press, 1972.

Mellor, D. H., and Alex Olivers, eds. *Properties*. Oxford: Oxford University Press, 1997.

Miller, Barry. "In Defence of the Predicate 'Exists,'" *Mind* 84 (1975): 338–54.

Miller, Barry. "'Exists' and Existence," *Review of Metaphysics* 40 (1986): 237–70.

Miller, Barry. *From Existence to God: A Contemporary Philosophical Argument*. New York: Routledge, 1992.

Miller, Barry. *A Most Unlikely God*. Notre Dame and London: University of Notre Dame Press, 1996.

Miller, Barry. *The Fullness of Being: A New Paradigm for Existence*. Notre Dame, IN: University of Notre Dame Press, 2002.

Mondin, Battista. *La metafisica di san Tommaso d'Aquino e i suoi interpreti*. Bologna: Edizioni Studio Domenicano, 2002.

Montagnes, Bernard. *La doctrine de l'analogie de l'être d'après Saint Thomas d'Aquin*. Louvain, Belgium: KU Leuven, 1963.

Montagnes, Bernard. *The Doctrine of the Analogy of Being According to Thomas Aquinas*. Translated by E. M. Macierowski. In Marquette Studies in Philosophy 25. Milwaukee, WI: Marquette University Press, 2004.

Moore, G. E. "Is Existence a Predicate?" *Proceedings of the Aristotelian Society Supplementary* 15 (1936): 175–88.

Nietzsche, Friedrich. *The Gay Science*. Translated by W. Kaufmann. New York: Vintage Books, 1974.

Nietzsche, Friedrich. *On the Advantage and Disadvantage of History for Life*. Translated by Peter Preuss. Indianapolis, IN: Hackett Publishing, 1980.

Nietzsche, Friedrich. *Beyond Good and Evil*. Translated by W. Kaufmann. New York: Vintage Books, 1989.

Nietzsche, Friedrich. *On the Genealogy of Morals*. Translated and edited by W. Kaufmann and R. J. Hollingdale. New York: Vintage Books, 1989.

Novalis. *Fichte Studies*. Translated by J. Kneller. Cambridge: University of Cambridge Press, 2003.

Nuzzo, Angelica. *Hegel and the Analytic Tradition*. London: Continuum, 2011.

Owens, Joseph. *The Doctrine of Being in the Aristotelian Metaphysics*. Toronto: Pontifical Institute of Medieval Studies, 1951.

Patt, Walter. "Aquinas's Real Distinction and Some Interpretations," *The New Scholasticism* 62, no. 1 (1988): 1–29.

Phillips, Richard Percival. *Modern Thomistic Philosophy*. London: Burns, Oates & Washbourne, Vol. I, 1934, Vol. II, 1935.

Pieper, Josef. *The Silence of St. Thomas*. Translated by D. O'Connor. London: Faber and Faber, 1957.

Plato. *Apology*. Translated by G. M. A. Grube. In *Plato: Complete Works*. Edited by J.M. Cooper. Indianapolis, IN: Hackett Publishing, 1997.

Plato. *Parmenides*. Translated by M. L. Gill and P. Ryan. In *Plato: Complete Works*. Edited by J.M. Cooper. Indianapolis, IN: Hackett Publishing, 1997.

Plato. *Republic*. Translated by G. M. A. Grube. Revised by C. D. C. Reeve. In *Plato: Complete Works*. Edited by J. M. Cooper. Indianapolis, IN: Hackett Publishing, 1997.

Plato. *Sophist*. Translated by Nicholas P. White. In *Plato: Complete Works*. Edited by J. M. Cooper. Indianapolis, IN: Hackett Publishing, 1997.

Polansky, Ronald M. *Aristotle's* De Anima. Cambridge: Cambridge University Press, 2007.

Preston, Aaron. *Analytic Philosophy: The History of an Illusion*. London: Bloomsbury, 2010.

Prior, A. N. "Determinables, Determinates, and Determinants I," *Mind* 58 (1949): 1–20.

Prior, A. N. "Determinables, Determinates, and Determinants II," *Mind* 58 (1949): 178–94.

Prior, A. N. "Is the Concept of Referential Opacity Really Necessary?" *Acta Philosophica Fennica* 16 (1963): 189–99.

Quine, W. V. O. "On What There Is," *Review of Metaphysics* 2, no. 5 (September 1948).

Quine, W. V. O. *From a Logical Point of View*. Harvard, MA: Harvard University Press, 1963.

Quine, W. V. O. "Existence and Quantification," in *Fact and Existence: Proceedings of the University of Western Ontario Philosophy Colloquium* 1966. Edited by Joseph Margolis. 1–19. Toronto: University of Toronto Press, 1969.

Quine, W. V. O. *Ontological Relativism and Other Essays*. New York: Columbia University Press, 1969.

Redding, Paul. "The Curious History of Hegel, Analytic Philosophy and the Return of Modal Metaphysics." In *Filosofia & Interdisciplinaridade: Festschrift em homenagem a Agemir Bavaresco*. Edited by Jozivan Guedes. 748–68. Porto Alegre: Eidtora Fi, 2015.

Redding, Paul. "Hegel and Sellars's 'Myth of Jones': Can Sellars Have More in Common with Hegel than Rorty and Brandom suggest?" In *Wilfrid Sellars, Idealism and Realism*. Edited by Patrick J. Reider. London: Bloomsbury, 2017.

Reinhold, Karl Leonard. "Eighth Letter: Continuation of the Preceding Letter: The Master Key to the Rational Psychology of the Greeks." Translated by James Hebbeler. In *Letters on the Kantian Philosophy*. Edited by K. Ameriks. 104–23. Cambridge: University of Cambridge Press, 2005.

Renard, Henri. *The Philosophy of Being*. Milwaukee, WI: The Bruce Publishing Company, 1948.

Rockmore, Tom. "Analytic Philosophy and the Hegelian Turn," *The Review of Metaphysics* 55, no. 2 (2001): 339–70.

Rockmore, Tom. *Hegel, Idealism, and Analytic Philosophy*. New Haven, CT: Yale University Press, 2005.

Roenisch, Frederick. *Early Thomistic School*. Dubuque, IA: The Priory Press, 1964.

Rorty, Richard, editor. *The Linguistic Turn: Essays in Philosophical Method*. Chicago, IL: University of Chicago Press, 1967.

Rorty, Richard. "Wittgenstein, Heidegger, and the Reification of Language." In *Essays on Heidegger and Others: Philosophical Papers*, Vol. 2. 50–65. Cambridge: University of Cambridge Press, 1991.

Russell, Bertrand. "On Denoting," *Mind* 14 (1905): 479–93.

Sacred Congregation on Study, *Acts of the Holy See*, ["The 24 Theses"], Year 6—Vol. 6, July 27, 1914, Rome, Vatican Polyglot Publishing, 1914, 383–6. http://www.vatican.va/archive/aas/documents/AAS%2006%20%5B1914%5D%20-%20ocr.pdf.

Sartre, Jean-Paul. *Being and Nothingness*. Translated by H. E. Barnes. New York: Washington Square Press, 1984.

Scalambrino, Frank. "From a Phenomenology of the Reciprocal Nature of Habits and Values to an Understanding of the Intersubjective Ground of Normative Social Reality," *Phenomenology and Mind* 6 (2014): 156–67.

Scalambrino, Frank. Phenomenological Psychology, *Internet Encyclopedia of Philosophy*. http://www.iep.utm.edu/phen-psy/, 2015.

Scalambrino, Frank. *Philosophical Principles of the History & Systems of Psychology*. London: Palgrave Macmillan, 2018a.

Scalambrino, Frank. "Where Is the Twilight Zone?" *Philosophy and the Twilight Zone*. Chicago: Open Court, 2018b.

Scalambrino, Frank. *Full Throttle Heart: The Rapture & Ecstasy of Nietzsche's Dionysian Worldview*. Castalia, OH: Magister Ludi Press, 2019.

Schelling, F. W. J. *Ideas for a Philosophy of Nature*. Translated by E.E. Harris. Cambridge: University of Cambridge Press, 1989.

Schelling, F. W. J. *System of Transcendental Idealism*. Translated by P. Heath. Charlottesville, VA: University of Virginia Press, Introduction, 2001.

Schelling, F. W. J. *Philosophical Investigations into the Essence of Human Freedom*. Translated by J. Love and J. Schmidt. Albany, NY: SUNY Press, 2006.

Schelling, F. W. J. *The Grounding of Positive Philosophy: The Berlin Lectures*. Translated by B. Matthews. Albany, NY: SUNY Press, 2007.

Schelling, F. W. J. *On the Divinities of Samothrace*. Translated by F. Scalambrino. Castalia, OH: Magister Ludi Press, 2019.

Schopenhauer, Arthur. *The World as Will and Representation*. Vol. 1. Translated by E. F. J. Payne. New York: Dover Publications, 1969.

Schopenhauer, Arthur. *On The Fourfold Root of the Principle of Sufficient Reason*. Translated by E. F. J. Payne. LaSalle, IL: Open Court Press, 1974.

Schopenhauer, Arthur. *On Philosophy at the Universities*. Translated by F. Scalambrino. Castalia, OH: Magister Ludi Press, 2020.

Smith, Gerard and Littie H. Kendzierski. *The Philosophy of Being: Metaphysics I*. Milwaukee, WI: Marquette University Press, 1990.

Tavuzzi, Michael. "Aquinas on the Preliminary Grasp of Being," *The Thomist* 51, no. 4 (1987): 555-74.
Tavuzzi, Michael. "Hervaeus Natalis and the Philosophical Logic of the Thomism of the Renaissance," *Doctor Communis* 45 (1992): 132-52.
Tooley, Michael. "Introduction." In *Particulars, Actuality, and Identity over Time*. Edited by M. Tooley. vii-1. London: Garland Publishing, 1999.
Torrell, Jean-Pierre. *Saint Thomas Aquinas, Vol. 1: The Person and His Works*. Translated by Robert Royal. Washington, DC: The Catholic University of America Press, 1996.
Twetten, David. "How Save Aquinas's 'Intellectus essentiae Argument' for the Real Distinction between Essence and Esse?" *Roczniki Filozoficzne* 67, no. 4 (2019): 129-43.
Unger, Peter. *Empty Ideas: A Critique of Analytic Philosophy*. Oxford: Oxford University Press, 2017.
Vallicella, William. *A Paradigm Theory of Existence*. New York: Springer, 2002.
Wernaer, Robert M. *Romanticism and the Romantic School in Germany*. London: D. Appleton & Company, 1910.
Wilhelmsen, Frederick D. *Man's Knowledge of Reality: An Introduction to Thomistic Epistemology*. Upper Saddle River, New Jersey: Prentice Hall, 1956.
Williams, C. J. F. *What Is Existence?* Oxford and New York: Oxford University Press, 1982.
Williams, C. J. F. *Being, Identity, Truth*. Oxford and New York: Oxford University Press, 1992.
Williams, C. J. F. "Being." In *Blackwell Companion to Philosophy of Religion*. Edited by Philip Quinn and Charles Taliaferro. Malden, MA: Blackwell, 2000.
Wippel, John. *The Metaphysical Thought of Thomas Aquinas: From Finite Being to Uncreated Being*. Washington, DC: Catholic University of America Press, 2000.
Wittgenstein, Ludwig. *On Certainty*. Translated by Denis Paul and G. E. M. Anscombe. Oxford: Basil Blackwell, 1969.
Wittgenstein, Ludwig. *Philosophical Investigations*. Edited by P. M. S. Hacker and Joachim Schulte. Malden, MA: Blackwell Publishing, 2009.
Wuellner, Bernard. *Summary of Scholastic Principles*. Chicago: Loyola University Press, 1956.
Zöller, Günter. "German Realism." In *The Cambridge Companion to German Idealism*. Edited by K. Ameriks. 200-18. Cambridge: Cambridge University Press, 2000.

Index

accident 24, 26, 27, 28–32, 34, 38
act of being 27, 38, 133, 136–8
actuality (Thomism) 23, 33
actus essendi 15, 16, 27, 32–3, 137
analogy 9
Analytic Philosophy, features of 88–9
apprehension 7, 10, 13–14, 20, 30; *See also* simple apprehension
Aristotle 2–4, 8, 14, 28–30, 33, 41, 44, 50–6, 58, 60–1, 103, 123, 149, 154

being of reason 16–17, 34–8
Bradley, F.H. 83–5
British Idealism 83–5

Cambridge properties 94, 114–18
Canon 40–1, 43–4, 47–9, 64–5, 67, 70, 74–5, 78, 81–2
Copernicus, Nicolaus 42
Critique of Practical Reason 50
Critique of Pure Reason 4, 39–40, 43, 47, 48, 50, 57, 64, 66–7, 81, 141, 151
Critique of the Power of Judgment 49–50, 79
and determining Power of Judgment 49, 53
and Reflecting Power of Judgment 49, 60

De Beauvoir, Simone 46, 77
Deleuze, Gilles 46–7
Derrida, Jacques 46, 140
Descartes, Rene 46, 69, 121
distributive predicates 122–3
domain 47–9, 51, 82, 143–4

esse commune (Thomist principle of entity) 33–4
essence 8, 15–16, 21–3, 26, 33–4, 127–8, 137, 138–9, 150
existence Distinguished from Being by Thomists 133–4
Existentialism 47, 70–1, 73, 75–6

Fabro, Cornelio 11
Fichte, Johann Gottlieb 66–72
Ficino, Marsilio 46

German Idealism 65, 67–8, 70–1, 74–5, 82
German Romanticism 65, 68, 70–1, 74–5, 82, 143
Gettier Cases 85–8
God 9, 22, 34, 62–3

Hegel, G.W.F. 59, 66, 69, 71–4, 76–7, 83, 140
Heidegger, Martin 45, 47, 77
Heraclitus 1–2, 142
hermeneutics 12, 47, 75–6
Hobbes, Thomas 69
Hölderlin, Friedrich 66, 68–74
Homeric Contest 45, 65–8, 70–2, 74, 82
Husserl, Edmund 78, 142
hyperbolic objectivism 13–14, 125, 133–5
hyperbolic subjectivism 11–12, 14, 125–7, 131

incommensurability 41–4, 129, 131, 143–4

Jacobi, Friedrich Heinrich 66

Kant, Immanuel 3–4, 12–13, 39–41, 43–5, 47–70, 72, 74–82, 126–31, 139, 141–2, 145, 151, 153
Kierkegaard, Soren 71, 76

logical intentions (First and Second) 36–7, 52–3, 58
Logical Positivism 85

Mendelssohn, Moses 66
Moore, G.E. 84–5

Nietzsche, Frederich 45–7, 71, 76, 140
noetic process 50, 55, 57–64, 67–8, 71–2
noumenon 8, 126
Novalis 66, 70–1

Organon 40, 43, 48–9

Phenomenology 47, 71, 75
Plato 1, 2, 46, 97–9, 101, 110–11, 113, 118, 120–1, 140, 152
potentiality 16, 28, 54–5, 61, 131
predicates 93. *See also* distributive predicates
Prolegomena to Any Future Metaphysics 43, 47–8
principle of actuality 43, 48–50, 130–1, 144; *See also* Actuality (Thomism)
principle of non-contradiction 12, 19, 43, 48–9, 126, 130, 132, 144

Quine, W.V.O. 13, 110–12, 152–4

Reinhold, Karl Leonhard 66–7, 70
Real Distinction 10, 32
Roselli, Salvatore 11–13
Russell, Bertrand 13, 84–5, 104–9

Schelling, F.W.J. 45, 66, 68, 70–4
Schopenhauer, Arthur 45, 66, 71–4, 140
second-order properties 100–2
self-subsisting being 7, 8, 33–4
simple apprehension 21–5
Spinoza, Benedict 66, 70
substance 8, 15–16, 26–34, 38, 58, 133

thing-in-itself 56, 141–2, 144
transcendental intuition 57–8, 61–2, 82
transcendental logic 40, 43, 48–9, 51, 67, 82, 144
transcendental method 4, 39–44, 47, 49, 59, 62, 64–5, 67–9, 75–6, 79, 80–2, 131
transcendental unity of apperception (TUA) 44–5, 48–9, 58–65, 67–75, 77–9, 81
trolley problems 141
two ultimate questions in the philosophy of being 44–5, 60, 78, 80–1, 139
Twenty-four Theses 11–13

Williams, C.J.F. 92–4, 97, 98–9, 101, 102–4, 112, 114, 117, 121

www.ingramcontent.com/pod-product-compliance
Lightning Source LLC
Chambersburg PA
CBHW070638300426
44111CB00013B/2152